Britain and Ireland

For Kay

my constant and faithful travelling companion

Britain and Ireland
A celebration of people and places

Peter Orr

Tynron Press
Scotland

© Peter Orr 1991

First published in 1991 by
Tynron Press
Stenhouse
Thornhill
Dumfriesshire DG3 4LD

ISBN 1-85646-025-8
All rights reserved

The author wishes to thank Peter Hardaker for the use of his picture of 'Sunrise at Whitby' on the front cover

Cover design by Christina Fong
Typeset by Linographic Services Pte Ltd
Printed in Singapore by General Printing Services Pte Ltd

Contents

PART ONE: ENGLAND

1. There'll Always be an England ... 3
2. Southern England ... 5
3. The Channel Islands ... 7
4. The South Coast ... 15
5. London ... 25
6. The Thames Valley ... 31
7. Shakespeare Country ... 37
8. The West Country ... 41
9. East Anglia ... 46
10. Ask Where's the North ... 53
11. South Yorkshire ... 55
12. The Peak District ... 58
13. North Yorkshire and Cleveland ... 63
14. Men of the Northlands ... 74
15. The North-West ... 81
16. Towards the Border ... 86

PART TWO: SCOTLAND

17. Fair Caledonia ... 93
18. Southern Scotland ... 95
19. The Trossachs and Beyond ... 98
20. Aberdeen and Royal Deeside ... 102
21. The Western Isles ... 107

PART THREE: WALES

22. Cara Wallia ... 117
23. North Wales ... 119
24. Central and South Wales ... 124

PART FOUR: IRELAND

25. I Am of Ireland ... 131
26. Northern Ireland ... 135
27. Dublin ... 137
28. Wexford and the South-East ... 139
29. Cork and Kerry ... 144
30. Clare and Galway ... 147

Last Words ... 151

Bibliography ... 153

Preface

> I cannot rest from travel: I will drink
> Life to the lees ...

Some journeys are undertaken for reasons of necessity; others are prompted by such various motives as the pursuit of pleasure, escape from a drab environment, or sheer curiosity. It is with such basically unnecessary journeys, ultimately the most rewarding form of travel, that this volume is concerned. It is not, nor is it intended to be, a conventional guidebook; there is an abundance of such publications, many of them penned by writers abler and more experienced than myself. No, this is simply a book recording personal experiences, a chronicle of explorations, and a recalling of the multitude of comforts afforded by people and by landscapes to a traveller who happens to write on the subject for the *Daily Telegraph* and the *Yorkshire Evening Press*. To the travel editors of those English newspapers, and to the editorial staff of *Agenda*, the *Arts Review*, BBC Radio, Channel Four Television, the *Evening Gazette*, *Kirkleatham Parish News* and *Studio Sound*, the author owes a debt of gratitude for both encouragement and forbearance, generously extended and warmly welcomed. I am only too conscious of my own inadequacy in conveying sensations of intense delight in so many remarkable discoveries, and in just remembrance of dear friends who have shared our journeys and cheered us on our pilgrimages through these islands. The best that can be said of this book is that it is a personal miscellany, recording years of cheerful explorations, and that most of it is true.

The fleeting impressions contained in these pages have been accumulated in haphazard fashion over the course of a lifetime. There are ups and downs, hills and valleys: that is to say, the picture contains warts and all. Of course, there is much that is left untouched, and a discerning visitor to these islands could quite easily avoid all the places mentioned here and still enjoy a memorable voyage of exploration. I can but echo Tennyson's words:

> I am a part of all that I have met;
> Yet all experience is an arch wherethro'
> Gleams that untravell'd world, whose margin fades
> For ever and for ever when I move.

Readers may, with justice, complain that I have shown insufficient regard for certain regions — Wales, the Lake District and the West Country among them. Although I have frequently wandered through those domains with wonder and admiration for their manifold attractions, yet, rightly or wrongly, I elected to focus attention on those places which I have come to know and love best. So there, with apologies to all Welshmen, Lakelanders and Westcountrymen whom I may unwittingly have offended, I rest my case.

Thanks are due to Caledonian MacBrayne, Thomas Cook Ltd, Friends of the Settle-Carlisle Line, the Irish Tourist Board, the Northern Ireland Tourist Board, North Sea Ferries, Ryedale District Council and Thanet District Council for permission to reproduce maps and photographs.

A travel writer's lot is certainly not a life of drudgery. Enjoyable on the whole, it can also be quite exhausting. But, as the man said, it is better than working. It also confers the advantage of seeing more places in a single year than the average tourist manages in a decade. My hope is that I have managed to conjure up something of the magic and mystery of our wanderings through these islands over the course of so many years.

                                                      Peter Orr
                                        Guisborough, Cleveland, 1991

BRITAIN AND IRELAND

PART ONE
ENGLAND

ENGLAND

There'll Always be an England

In the 19th century, the poet William Blake wrote of 'England's green and pleasant land'. Nearer to our own time, Rudyard Kipling, born in Bombay, India, expressed this rosy view of the land that was really his home:

> Our England is a garden that is full of stately views,
> Of borders, beds and shrubberies and lawns and avenues,
> With statues on the terraces and peacocks strutting by;
> But the Glory of the Garden lies in more than meets the eye.

There lingers in the imagination of many people an almost mythical England, composed of quiet country lanes running between banks of wild flowers, distant tapping of croquet mallets on the lawn of the manor house, innocent damsels and their swains taking tea at the vicarage, emblems of that gentle, well-ordered world suggested by the writings of Jane Austen, Elizabeth Gaskell, Rupert Brooke and John Betjeman, a world in complete antithesis to the harsh and cruel urban society depicted in the pages of Charles Dickens and George Orwell. Modern life, on the whole, has not dedicated itself to the preservation of picture-book scenery, but rather to the pursuit of wealth. Motorways have carved their tracks through once peaceful countryside, and many a secluded rural village has found itself invaded by workers from the cities seeking a small patch of green to call their own. In 1990, the *Observer* reported that 'Britain's rural housing crisis is now so deep that a dozen new homes will have to be built in every village in England and Wales in the next five years to solve the shortage.' The report goes on to say that 'by 1995 almost 200,000 village households will need housing'. Dormitory towns and villages have mushroomed everywhere, providing homes for a population which is absent during the day, the new race of commuters. They grew up with the railways, and really came into their own with the motor car. The Industrial Revolution turned Britain from a largely rural to a predominantly urban civilisation; yet, for many, the village remains an ideal place for living, the parish church still the focal centre of community life. England, after all, has an Established Church, which it owes to King Henry VIII. That same monarch must also assume some share of responsibility for the ruined ecclesiastical buildings to be found throughout the country, following the dissolution of the monasteries. That is a chapter of history familiar to English schoolchildren. But there are other, earlier remains which tell of more primitive forms of worship: the stone circles, the 'henges', are reminders of days long before St Augustine landed in Kent to fulfil his mission of bringing Christianity to England.

Then there are the great houses and gardens throughout the land, many of them now opened to the public by their owners, the impoverished gentry anxious to generate additional income towards the upkeep of these stately piles. In such surroundings, the visitor can sense that he is privileged to stand on one of many historic sites to be found up and down the country, where high drama has been enacted in former times, but whence the personages have long since departed, gone with the wind. Gone with the wind, too, from estates and forests throughout the land, are thousands of ancient trees, felled by the storms of 1987 and 1990; and, not so many years ago, Dutch Elm Disease stripped the countryside of many attractive specimens.

The English have a worldwide reputation for insularity, a quality best illustrated in a story told by an American columnist, George Will. According to Will, a porter at Waterloo Station in London once boasted to a newspaper reporter that his grandfather had been 'among those who defeated Napoleon on this very spot'. Now, as every true Anglophile knows, the Battle of Waterloo was fought on the playing-fields of Eton, one of the recognised breeding-grounds of that curious species of humankind, the English gentleman.

The English gentleman has been accurately depicted as 'a man with a passion for horses, playing with a ball, probably one broken bone in his body, and in his pocket a letter to *The Times*'. He is, in Daniel Defoe's words, one of 'your Roman-Saxon-Danish-Norman English'. His happy breed can be seen at the Lord's Test in June, at the Epsom Derby in the same month, at the Henley Regatta in July, at similar events taking place throughout the year in various parts of the realm and, less commonly these days, unless the sovereign is present, at church on Sundays.

> England! with all thy faults I love thee still ...

wrote William Cowper, and was echoed by Lord Byron, who continued with a list of items that he could forgive and forget: taxes (when they're not too many), the nation's debt, our cloudy climate, and our chilly women. Forgiving and forgetting, Byron found that he could also

> ... greatly venerate our recent glories,
> And wish they were not owing to the Tories.

Yet England, the 'mother country' to so many exiles, and even to some who have never set foot on its shores, has something that calls its natives home from distant journeys. William Wordsworth was one who acknowledged the potency of such a summons:

> I travelled among unknown men.
> In lands beyond the sea;
> Nor, England! did I know till then
> What love I bore to thee.

Southern England

... bright and fierce and fickle is the south ...

For 22 years, we had the good fortune to live in a village in semi-rural Buckinghamshire, little more than a mile from the River Thames. Wooburn Green actually has its own village green, on which there is a fair every year and where, on public holidays and in fine weather, there may be seen the time-honoured, colourful rituals of morris dancers, and stirring contests between rival tug-o'-war teams, each side straining on the rope in desperate efforts to topple the opposition. Before arriving there, we had endured the common lot of those whose work is in London. That can be a nomadic kind of existence, as many city-dwellers have discovered. We were not, I believe, altogether atypical in our movements: we began in Maida Vale, not far from the canal where there were boats taking leisurely trips through Regent's Park. From there, we migrated to South Kensington, convenient for Harrods, for the Albert Hall where the promenade concerts are held each summer, and for the Victoria and Albert, Science and Natural History Museums. Thence to Edmonton, where we lived for some months in Lamb's Cottage, home of Charles Lamb from May, 1833, until his death in December of the following year. Not far away was White Hart Lane, the home ground of one of England's most famous football teams, Tottenham Hotspur. We were there in their great year, when they won the Cup and League double. A brief period at Wimbledon followed, just over the road from the broad spaces of Wimbledon Common and, beyond, Richmond Park with its herds of deer. After that began our gradual retreat to the outer suburbs of Greater London, first to the 'leafy lanes in Pinner' mentioned in John Betjeman's poem, 'The Metropolitan Railway', and then to the southern side of the river, to Erith in Kent.

> There are men in the village of Erith
> Whom nobody seeth or heareth,
> And there looms on the marge
> Of the river a barge
> That nobody roweth or steereth.

Eventually, by a circuitous route, we arrived in Wooburn Green which, standing as it does within thirty miles of London, cannot escape for ever the inevitable consequences of such proximity. Like other villagers in that pleasant area of South Buckinghamshire, we have watched our home grounds trampled down by hostile feet. Thus runs a familiar lament in south-east England, that corner of the country where so much of the nation's business and entrepreneurial activity, and such a large share of its wealth, seem to be concentrated. Daily battles are fought between the conservationists and the developers. Even now, the people of Kent brace themselves against the day when the Channel Tunnel, linking Britain to France, will open for business. The route from London to Bristol is now known as the 'Western Corridor', with schemes for development taking shape all the way alongside the motorway that links the two cities. Oh, yes, the English countryside is still there, the rural expanses depicted in song and story, but the encroachment continues. As Philip Larkin put it, in his poem 'Going, Going', there used to be reassurance in

> The sense that, beyond the town,
> There would always be fields and farms ...

But now comes the feeling

> That it isn't going to last.

Larkin, a poet noted for what some people, rather myopically, saw simply as incorrigible pessimism, looked to the disappearance of the England he once knew:

> The shadows, the meadows, the lanes,
> The guildhalls, the carved choirs.

These fears are given substance by the gales of 1987 and 1990, which wrought appalling devastation in the woods and forests of southern England, uprooting thousands of ancient trees. And justified misgivings are fuelled by reports such as that which appeared in *The Times* early in 1990: 'Hedgerows are a feature of the British landscape, yet they are disappearing at the rate of 4,000 miles a year, swallowed up by developers and intensive farmers and robbing wildlife of natural sanctuary.' Four thousand miles a year! Small wonder that Philip Larkin regarded the ecological catastrophe as dangerously imminent:

> I just think it will happen, soon.

Of recent years, a wave of nostalgia has made itself manifest, its ripples spreading back to the farthest extent of living memory and beyond, as far back as the beginnings of photography, which conferred on man the ability to preserve for subsequent generations a visual record of places as they were. Almost every bookshop in Britain now stocks souvenirs of the locality, in picture and in print. *As It Was* is the title of a collection of photographs of old Bourne End and its environs, a pleasant part of South Buckinghamshire by the Thames. There are shots of elegant Victorian tea-parties, large private estates with their bands of faithful retainers, roads almost empty of traffic, and evidence of a different kind of lifestyle, largely devoid of the bustle and clamour which became increasingly difficult to escape during the twenty years we inhabited that once lovely and unspoilt countryside. But, as Tennyson wrote in what must be one of the best of all travel poems, 'Ulysses':

> Tho' much is taken, much abides ...

Indeed, as I trust the pages which follow will disclose, there endures still a multitude of scenes to lure and captivate visitors to these shores.

The Channel Islands

For many years, I have persistently avoided the idea of going to the Channel Islands. If one is prepared to pack luggage into the car and take a ferry across the Channel, then why not go the whole hog and end up in France? Such was my thinking, anyway. I also believed that I should find nothing other than tomatoes, cows, new potatoes, daffodils and cheap drink and cigarettes. Only recently was I persuaded otherwise and brought to confess the error of my ways. Now, I am more than ready to recognise the Channel Islands for what they truly are, British jewels lying just off the French coast.

Regarded collectively, the Channel Islands appear as an oddity: closer to France than to England, yet belonging to the United Kingdom with, effectively, self-governing status except in matters of defence and overseas diplomatic representation, they do not fit easily into any preconceived pattern. Of course, as is well known, they offer escape from punitive taxes and duties levied in mainland Britain, which explains the presence of numerous 'tax exiles'. Prices of alcoholic beverages, tobacco and other luxuries are an incentive to draw tourists there, but there is so much more than just material benefits to be enjoyed in these beguiling islands, with an amazing diversity of recreational activities readily available. Regarded individually, they present a succession of varied pleasures unlike any encountered elsewhere. Somehow, the scale of things seems to have been upset, and their diminutive size has been turned into positive advantage. Apart from the principal towns, there is no danger of congestion, and no trepidation, such as I experienced once or twice in Malta, that if you go too far or too fast you are in imminent danger of tumbling into the sea. The weather is generally kind, too. Spring comes early, and summer goes on a bit longer; swimming in the sea in late September was utterly delightful. I am sure that there must be drawbacks which a longer sojourn would disclose but, as a first-time, short-stay tourist, I can honestly say that I could find no serious complaint on any count.

Jersey, Guernsey, Alderney, Sark: the roll-call summons back half-forgotten geography lessons. Now, in riper years, I must add Herm and its neighbour, Jetthou; Lihou, smallest of the inhabited islands, accessible by causeway from Guernsey at low-water; Brechou, just off Sark; Burhou, with a refuge hut for stranded yachtsmen who fail to reach safe anchorage in Alderney; and Les Eccrehous, three rocky islets once notorious for smuggling.

English is spoken everywhere (though Norman French is still the language of lawyers), British currency is accepted, there is no quarantine for animals from Britain, and driving is on the left. Yet British visitors are confronted by sights obviously different from those of the mainland: French street names, blue pillar boxes, yellow telephone kiosks, tiny road signs, few and far between, all characteristic of the Channel Islands, lying almost in French embrace just west of the

Cherbourg peninsula. It is curious that they appear on the Michelin Motoring Atlas of France, but *not* in the Ordnance Survey Motoring Atlas of Great Britain. Formerly part of the Duchy of Normandy, their inhabitants chose to remain British (after all, their own William had conquered England); the islands were taken by the Germans in 1940, and there are museums to remind visitors of those darker days.

The big three, Jersey, Guernsey and Alderney, are served by ferry, hydrofoil and aircraft from Britain and France. We crossed from Poole by British Channel Islands Ferries aboard the *Havelet*, an agreeable, if rather basic, ship. A strong south-westerly prompted the bartender to remark that it was 'an interesting sea-state', and explained why I was one of only five in the dining-room where I had melon, a huge plate of scampi, then cheeses and creme caramel. Actually, I enjoyed the trip, but then I like the sea and am partial to eccentric vessels. The flagship, *Rozel*, proffers more sophisticated comforts.

This was our first visit to these captivating islands, but certainly not intended to be the last. Outside the towns, roads are almost empty, and have that soothing character of country lanes. The climate is generally kind, and in late September we encountered midsummer weather. '82 degrees in Jersey yesterday,' I boasted on arriving in Guernsey. '83 here!' snapped the Guern I was addressing. Yes, there is inter-island rivalry, but enough water separates them to keep the peace.

Finance, food, fun and, less significantly now, farming: not the whole story, but a reasonable indication of what to expect. We ate as well as we have eaten anywhere, wallowed occasionally in unaccustomed luxury, and wondered why we had never travelled that way before.

In Jersey, we stayed at a first-class guesthouse, the Panorama, its front door on St Aubin's precipitous High Street, a pleasing garden at the rear affording splendid views across the bay to St Helier. One balmy evening, we sat there at leisure, enjoying spectacular fireworks on the esplanade a couple of miles away: there is always something of interest happening in Jersey. Rooms were comfortable and well-equipped: besides the usual features — shower, fridge, colour television, kettle for tea and coffee — we found an unexpected novelty, a microwave oven. That was a kindly thought, but not the Rubik cube, which promised torture. In the morning there appeared a most remarkable breakfast menu: fruits, cereals, eggs, bacon, sausage, tomato, beans, mushrooms, smoked haddock, kipper, smoked mackerel, welsh rarebit and a serious temptation, crumpets with bacon and maple syrup. Our cordial hosts, Mr and Mrs Squires, advertise eighty different varieties of tea, served in the conservatory with cakes and Jersey cream. A super place, and excellent value: we loved it. Telephone: 0534 42429.

Just down the road, following the course of a disused railway track, is the Corbière Walk, a gentle, undemanding stroll along a wooded route, pleasantly embellished with clumps of hydrangeas and a blaze of fuchsias. Even more colourful and arresting is the Eric Young Orchid Foundation, close to Victoria Village; not the easiest place to find, since planning regulations forbid all but the smallest signs. However, the quest is well worth extra effort, and a friendly milkman finally directed us to this ravishing collection of exotic plants, open Thursdays, Fridays and Saturdays from 10 to 4 all year (except bank holidays). It is a veritable wonderland of sights and scents, colours and shapes, a rare and memorable delight not to be missed. Then there is Samares Manor, 14 acres of ornamental gardens, open daily from 10 to 5, end of March to end of October. A splendid place, but looking distinctly parched by drought when we were there. The rocky north coast affords dramatic contrast to the green lushness of the interior; then, in the west, are several good coastal walks. As television addicts know, this is Bergerac country so, before setting out, I consulted my old friend Terence Alexander, known to viewers as Charlie Hungerford. After eight years of *Bergerac*, Terry thinks Jersey marvellous, and will miss it now the series has come to an end. He and his wife, actress Jane Downs, are regulars at Bistro Frère (telephone: 0534 61000), an admirable establishment at Rozel, in the north-eastern corner, looking at France. We took their advice and had really memorable seafood from a temptingly imaginative menu, while eavesdropping on a party of amiably noisy businessmen at the next table. 'The great thing about Jersey,' one pronounced, 'is that you don't come here for the beach or the weather, you come here for a meal.' Another had his mind on different pleasures: 'Where shall we go this evening? Are there any naughty places in Jersey?' This is really like *Bergerac*, I thought. In fact, downtown St Helier, as I discovered, is full of familiar sights: Pizzaland, Marks & Spencer, W H Smith and busy evening traffic. 'When it rains, it's just like Manchester,' Terence Alexander admitted. I took refreshment there in an unpretentious and old-fashioned pub, whose prices were an agreeable surprise, and admired the gentle tact of the Minaz Indian Cuisine: 'We reserve the right to refuse admission without reason. This is not intended to offend.' The Opera House, opened by Lillie Langtrey in 1900, is a joy, red plush and gilt within, and gentlemen in evening dress taking the tickets. We ate at the Old Courthouse in St Aubin, just along from the harbour, good on atmosphere, with solid stone walls and floors, a promising menu, canned music and distinctly sluggish service. But nobody was in a hurry.

I left Britain with a special recommendation from my dentist, a young lady of considerable discernment, as I now recognise. For a special celebration, I can think of nowhere better than Longueville Manor, St Saviour. The setting is gracious, but the manor has a pleasant feeling of being lived in. We were pampered, and thoroughly enjoyed the set dinner. I had wild mushroom consomme with poached quail's egg, followed by grilled sea bass with oyster and chervil, then cheeses, and exquisite barquettes of nectarine and raspberries. The whole meal was elegantly presented, the wine list extensive, but not cheap, service attentive, but not embarrassingly so, and tasteful flower arrangements everywhere. All in all, an evening to remember with a glow of pleasure. Telephone: 0534 25501.

We approached Jersey by sea on a perfect evening of late summer, when the setting sun tinged the rocky outlines of the island's shore with a warm, pink glow. Little bays opened up the vistas inland, and lights began to twinkle from dwellings set high up on the cliffs. At first sight, it appeared the most inviting of places. Nothing during our brief stay there in any way contradicted that initial impression. Indeed, our expectations were generously surpassed.

Although the area of Jersey is only 45 square miles, there are more than 500 miles of roadway on the island, generally uncrowded, except on main routes around St Helier, with a speed limit of 40; car hire is inexpensive, petrol cheap.

It is the southernmost of the Channel Islands, only 14 miles from the French coast. There are quite extraordinary tides, up to 40 feet, and at low water seaweed (called there *vraic*) is gathered on the beaches, to be used as fertiliser. Sightseeing is fascinating and varied, there are wonderful walks, and ample opportunities for bathing. If you have long wanted to adopt a snail, then you can do so at Jersey's zoo, though of course you will not be allowed to take the creature home with you. Snails, incidentally, are the basis of an ancient Jersey cure for coughs: at least, that is what I am told! We also noted a butterfly farm, and a lavender farm. Gastronomically, Jersey deserves classification as a kind of gourmet's paradise. The *Jersey Evening Post* has columns of advertising headed 'Lost Dogs', 'Lost Cats' and, reassuringly, 'Cats Found'. A happy island.

Too soon we departed, our destination Guernsey. The regular midday gun greeted our arrival in St Peter Port, once the haunt of shipwreckers and privateers, today a charming town of pleasing aspect, rising from the water's edge, with a proliferation of jewellers' shops along its cobbled streets, and an establishment with 'Samuel Pepys' writ large over the window, but no diaries for sale within. Negotiating traffic at rush-hour and parking in St Peter Port can prove tricky, but it is easy to escape from the press.

We found the ideal refuge at the Hotel St Pierre Park, an award-winning hotel just a few minutes' drive from town, set in 40 acres, containing a 9-hole golf course, a tennis court and a small lake with a fountain, illuminated at night. There are three restaurants, a health and beauty salon, and a small gymnasium among its many attractions. Taking an early morning dip in their indoor pool, I was amused to see a number of inquisitive ducks peering curiously through the glass windows, obviously entranced by the sight of humans engaged in odd aquatic sports. St Pierre Park is one of the most comfortable hotels I have encountered, and the staff went out of their way to be helpful. As in Jersey, English newspapers were delivered with breakfast — unlike what happens in some remote parts of Scotland, where they arrive with lunch. Telephone: 0481 28282.

Like Jersey, Guernsey has its Battle of Flowers, a gay and colourful pageant. One popular tourist attraction which was commended to our attention is the Little

ANCRESSE BAY
FONTENELLE BAY
PEMBROKE BAY
LE GRAND CAMP
CHOUET BAY
LADIES BAY
GRAND HAVRE
Rousse
L'Ancresse Common
Fontenelle
BEAUCETTE MARINA
La Moye
Clos du Valle
MIELLETTE BAY
VALE
Bordeaux
PORTINFER
Belly Board Surfing
PORT SOIF
La Passée
Les Vardes
L'Islet
Pleinheaume
Ville Baudu
BORDEAUX HARBOUR
Les Grandes Rocques
Vingtaine de l'Epine
VALE
de Carteret
Oatlands Craft Centre
The Bridge
Bailiffs
ST SAMPSON'S HARBOUR
ST SAMPSON
St Clair
Lilyvale
Go-Kart Track
Richmond Corner
SPUR POINT
King George V Sports Field
Les Quartiers
La Ramée
LONGSTORE
Le Villocq
BELLE GREVE BAY
Sailing
LA SALERIE
ST. JOHN AMBULANCE & RESCUE SERVICE
Beau Sejour Centre
Preel
St Pierre Park
HARBOUR
Castle Cornet
King's Club
ST PETER PORT
ST ANDREW
HAVELET BAY
BATHING POOLS
Bailiff's Cross
PRINCESS ELIZABETH HOSPITAL
La Vallette
Military Museum
Aquarium
Le Four Cabot
Fort George
LES TERRES POINT
SOLDIERS BAY
Les Huriaux
German Underground Hospital
Les Hubits
Village du Putron
Carmel
Les Blicqs
La Bellieuse
LE BECQUET
ST MARTIN
FERMAIN POINT
FERMAIN BAY
Le Chêne
La Villette
LA RICOU
Les Nicolles
LA ROCQUE AU PIEGNE
La Fosse
Calais
PIED DU MUR (MARBLE BAY)
Moulin Huet Pottery
LA DIVETTE
MOULIN HUET BAY
PETIT PORT
Jerbourg Point
PETIT BOT BAY
LE JAONNET BAY
Icart Point
SAINTS BAY
SAINTS HARBOUR (MOORINGS)
LE CREUX AU CHIEN (CAVE)
ST MARTIN'S POINT
TELEGRAPH BAY

GUERNSEY

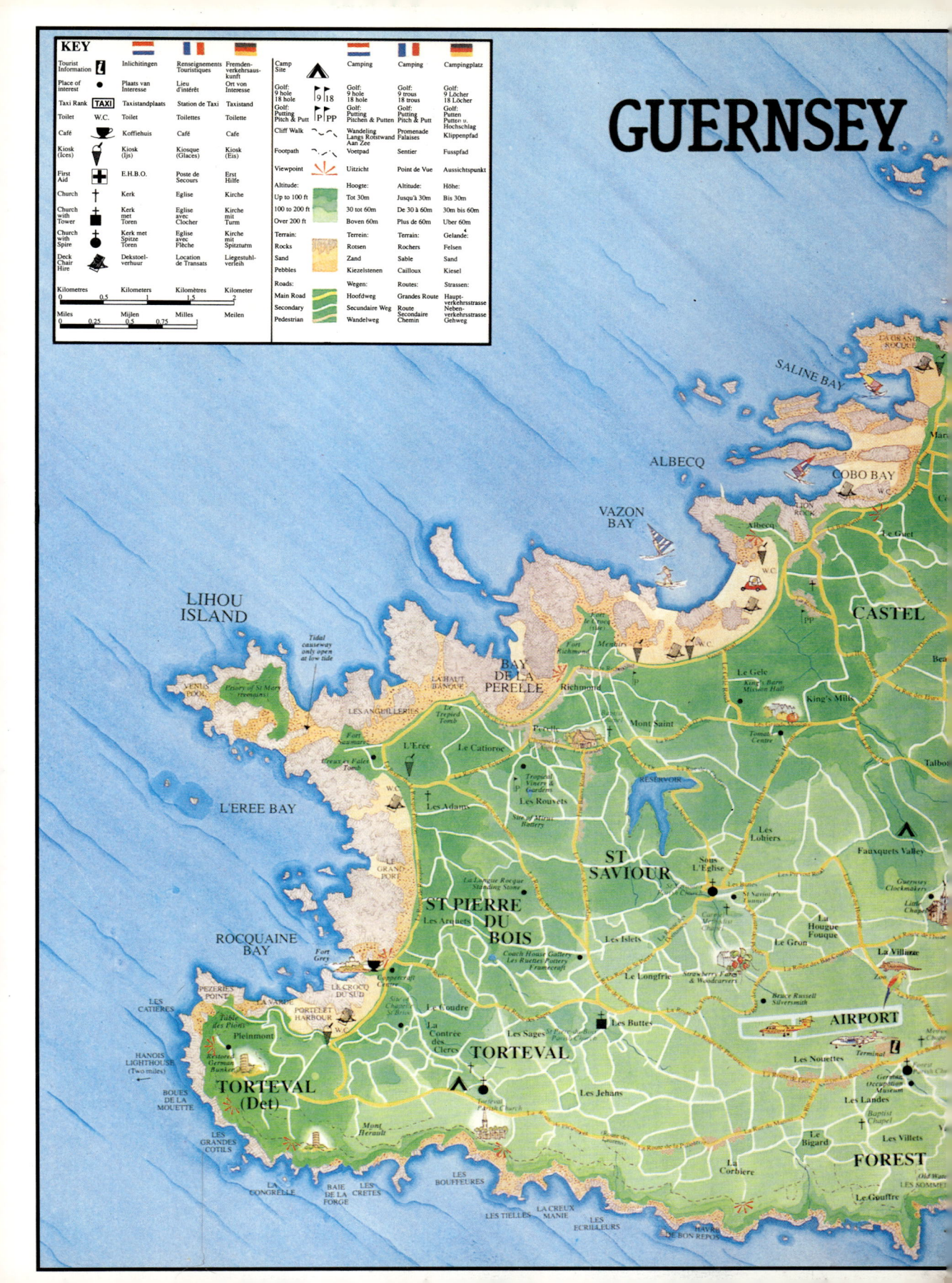

KEY

		Inlichtingen	Renseignements Touristiques	Fremdenverkehrsauskunft
Tourist Information	🅘	Inlichtingen	Renseignements Touristiques	Fremdenverkehrsauskunft
Place of interest	●	Plaats van Interesse	Lieu d'intérêt	Ort von Interesse
Taxi Rank	TAXI	Taxistandplaats	Station de Taxi	Taxistand
Toilet	W.C.	Toilet	Toilettes	Toilette
Café	☕	Koffiehuis	Café	Cafe
Kiosk	🍦	Kiosk (Ijs)	Kiosque (Glaces)	Kiosk (Eis)
First Aid	✚	E.H.B.O.	Poste de Secours	Erst Hilfe
Church	✝	Kerk	Eglise	Kirche
Church with Tower	✠	Kerk met Toren	Eglise avec Clocher	Kirche mit Turm
Church with Spire	▲	Kerk met Spitze Toren	Eglise avec Flèche	Kirche mit Spitzturm
Deck Chair Hire	🪑	Dekstoelverhuur	Location de Transats	Liegestuhlverleih

Kilometres 0 0.5 1 1.5 2
Miles 0 0.25 0.5 0.75

Camp Site	▲	Camping	Camping	Campingplatz
Golf: 9 hole 18 hole	9|18	Golf: 9 hole 18 hole	Golf: 9 trous 18 trous	Golf: 9 Löcher 18 Löcher
Golf: Putting Pitch & Putt	P|PP	Golf: Putting Pitchen & Putten	Golf: Putting Pitch & Putt	Golf: Putten Putten u. Hochschlag
Cliff Walk	〰	Wandeling Langs Rotswand Aan Zee	Promenade Palaises	Klippenpfad
Footpath	···	Voetpad	Sentier	Fusspfad
Viewpoint	☀	Uitzicht	Point de Vue	Aussichtspunkt
Altitude: Up to 100 ft 100 to 200 ft Over 200 ft		Hoogte: Tot 30m 30 tot 60m Boven 60m	Altitude: Jusqu'à 30m De 30 à 60m Plus de 60m	Höhe: Bis 30m 30m bis 60m Uber 60m
Terrain: Rocks Sand Pebbles		Terrein: Rotsen Zand Kiezelstenen	Terrain: Rochers Sable Cailloux	Gelande: Felsen Sand Kiesel
Roads: Main Road Secondary Pedestrian		Wegen: Hoofdweg Secundaire Weg Wandelweg	Routes: Grandes Route Route Secondaire Chemin	Strassen: Hauptverkehrsstrasse Nebenverkehrsstrasse Gehweg

SALINE BAY
LA GRANDE ROCQUE
ALBECQ
COBO BAY
VAZON BAY
CASTEL
LIHOU ISLAND
BAY DE LA PERELLE
King's Mills
L'ERÉE BAY
ST SAVIOUR
ST PIERRE DU BOIS
ROCQUAINE BAY
LES CATIÈRES
PEZERIES POINT
HANOIS LIGHTHOUSE (Two miles)
BOUES DE LA MOUETTE
TORTEVAL (Det)
TORTEVAL
AIRPORT
FOREST
LES GRANDES COTILS
BAIE DE LA FORGE
LES CRETES
LES BOUFFEURES
LES TIELLES
LA CREUX MANIE
LES ECRILLEURS
HAVRE DE BON REPOS
LE GOUFFRE

Chapel. This fascinating oddity has walls faced inside and out with coloured ceramics and seashells. At first sight, it looks like a model straight out of Disneyland, but half a dozen people can squeeze in at a time.

The beaches around the island are nothing if not enticing. A mere handful of folk were sunning themselves at Moulin Huet Bay when I made my way down to the alluring stretch of sand, rocks and water on a perfect morning. The previous evening, I had enjoyed swimming in L'Ancresse Bay as the sun was swiftly and dramatically declining towards the western horizon: a cool, but not chilling, dip. I must have cut quite a figure emerging from the sea, as I was propositioned by a girl young enough to have been my granddaughter. Most flattering, these Guerns!

'Renoir painted here, Victor Hugo wrote here,' the Guernsey Tourist Board proudly proclaims. I wish I could tell you about Victor Hugo's house there: on my last day in Guernsey, I tried to fit in a quick visit, but the stern custodian, who clearly thought that I was intent on denuding the property of its valuables, was less than helpful and obstinately refused me entry. We parted on fairly hostile terms, and I saw no more than the front door. A pity, since I am informed by friends more fortunate than myself that it is immensely rewarding. Perhaps some of my readers may fare better; let me warn them that the guided tour is obligatory, that it is impossible to join a tour already in progress, and that there is a rigid timetable from which no deviations are permitted.

Guernsey has much to commend it: lovely countryside and fine beaches; a charming capital, St Peter Port, where we attended Sunday morning service in the parish church; an arts festival, with theatrical presentations, and concerts in a hall formerly the Church of St James; and easy access to the smaller islands.

I flew to Alderney from Guernsey in one of Aurigny's nine Trislanders, an experience to be cherished in the days of jumbo jets. Aurigny is the French name for Alderney; Mick McCormick, now its commercial manager, has been with the airline for all its 21 years of operation. In 1988, they carried 306,000 passengers, and there is now regular commuter traffic between Jersey and Guernsey, as well as holiday flights from Southampton and Bournemouth. This was flying at its best, as far as I am concerned: I sat immediately behind the captain, with large windows affording views on every side. In earlier days of the airline, passengers had to be weighed, and then directed to embark alternately from each side, to ensure that the aircraft did not overbalance and tip up on the runway. Things have progressed since then, but being in a small, slow, friendly aeroplane at about 1,000 feet, able to see details of landscape and seascape spread out below, bestows a rare and pleasing sensation. So, I was in the best of humours when I arrived in Alderney, and nothing occurred all day to disturb that deep contentment. The island is, for me anyway, just the right size: small enough to drive around in an hour, yet large enough for the wanderer to lose himself. Mick was my genial guide: 'Alderney is the key to the Channel,' he observed as we surveyed immense forts, erected in Queen Victoria's time for defence against possible French invasion, and used later by German invaders. The native population had been evacuated, and under Nazi occupation Alderney became a forced labour camp. On a wall of St Anne's large, pink granite parish church, a tablet records the burial of 45 Soviet citizens who died there between 1941 and 1945.

'Good bathing, and a great place for bird-watching,' Mick observed as a grey heron flew overhead. The coast of France, just eight miles away, seemed almost within touching distance. Mick often takes his yacht there, landing on the Cherbourg Peninsula after a two-hour crossing, enjoying lunch, and getting back in time for the evening opening of the Yacht Club bar. The island can boast of many distinguished inhabitants: until his death, it was the home of actor Geoffrey Sumner, of *The Army Game*. He read the lesson in church, and helped to run the local museum. John Arlott, doyen of cricket commentators, lives there, and Ian Botham takes holidays in Alderney. Here can be seen the only working railway in the Channel Islands, with two miles of track, and rolling-stock including carriages from London's Bakerloo Line. Alderney has a population of 2,200; its main industry is tourism, with 600 holiday beds, in hotels, guesthouses and self-catering accommodation. Yet there are no crowds and no caravans are permitted. As on the other islands, seafaring is an important activity, and the visitor will observe innumerable vessels, from tiny pleasure craft to larger ships on more serious business. At Braye is an immense breakwater, originally designed to afford shelter to the British fleet, and there are formidable Victorian fortifications at strategic intervals around the coast.

St Anne is a welcoming sort of town, just the place for thoughtful loafing, which I consider to be just about the ideal way to spend the days of holiday time. There, I enjoyed a feast of crab and prawns in one of its many restaurants. Victoria Street is its principal thoroughfare, where Ebenezer Wrinklies, a food emporium, sells among other things, raw, unroasted coffee beans. Just off the main street, I found the Coronation Inn, established in 1868, and now serving Randall's real ale from Guernsey. There was a jolly sign outside the fish-fryer's: 'Good Buy Mr Chips'.

Alderney airport is just about as different from Heathrow as it is possible to be, almost deserted when I reported for my flight back to Guernsey. I flew back on board G-JOEY, the airline's mascot plane, which has prompted a series of children's books and attracted a host of enthusiastic admirers. So far as I know, no Boeing 747 has won that kind of affection!

Herm has something of magic about it: a tiny, Robinson Crusoe island, twenty minutes from St Peter Port aboard a sleek, comfortable catamaran. It would be easy to walk right round the island, without exertion, in a morning, but enticing diversions along the way tend to retard progress. On a day of bleaching sunshine, I made for Shell Beach, a stretch of shining sand where bathing is easy and, as its name indicates, pickings are good for shell-gatherers. Returning to view the tiny church, I ran into a wedding party. Cars are forbidden on Herm, so bride and groom departed in a balloon-festooned cart drawn by tractor. At the White House Hotel, overlooking the diminutive harbour, and with a view of neighbouring Jetthou, we enjoyed excellent duck casserole. Telephone: 0481 22159.

Only 1½ miles by 1½ miles, Herm rises from the blue waters a precious stone set in a silver sea; or so it seemed, on a September day of blissful warmth. The sea lapping the glorious beaches had that clarity reminiscent of tropical seas, and there was a distinct feeling that the march of time had been suspended. Just twenty minutes by comfortable catamaran from St Peter Port, it is a place apart. In a sense, it serves as an emblem for the Channel Islands: the scale is miniature, distances are small, nowhere is far from anywhere else, and over all hangs an air of untroubled serenity.

A tractor greeted our arrival on Sark, largest of the small islands, after 45 minutes in the rather cramped and crowded *L'Esprit de Serk* on the sea-crossing from Guernsey. Since there are no cars on Sark, the tractor-hauled carriage was our conveyance up the steep way from the harbour to the little village; well worth 35 pence. 'Sark's a funny place,' an informant on Guernsey had remarked. 'You either love it or you don't!' I hired a bicycle, and spent a blissful day of exploration along broad dirt-tracks, mercifully firm in dry weather, while my wife confessed to less than total enchantment after a 1-hour excursion by horse and carriage over terrain she judged rather severe. By bicycle, I found the undulations agreeable, and the prospect on reaching La Coupée breathtaking. Indeed, Sark's scenery is quite dazzling: rocky headlands thrusting boldly into clear, blue waters, which wind can whip into masses of foam; then, one comes upon sudden, unexpected bays with golden beaches. Sark is liberally supplied with places of refreshment, so, after strenuous pedalling past verges decorated with pink lilies and, in vivid contrast, scarlet fuchsias, I paused for a drink at a friendly little inn on a lane leading nowhere. Later, I cooled off in the pool at Aval du Creux Hotel, and treated myself to a generous plateful of scallops. Telephone: 0481 83 2036.

There is a nice story about an establishment renting bicycles on Sark. Dismayed by the appearance of a rival hirer, the owner of the older firm bribed boys to sabotage machines belonging to his adversary: 50 pence a puncture, £2 a bent wheel, a fiver if the bicycle was thrown into the harbour. His turpitude discovered, just retribution ensued.

The Dame of Sark (or Serk, as it is called by some) was a legend in her lifetime. Now she is gone, responsibility for the island falls on the shoulders of the Seigneur, or Lord of the Manor, Michael Beaumont Esquire. For sheer beauty of scenery, Sark probably carries off the palm, but the competition for that honour is fierce, and very little (perhaps just quirks of individual taste) separates the winner

14   *ENGLAND*

from the rest. The answer, I suppose, is to see them all, and make your own decision. That probably means you will want to go and see them all again, just to make sure!

Amid all the wild beauty lurks the odd feeling that Sark is a private, even secret place, and that the visitor should be careful not to disturb its tranquillity. For a lonely moment, cycling under the fierce September sun, I thought I loved this strange place; now, I wonder whether it was mere enchantment.

There are many ways of getting to the Channel Islands and, once there, much to see. Useful telephone numbers for information and reservations: Guernsey Tourist Board: 0481 23552, Jersey Tourist Board: 0534 78000, British Channel Island Ferries: 0202 681155, Condor Hydrofoil: 0305 761551, Isle of Sark Shipping Company: 0481 24059, Sealink: 0233 647047, Torbay Seaways: 0803 214397, Trident (for Herm): 0481 21379, Air UK: 0345 666777, Aurigny Air Services: 0481 82 2886, British Midland: 071 589 5599, Dan Air: 0345 100200, Guernsey Airlines: 081 549 1700, London City Airways: 071 511 4200, Sarnia Air: 0481 82 2283.

The South Coast

A fascinating and utterly absorbing film was shown recently on British television, shot from an aircraft making a circumnavigation of Britain's coast. For the armchair traveller, no better entertainment could be devised: here we were, sitting comfortably at home, yet being whisked along the seaboard at ever so many hundreds of miles an hour, and given a bird's eye view (there can be none better, surely) of beaches and towns and piers and harbours, all flitting across the astonished gaze in rapid and bewildering succession. Vicariously, one was able to enjoy the journey of a lifetime in such manner, and revel in many sights not revealed to the earthbound tourist.

Memorable indeed is the length of coastline stretching from the easternmost point of Kent, the North Foreland, to Plymouth Sound, in the south of the county of Devon. On the northern curve of that piece of Kent which bulges into the sea is Margate, long a popular resort for holidaymakers. It was from Broadstairs to Margate that Mr and Mrs Pooter came to play an unruly party game with their friends, Cummings and Gowing. Admirers of *The Diary of a Nobody*, by George and Weedon Grossmith, will recall the incident. Holiday towns along the coast are noted for their palaces of entertainment, their Winter Gardens and Beach Pavilions, and Margate's Theatre Royal claims to be the second-oldest theatre in the country. In the centre of town stands Tudor House, a timber-framed building which underwent extensive restoration in 1951, the year of the Festival of Britain. Now it houses a museum of local history and a display of seashells.

Round the head, and we are at Broadstairs and its Pavilion Theatre. Here Charles Dickens spent his vacations from 1836 to 1850, and wrote part of *Pickwick Papers*, as well as *Nicholas Nickleby*, *The Old Curiosity Shop* and *Barnaby Rudge*. There is even a building rejoicing in the name of Bleak House, where Dickens completed one of his most famous novels, *David Copperfield*. Broadstairs melts imperceptibly into Ramsgate, where histrionic diversions are to be found at the Granville Theatre. From Ramsgate, Sally Line runs a regular ferry service to Dunkirk, the port in northern France where, in May and June of 1940, more than 300,000 British and Allied troops were evacuated from the beaches by naval ships, backed up by an armada of small vessels from England.

Southwards lie Sandwich Bay and the town of Deal, where Julius Caesar and the Roman invaders are said to have landed in 55 BC. To the beaches of Kent, 500 years later, came Hengist and Horsa with their Saxon invaders. Then, in 597 AD, St Augustine arrived, to inaugurate his task of spreading Christianity through England. And it was from Deal, almost thirty years ago, that I took my very first day-trip to France, a jolly outing on board a venerable ship, the *Queen of the Channel*.

16   ENGLAND

The traffic between Britain and the continent of Europe continues to flow in a steady stream: in 1989, two million cars passed through Dover. That is some measure of its importance as a port. We have sailed from there more times than we care to remember, on ferries bound for Calais, Boulogne, Zeebrugge or Ostend. It was to the cliffs at Dover that Shakespeare, in *King Lear*, brought the blinded Gloucester, who hoped to end his wretched life there by leaping from the dizzy height.

Today there is growing awareness of ecological considerations: the Chairman of Dover District Council wrote to *The Times* in December, 1989, pointing to 'the investment that Dover District Council is making in the protection of the country-side, in particular, the chalk grasslands on top of the white cliffs: "We have adopted the theme of White Cliffs Country and we are spending £14 million on the White Cliffs Experience Heritage Centre"'.

The Cinque Ports were originally five in number, as their title would suggest: Hastings, Romney, Hythe, Dover and Sandwich. Later additions to the list were Winchelsea, Rye, Deal and Folkestone. The Warden of the Cinque Ports is now an honorific title, held after the Second World War by Winston Churchill.

Near Folkestone is the site of excavations for the Channel Tunnel. This is not a new project: when it was mooted in the last century, Theodore Hook produced a verse which, in the view of many people, should have been the last word on the subject.

> A tunnel underneath the sea, from Calais straight to Dover, Sir,
> That qualmish folks may cross by land from shore to shore,
> With sluices made to drown the French, if e'er they would come over, Sir,
> Has long been talk'd of, till at length 'tis thought a monstrous bore.

Many people view with understandable dismay what the future may hold for Kent when the Channel Tunnel is completed and traffic starts flowing through what was once known as 'The Garden of England'. Indeed, the Channel Tunnel has aroused passions in many parts of Britain. Not so very long ago, I was invited up to the bridge of one of the cross-Channel ferries operating between Dover and Calais. We were about halfway across, and the captain of the vessel pointed to the water below us, stirred by the bow-waves of the swiftly-moving ship. 'Somewhere down there,' he said, 'will be the tunnel. Now, suppose there's an accident just at this point — an explosion, a fire, a derailment, a collision — it's been known to happen elsewhere. But here, you're ten miles from either shore, and it's not going to be easy to get rescue services to the scene of the accident. You've got to think about the safety aspect of the thing.' I nodded my head in agreement as we sped on towards Calais in the sunshine. That was some time ago, but the ironic thing was that this conversation took place aboard the *Herald of Free Enterprise*, which capsized outside Zeebrugge harbour in March 1987, with the loss of 193 lives.

Inland Kent is not to be neglected. There is, of course, the magnificence of Canterbury Cathedral, symbol of the central authority of the Church of England since St Augustine became its first archbishop in the 6th century. Here, in 1170, Archbishop Thomas à Becket was murdered, and his shrine became a place of pilgrimage where, as Chaucer records so memorably at the outset of *The Canterbury Tales*,

> ... from every shires ende
> Of Engelond to Caunterbury they wende,
> The hooly blisful martir for to seke,
> That hem hath holpen whan that they were seeke.

Kent is a county richly endowed with great houses and historic sites. Westerham was the birthplace of General Wolfe, and his home is now named Quebec House, in acknowledgement of his daring capture of Quebec from the French in 1759; nearby is Chartwell, residence of Winston Churchill for more than forty years, now opened to the public; Ightham Moat, an enchanting medieval moated manor-house, which I fell in love with at first sight; Scotney Castle; Leeds Castle, a magnificent moated fortification, where we once spent the night as guests of the trustees, and found modern comforts in an ancient setting; Knole, near Sevenoaks, one of the largest houses in the land; Finchcocks, a fine 18th-century house where our friends Richard and Katrina Burnett have assembled an intriguing collection of keyboard instruments which Richard, a professional keyboard player, demonstrates most entertainingly on open days; Penshurst Place, with its imposing 14th-century hall, 62 feet long and 60 feet high; Sissinghurst Castle, once the home of Harold Nicolson and his wife, Vita Sackville-West, who created one of the most pleasing gardens you will find anywhere — the list is almost endless, and the pleasures prolific.

I have a special affection for Sussex: partly because my father was born there in the last year of the 19th century, and grew up in that county; partly because many of my happiest holidays have been spent there; but largely because it remains, despite the spread of commuter-land into its once rural calm, still a good place to be.

> If I ever become a rich man,
> Or if ever I grow to be old,
> I will build a house with deep thatch
> To shelter me from the cold,
> And there shall the Sussex songs be sung
> And the story of Sussex be told.

Those were the words of a writer who loved dearly the county of Sussex by the sea, Hilaire Belloc.

Rye is an entrancing spot on the river Rother, an inland town since the sea retreated in the 13th century. There are cobbled streets, half-timbered houses, and inviting inns. The George, a Trusthouse Forte hotel, and a coaching-inn in days gone by, contains oak beams said to have come from one of the vessels in the Spanish Armada of 1588. The museum in the Ypres Tower is open in the summer months, and the church with its famous clock is worth a visit. Henry James lived at Lamb House from 1898 to 1916; not far away is the Star, one of England's oldest inns. 'Very neat and old-maidish and quiet and comfortable,' was Logan Pearsall Smith's opinion of the place.

At Hastings, there is a charming little theatre called The Stables where, on several occasions, I have been invited to bring friends, a famous actress, a distinguished singer, and an eminent pianist, to present an entertainment of words and music to local audiences. For that reason, Hastings has a special place in our book of memories. Inland is Battle; near there, on 14 October 1066, at a little place called Senlac, was fought what history records as the Battle of Hastings. In that encounter, graphically depicted in the Bayeux Tapestry, William the Conqueror, Duke of Normandy, overcame the English forces under Harold II, and assumed the English throne as William I.

Bexhill did not appeal to the writer and dramatic critic, James Agate, who thought it a 'filthy hole, dull and, I gather, purseproud'. At Eastbourne, H G Wells found the 'sea air mingled with the taint of such crabs as have gone recently from here to that bourne from which no traveller returns'.

'Today, from Rottingdean to Newhaven is almost fully developed suburb, of great horror,' wrote Rudyard Kipling. If he could behold the scene today, his horror would be considerably magnified. Kipling lived in Rottingdean from 1897 to 1902, and there he wrote *Stalky & Co*, *Kim* and the *Just So Stories*.

From Rottingdean, the road runs close to the edge of the cliffs, with fine views of the South Downs and a sight of England's most famous girls' school, Roedean, on into Brighton, best-known of all Sussex resorts, 'the place to get husbands', or so Lydia avowed in *Pride and Prejudice*. Just an hour by electric train from London, it became the home of quite a number of distinguished actors and actresses, Laurence Olivier among them. The town's most notable architectural feature is undoubtedly the Royal Pavilion, a bizarre pleasure-dome in an oriental style dictated by the Prince Regent, later King George IV. 'The Pavilion at Brighton is like a collection of stone pumpkins and pepper-boxes,' was the verdict of William Hazlitt. 'Any thing more fantastical, with a greater dearth of invention, was never seen.'

When I was a teenager, I used to spend my holidays in Brighton with my father's sister Maud, an amazingly hospitable aunt. She, and other inhabitants of the town, used to speak disparagingly of 'those wretched day-trippers'; and around the time of what was then observed as the August Bank Holiday, they were wont to use even stronger language in their descriptions of unruly hordes spilling out of green trains of the Southern Railway and green coaches of the Southdown Bus Company, all intent on a jolly day out by the seaside. They do not share the disposition of Matthew Arnold, who reported: 'Brighton makes me bilious.' More optimistically, they find themselves in sympathy with Thackeray, who wrote of 'Kind, cheerful, merry Dr Brighton.'

There is abundant diversion to be found in and around Brighton: once the prime attractions of the seafront were two busy piers, Palace Pier and West Pier, each with a theatre at the end. Times change, and now attention has shifted eastwards to the huge, modern marina. The beach is largely pebbles, but the seafront is several miles long, and there are bracing walks under or along the cliffs. Some of my favourite golf-courses belong to that locality, with sweeping views of the coast in one direction, and fine prospects northwards to the South Downs. One of the best viewpoints in southern England is at Devil's Dyke, a few miles outside Brighton. The story goes that the devil, in pursuit of one of his wicked schemes, began to dig a dyke, or channel, to let in the sea and flood the surrounding countryside. It is said that an old lady who lived in a nearby cottage, alarmed by the noise, came out with a candle to investigate. The devil took the light to be that of the dawn, desisted from his labours and fled, leaving a huge trough gouged out of the downland chalk. From the top of Devil's Dyke, on a clear day, it is possible to see Windsor Castle, some fifty miles away. From that same vantage point, we have watched admiringly the carefree movements of hang-gliders, rising and falling gracefully on the air currents.

Some years ago, I was involved in recording a set of those well-known fairy tales by the brothers Grimm, with an eminent actor and his actress wife. I spied the opportunity for a pleasant rural outing, since Paul and Joy, very sensibly, live in the Sussex countryside, and it seemed like a good idea to investigate recording facilities in their area, rather than bring them all the wearying way into London. As I say, it seemed like a good idea at the time. The yellow pages yielded some promising leads, and subsequent telephone enquiries produced earnest assurances that all stipulations, including my insistence on a really quiet location, could very easily be met. Thus encouraged, I set out to make a reconnaissance.

My first call was at a large house, set back a little way (but only a very little), from a very busy trunk road. The owner, an entirely amiable, but rather vague gentleman, greeted me and led the way into the garage. I should mention, in fairness to him, that it was a double garage.

'Well, here it is,' he announced confidently. 'This is the studio, and that,' (he motioned towards a flimsy partition, standing precariously at the far end) 'that is the control-room.' I was conscious of a sinking feeling: it was not a promising start.

'May I see inside the control-room?' I asked, raising my voice in order to be heard over the thunder of a passing lorry. My host seemed not to be aware of the traffic noise. Perhaps he is deaf, I thought. Certainly, on the basis of our brief telephone conversation, I had not expected him to be quite so elderly and so obviously frail.

We peered round the partition into the so-called control-room. There was a simple workbench (dirty), a small window (also dirty), offering a dim view into the garage (sorry — studio!), an ancient-looking tape-recorder on the floor, various lengths of cable and a mysterious object which I took to be the remains of an early wireless set.

My host picked up the aforesaid mysterious object and dusted it off. Then, obviously, he thought some sort of comment was required. 'This,' he proclaimed with every appearance of seriousness, 'this is the mixer.'

'Ah ... yes,' I said. I could not think of anything else to say. We looked at it for a little while in a kind of reverent silence, and then he began to rotate the knobs, evidently anxious to convince me that the mixer was in good working order. One of the knobs fell off. He picked it up and tried to push it on again.

'This one is for the bass,' he announced.

'For the bass?' I echoed. 'Ah ... yes.' I was aware that I was beginning to repeat myself, but I was running out of ideas. There was another awkward silence while we both contemplated this product of fairly modern technology. He turned it round in his hands, to afford me a better view; I thought he was going to drop it. Eventually, I decided that it was time to attempt a question: he seemed to expect some sort of comment. 'At what frequency does it roll off?' Not a very elegant way of putting it, I know, but I thought it would serve. He considered the question carefully, and then, with a bewildered expression, asked me to repeat it. I tried a different formula; 'At what frequency does attenuation start with that control?' I asked, pointing to the wobbly knob. Another silence ensued. 'Or even boosting, perhaps?' I added hopefully.

'Well, now,' he said, looking a little hurt by my insistence. 'I think you're getting a bit technical for me.'

Having exhausted the possibilities of the garage-studio, we retired to the house for a mug of tea. I explained as kindly as I could that his premises were not really suited to my particular needs. 'There are certain noise problems.' I pointed to the road, just a few yards away.

'Oh, really,' he said disbelievingly. Clearly, he was disappointed by my lack of enthusiasm. After a pause, he changed to another tack: apparently, he had a friend, also in the recording business, whose studio was actually a caravan in the middle of a field, miles away from anywhere. When I pressed him as to the exact location of this caravan-cum-studio, it transpired that it was quite close to Gatwick Airport. Very probably in line with the main runway, I thought grimly, as I left in something of a hurry.

A few miles away, I found a much more promising venue, a studio which looked like a studio, with an impressive array of up-to-date equipment. 'Yes, dead quiet it is here,' the owner said. 'Absolutely soundproof.' We listened approvingly to the silence that reigned there. It really was quiet. I made a booking for a session some weeks later, and departed full of confidence.

And that should have been the end of the story, adding further credibility to the old phrase, all's well that ends well. Unfortunately, things did not turn out quite like that. We arrived on the appointed day, Paul with his crossword, Joy with a magazine. It was fortunate that they had come thus provided, for it was to prove a tedious morning, with many a false start. The first thing to disturb the peace of this 'dead quiet' studio was an enormous roaring noise, accompanied by violent vibrations. 'What on earth is that?' I asked, more than a little unnerved. 'Oh, that'll be the 10.15 to London,' came the reply. 'Soon be gone. The station's just behind the studio, you know.' I did not know.

I shall not weary the reader with an account of subsequent mishaps, but merely mention that it was one of the worst days in all my years as a record producer. Somehow, we got through, I know not how, but the experience left me a sadder and a wiser man. Not sad enough, nor wise enough, unfortunately, to foresee and avoid an even worse disaster which befell me later in Newcastle. But that is another story altogether.

There are many remarkable sites in Sussex, houses, castles and gardens, some under the care of the National Trust: Bodiam Castle, built in 1385 on the border with Kent; Sheffield Park Gardens, and the Bluebell Railway; Bateman's at Burwash, Kipling's home from 1902 to 1936; Nymans Garden at Handcross; and Petworth Park, a 700-acre deer-park surrounding Petworth House, where the poet Wilfrid Scawen Blunt was born on 17 August, 1840, and which now contains an important collection of pictures, many by Turner and Van Dyck.

Bognor has enjoyed immense popularity as a seaside resort. It became known as Bognor Regis, following royal patronage. A legend, which I hope to be true, records the last words King George V was heard to utter: 'Bugger Bognor!' There is a Sussex proverb which says: 'While one half of Chichester goes to sleep, the other half goes on tiptoe for fear of waking 'em up.' Chichester merits a visit, not just for its 11th-century cathedral, and its Roman amphitheatre, uncovered in 1935, but for the Festival Theatre, opened under the direction of Sir Laurence Olivier, in 1962. Here, it may be said, were sown the seeds of the National Theatre, and Chichester was an arresting modern example of 'theatre-in-the-round'.

The next county on this coastal route is Hampshire, which also includes the Isle of Wight. Portsmouth contributes vivid reminders of British naval history. 'There's the *Ark Royal*,' exclaimed one of the passengers crowding the decks of our Brittany Ferry as it made its way cautiously into Portsmouth Harbour. All around were grey hulls of modern naval vessels, some making ready to put to sea. They are the warships of our own day, but at Portsmouth the visitor can also see, from the navy of Henry VIII, the *Mary Rose*, which sank in 1545 and was brought to the surface in 1982. I can still recall the excitement we felt watching the live television pictures of the first sight of that wooden hull rising out of the waters again after more than four hundred years of briny immersion. Nelson's flagship at the Battle of Trafalgar in 1805, the *Victory*, and HMS *Warrior*, an 'ironclad' from 1860, are there, too.

In 1958, before jumbo jets had displaced the great ocean liners, and when transatlantic voyages were more common than in these days of rapid air transit, we embarked on the *Queen Mary* at Southampton, bound for New York. I have crossed the Atlantic many times since then, but never in such leisured and agreeable fashion as we experienced on board the Cunard vessel. Those days are gone for ever, the days of which Rudyard Kipling wrote:

> Yes, weekly from Southampton
> Great steamers, white and gold,
> Go rolling down to Rio ...

I was in Bournemouth in the summer of 1952, with the Marlowe Dramatic Society of Cambridge University. We were presenting Shakespeare's *Romeo and Juliet* in the Palace Court Theatre, with a cast including several people who went on to make names for themselves in the professional theatre — Peter Hall, John Barton, Tony Church, Roderick Cook. The date, 1952, is important in the context of the story I am about to tell. It happened on a Wednesday afternoon: we were giving a matinee performance on one of the hottest days of the year and the audience, understandably, was distinctly thin. Most of Bournemouth's holidaymakers preferred the beach to the Bard on such a day. A trio of elderly ladies in the orchestra pit valiantly made their way through an arrangement of Tchaikovsky's *Romeo and Juliet*, and then the curtain rose. The opening scene of the play, as most of my readers will recall, is the occasion of a quarrel between supporters of the two warring families in Verona, the Montagues and the Capulets. On their deadly enmity, of course, hangs the issue of the drama. I had been entrusted with the minor role of Sampson, a servant in the house of Capulet, who actually provokes the squabble by biting his thumb at two servingmen of the house of Montague. Biting the thumb, I should explain, was considered an extremely rude and offensive gesture in Elizabethan times. Anyway, I thought I did rather well, in a most insulting manner. Be that as it may have been, the result is a violent brawl, into which are drawn citizens of both parties, then Benvolio and Tybalt (enacted by Peter Hall), Old Capulet and Old Montague, with their wives and, finally, to quell the riot, Prince

Escalus with his train.

Well, on the particular Wednesday afternoon of which I speak, the opening scuffle became more than usually animated; in fact, you could say that it began to get out of hand. A charitable interpretation would ascribe such disorder and indiscipline to a keen desire on the part of the performers to gain the interest of what was a small and obviously lethargic audience. Whatever the cause, the effect was certainly dramatic. One of the female citizens (should we call her a citizeness?) was played by a young lady whose name was Rosa. She was to become a veritable damsel in distress for, as the commotion grew, a hand reached out and seized her. Unhappily, the owner of the hand lost his balance and, in an effort to maintain his equilibrium, he clung desperately to the fabric of Rosa's dress. There was a sort of tearing noise and, quite abruptly, the dress parted company with its owner. For a brief instant, on a summer's afternoon in Bournemouth in 1952, Rosa stood stark naked before an audience who suddenly began to take genuine interest in the proceedings.

I know not how, but word spread around town like wildfire, and long before the curtain was due to rise on the evening's performance, a considerable queue had formed, largely composed, I suspect, of people who had never before in their lives thought of going to see a play by Shakespeare. Of course, they were doomed to disappointment: the spectacular, but unrehearsed happening of the afternoon was not repeated. As I say, it was in 1952, and that sort of thing just did not occur in the theatre — at least, not during the course of a Shakespearean tragedy. But we shall remember Bournemouth, and I like to think that perhaps a few of Bournemouth's theatregoing public will remember us.

Dorset is among the most attractive of English counties, on account of its varied coastline and the rural charms to be found inland. Thomas Hardy, the poet and novelist, author of the *Wessex Tales*, *Tess of the d'Urbervilles* and *The Mayor of Casterbridge*, was born in Higher Bockhampton, Dorset, on 2 June, 1840. We sailed from Poole Harbour recently on board a vessel of British Channel Island Ferries, bound for Jersey. It is a spectacular departure, with sight of Brownsea Island, where Robert Baden-Powell, hero of Mafeking, put into practice the principles of scouting for boys; then, clearing the harbour, the ship passes Studland Bay, The Foreland, Swanage Bay, Peveril Point and Durlston Head, as grand a show as any photographer could wish. At Lulworth Cove begins one of the most picturesque and dramatic stretches of coastline in England: Durdle Door, Weymouth, where ferries and hydrofoils leave for France and the Channel Islands, Portland Bill, and then the singular spectacle of Chesil Beach, a deposit of shingle some 200 yards in width, and 16 miles long. Lyme Regis is perhaps best known today as the location for the film of *The French Lieutenant's Woman*, but it has a longer history than that. On its curving breakwater, the Cobb, the Duke of Monmouth landed in 1685, to mount a rebellion against the Catholic King James II.

Monmouth's revolt was short-lived, however, for he was defeated at Sedgemoor, 5 miles from Bridgwater in Somerset, in July of the same year, and taken to London, there to be executed on Tower Hill.

A little way on, into the county of Devonshire, begins what is known as the English Riviera: Dawlish, Torquay (where my parents spent their honeymoon more than half a century ago), Paignton and Brixham, where William of Orange landed in 1688, and where Henry Francis Lyte was a minister for 25 years, during which time he wrote one of the most famous of all hymns:

> Abide with me; fast falls the eventide;
> The darkness deepens; Lord, with me abide;
> When other helpers fail, and comforts flee,
> Help of the helpless, O, abide with me.

And so to Plymouth, the famous old seaport of Devon, standing between the estuaries of the Plym and the Tamar. There it was, on 19 July 1588, that the English fleet, under the command of Lord Howard of Effingham, put to sea against the Spanish Armada of Philip II. There, too, if we are to trust in legend, Sir Francis Drake played bowls on Plymouth Hoe as the enemy ships approached English shores. The legend lives on:

> Drake he's in his hammock till the great Armadas come

wrote Sir Henry Newbolt;

> Slung atween the round shot, listenin' for the drum,
> An' dreamin' arl the time o' Plymouth Hoe.

As modern seafarers, enjoying much more comfortable and reliable journeys than the sailors in days of old, we make frequent use of Brittany Ferries for the crossing to Roscoff, in Brittany. The same company also has a service from Plymouth to Santander in the north of Spain, a peaceful voyage and a warm welcome at each end, four centuries after the Armada.

London

London, thou art the flower of cities all.

Thus wrote the Scottish poet, William Dunbar, in the early part of the 16th century. Times change, and opinions shift: Mr Woodhouse, in Jane Austen's *Emma*, pronounced thus: 'Nobody is healthy in London, nobody can be.' And for Shelley,

Hell is a city much like London
A populous and smoky city.

Today London, like cities the world over, has become a victim of the internal combustion engine. Urban pollution, with all its concomitant dangers, inconvenience and unpleasantness, is something that city-dwellers are still trying to come to terms with, in the absence of any obvious and immediate solution.

For much of my youth, I was convinced that Piccadilly Circus was the hub of the universe, the centre around which everything revolved. I remember well joining the huge crowds that gathered there in 1945 to celebrate the end of the War. The streets of London, for all I knew, could well have been paved with gold; certainly, there was something of magic about the great stores: Harrods, Gamages, Liberty, and those inseparable pairs, Derry and Tom, Bourne and Hollingsworth, Swan and Edgar, Fortnum and Mason, Dickens and Jones, Waring and Gillow, Marks and Spencer. The last time I was there, I was made aware of how times have moved on. In the concourse of Piccadilly Circus underground station, there is a shop selling ties: it is called 'Get Knotted'.

The Piccadilly Line of the London Underground now reaches as far as Heathrow, London's principal airport, once (and not so very long ago), a village surrounded by farmland. Arriving and departing passengers may still catch a glimpse through the windows of their aircraft of green fields below them, or the spire of Hounslow Church, but journeys to and from the airport can now be accomplished underground, with nothing but the dark walls of tunnels for scenery. At Osterley Park, a National Trust property not far from Heathrow, there are 140 acres of parkland, resplendent with magnificent cedars of Lebanon. The mansion, much of it the work of Robert Adam, has real style and elegance, forming an unexpected oasis of calm amid the turmoil of London's western suburbs.

The City of London, that square mile which contains the Bank of England and numerous other institutions dedicated to matters financial, has some of the most fascinating churches in the realm, enough to satisfy the curiosity of the most ardent students of ecclesiastical architecture. Supreme among them all is Wren's great creation, St Paul's, which stands at the top of Ludgate Hill. This is the Londoners' church, whereas Westminster Abbey belongs to the nation. Monarchs are crowned in state at the Abbey, but the funeral service for the greatest Englishman of our time, Sir Winston Churchill, was held at St Paul's.

Passing St Paul's just the other day, I was delighted to come upon a street which had escaped my notice on previous occasions: it bore the name, Ave Maria Lane. St Paul's stands proudly at the top of Ludgate Hill, looking down Fleet Street, once the street of newspapers, most of which have now moved away. A few minutes' walk away, set back from the bustle of Fleet Street, St Bride's is one of the many appealing churches in London, each with its own parochial function, its own notable annals, its own distinctive architecture.

England's capital has been celebrated through the ages, in prose and verse, by many writers. Much has been said, and written, of Chaucer's London, Shakespeare's London, Dickens's London. To the Romans, the town on the Thames was Londinium; to others, Lud's Town. Today, the Museum of London, at the Barbican, offers a comprehensive and enthralling exposition of London's past. This is something not to be missed by anyone interested in the tale of a great city.

London was not always a single place, a complete entity. Stow's *Survey of London*, published in 1598, described the twenty-six wards within and without the wall. Indeed, what we know today as Greater London contains two cities, the City of London and the City of Westminster, together with a number of boroughs, many of which have swallowed up individual villages. A spirited fantasy by G K Chesterton, *The Napoleon of Notting Hill*, imagines the revival of the separate identities of the boroughs: a Charter of the Cities renews local pride and evokes again the potent magic of place-names: Barons Court, Ravenscourt, Hammersmith, Kensington, Notting Hill, Bayswater. It is a highly entertaining tale and, at the same time, a fable for our own age, an elegaic recalling of a London long gone, of a London which, perhaps, only existed in the imagination of two childlike figures of Chesterton's story, Auberon Quin and Adam Wayne.

'Earth has not anything to show more fair,' wrote Wordsworth of the view from Westminster Bridge in 1807. A contrary impression is conveyed by Dickens at the opening of his great novel, *Bleak House*: 'London. Michaelmas Term lately over, and the Lord Chancellor sitting in Lincoln's Inn Hall. Implacable November weather ... Fog everywhere. Fog up the river, where it flows among green aits and meadows; fog down the river, where it rolls defiled among the tiers of shipping, and the waterside pollutions of a great (and dirty) city. Fog on the Essex marshes, fog on the Kentish heights.'

London has many faces, some smiling, others less amiable. I first came to know it in wartime: that was London of the blackout, the Blitz, bombing and barrage-balloons. The city suffered much devastation from Goering's *Luftwaffe*; not since the Great Fire of London broke out in Pudding Lane on the night of 2nd September 1666, had the city been exposed to such threat of extinction. Samuel Pepys, in his diary, records that earlier disaster when he 'walked to the Tower and there got up on one of the high places, and there I did see the houses at that end of the bridge all on fire, and an infinite great fire on this and the other side the end of the bridge. The Lieutenant of the Tower tells me that it begun this morning in the King's baker's house in Pudding Lane, and that it hath burned down St Magnes Church and most part of Fishstreete already. We saw the fire as one entire arch of above a mile long, a most horrid malicious bloody flame. It made me weep to see it. The churches, houses, and all on fire and flaming at once, and a horrid noise the flames made, and the cracking houses at their ruin.'

This was the Great Fire of London, which destroyed much of the city Shakespeare and Chaucer would have known. A memorial to this terrible chapter in London's history, the Monument, affords to those energetic enough to ascend steps to the top, a panoramic view of the area which Pepys, more than three centuries ago, saw engulfed in flames.

> 'But Lord, what a sad sight it was by moonlight to see the whole City almost on fire — that you might see it plain at Woolwich, as if you were by it.'

Modern London is a cosmopolitan city. Today, in its streets, you can hear a fascinating repertoire of languages. Soho, just a step from Piccadilly Circus, contains elements both romantic and seedy. For many years, it boasted a large Italian population: Signor Parmigiani, now gone from Old Compton Street, used to stock the best gorgonzola outside Italy; Del Monico, alas no more, had a formidable array of wines, among which was one of amazing cheapness and uncertain origin, which we used to refer to unkindly as 'plasma'. Soho has always been famous for its enormous variety of eating establishments, and it jauntily maintains that reputation to this day. French and Italian food have always been easily available there, but now Soho can honestly claim to present a complete international cuisine. I have enjoyed many an excellent Indian meal there in my time, and a walk along Gerrard Street these days will reveal a proliferation of Chinese shops and restaurants.

There is another side to Soho, in the shape of purveyors of pornography, strip-clubs and sex-shops, apparently a booming industry in recent years. Much amusement could be derived from perusal of cards displayed in the windows of newsagents, offering a range of mysterious services and commodities: 'Fine Italian chest for hire, with interesting features'; 'Greek typewriter available with unusual keys'; 'French lessons given by expert in techniques'; ubiquitous advertisements for models and, with a touch of humour, a note which read simply: *Honi soit qui mal y pense*, followed by a Gerrard telephone number. I like the story of a very respectable schoolteacher, a maiden lady resident in Soho who, on retirement, decided that she would like to continue her career a little longer by giving private lessons in her home. So she put an advertisement in the local shop window, announcing that she was available to give French lessons, French being her subject. She was quite unable to follow the drift of the strange replies elicited by her innocent promulgation. There is a generous measure of humour in such misunderstandings. Nowadays, the writing on the walls seems not to contain quite as many rude words as was previously the case. One of many examples of odd pieces of graffiti to be found in Soho is this, which I came across in a public lavatory: 'I used to be very indecisive, but now I'm not so sure.'

Among the more entertaining activities on show in London's streets are the various markets. Petticoat Lane, Portobello Road, Berwick Market are all famous attractions; then, there is a Sunday morning flower market at Columbia Road in Shoreditch. The sights, the sounds and even the odours of London's streets have a peculiar potency, a capacity to evoke a whole range of sensations. The smell of fish has gone from Billingsgate, and Covent Garden no longer accommodates the fruit and vegetable market, which has moved to Nine Elms, Battersea. But Covent Garden still has many attractions, having undergone something of a transformation in recent years. The London Transport Museum and the Theatre Museum are both rewarding and, for music-lovers, there is the Royal Opera House, one of the world's most famous houses, known to the regulars simply as 'The Garden'.

London's parks and gardens are justly admired. Regent's Park is my favourite among all of London's great open spaces. To begin with, it has an open-air theatre where, in my youth, I saw Robert Atkins in Shakespeare. Then, there is the London Zoo, one of the capital's chief attractions for a boy brought up in a northern town where such things were unheard of. There is a tale related to me by a former colleague, who was in the park to gather effects for a recording of *The Wind in the Willows*. While leaning over the balustrade of one of the bridges that grace the park, dangling a microphone on the end of its lead to capture the noise of ducks on the water, he was approached by a park-keeper who, with the courtesy that used to belong to uniformed officials in England, enquired what he might be doing. My friend explained that he was recording the sound of ducks quacking. The park-keeper nodded sympathetically. 'I thought it was something like that, sir,' he said. 'But the lady over there,' and he pointed to someone on a park bench a little way off, a person who looked very like the grandmother of the famous cartoons by Giles; 'she told me you were fishing by electricity.'

Not only the parks, but many a private home attracts the attention of passers-by to its floral displays. Close by Holland Park tube station where, as a commuter from Buckinghamshire, I used to park my car in years gone by, there was in springtime a gorgeous magnolia in front of someone's house. Its season of full flowering was brief, but its beauty remains an ineffaceable memory.

London is a great place, too, for window-visiting, dropping in, unseen and unexpected, on someone else's daily routine. There is an admirable tendency, on the part of people who occupy rooms on upper floors of buildings, not to draw their curtains in the evening, thus giving free rein to the peeping Toms of this world, among which number I am one.

A bus-ride along Holland Park Avenue of a winter's evening had me peering into lighted windows, and catching fleeting glimpses of other lives going on in cozy rooms. It was like a curtain being drawn aside for an instant on a scene from a play, a drama whose beginning and end will remain for ever unknown to me. Below, in the streets bulging with rush-hour traffic, homeward-bound, quarrelsome motorists traded insults with each other, and pedestrians risked injury or death with apparent nonchalance. The English are noted for their eccentricity, it is said. 'Mad dogs and Englishmen / Go out in the midday sun', wrote Noel Coward, and was right. On a bleak day in December, I saw people sitting aloft on the upper deck of an open-top bus, careless of the chill airs.

Not to be ignored, of course, is London's river, the Thames, a watery thoroughfare rich in historical reminders and architectural delights, which are best glimpsed from the water, on pleasure boats that ply in summer months downstream to Greenwich, the *Cutty Sark* and the Maritime Museum, and upstream to Hampton Court, Cardinal Wolsey's grand palace. HMS *Discovery*, Captain Scott's vessel, is moored along the Embankment by Temple Station; the schooner *Kathleen and May* can be seen near Southwark Cathedral, and opposite the Tower of London HMS *Belfast*, a retired cruiser of the Royal Navy.

Old customs die hard, and many a ritual observance adds an extra dimension to life in this city with such long and dramatic history. Some sights are familiar enough: the Chelsea Flower Show, the changing of the guard at Buckingham Palace, the Lord Mayor's Show, the state opening of Parliament and a host of others, a recent and notable addition being the London Marathon. On 30 January 1649, 'the man Charles Stuart', as he was named in the warrant issued by the regicides, was brought from the Tower of London to Whitehall, for decapitation by the 'bright axe'. The anniversary of the execution of King Charles I is marked every year; in 1990, members of the English Civil War Society walked along the same route that the king took to the scaffold, from St James' Palace to the Banqueting House in Whitehall, where a short service was held in commemoration.

In 1955, I went to work in the King's Cross district of London, as a schoolteacher. In 1987, we moved house to the north of England, 250 miles from the metropolis. During the intervening 32 years, most of my time was spent in London, pursuing a variety of occupations, making friends in many circles, and engaging in such diverse activities as boating on the Serpentine, listening to music in concert-halls, lazing in a deckchair in a park with the pleasing sound of a brass band borne on the summer air, joining thousands of other commuters in the daily struggle to and from the office, enjoying treasures on display at the British Museum, the National Gallery, the Tate Gallery and elsewhere, drinking in London pubs, eating at restaurants, running a record society, taking indoor golf lessons in the lunch-hour at a large department store, cursing the inefficiency of the railways and the unreliability of bus services, sitting on committees, assuming chairmanship of the Apollo Society, among whose founders was Peggy Ashcroft, watching Margot Fonteyn dance and hearing Kirsten Flagstad sing at Covent Garden, seeing Ralph Richardson, John Gielgud and Laurence Olivier on stage, going to the cinema, visiting London's marvellous churches, contemplating the Thames and its traffic, working, playing, sightseeing, idling — half a lifetime of memories.

Nowadays, I am but an occasional visitor to the streets of London. Just recently, I went to lunchtime service again at St Giles-in-the-Fields, on the very day that the rector, my old friend Gordon Taylor, was celebrating his 75th birthday. Then over the road to lunch at the Kantara Taverna, at the top of Shaftesbury Avenue, where I had the pleasure and privilege, over the years, of entertaining Vivien Leigh, Peggy Ashcroft, Donald Wolfit, C Day Lewis, Sylvia Plath, Stevie Smith and so many others. *O memoria praeteritorum bonorum!* No longer do I belong to that restless, busy, metropolitan life. When the melancholy fit comes on, I find myself in tune with a sentiment registered by Samuel Rogers in the last century:

> To anyone who has reached a very advanced age, a walk through the streets of London is like a walk in a cemetery. How many houses do I pass, now inhabited by strangers, in which I used to spend such happy hours with those who have long been dead and gone.

Such thoughts are for the dying year, when leaves have fallen from the trees, but this is not the note on which to end a chapter on Britain's capital city. Spring offers brighter notions, well caught by Alfred Noyes in that excellent piece of advice:

> Go down to Kew in lilac-time (it isn't far from London) ...

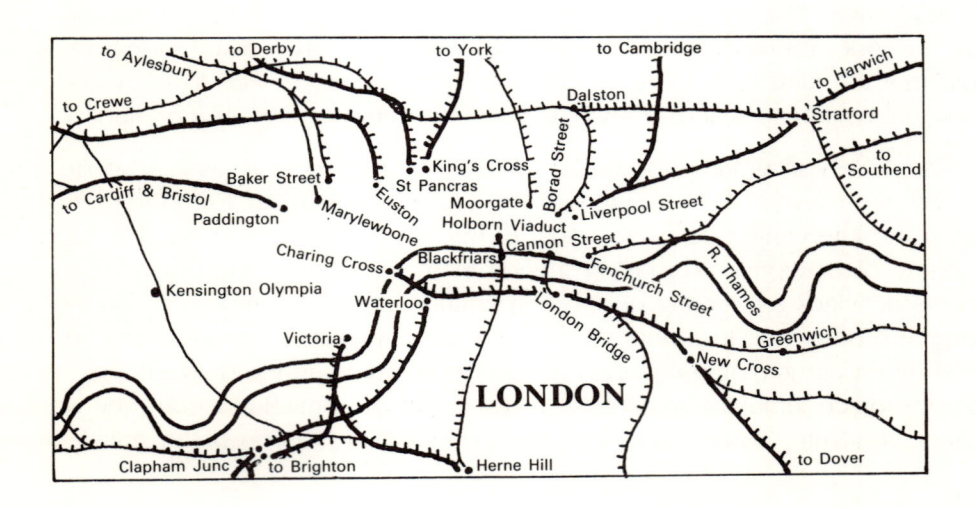

The Thames Valley

Sweet Thames, run softly, till I end my Song.

Spring and autumn are the seasons for visiting the Thames Valley, although winter in grudging benevolence sometimes extends the favour of crisp, clear, sunlit days, when walking in the Chilterns proves one of the most delightful experiences imaginable. For 22 years, we lived in Wooburn Green, in the Wye Valley (hence the name Wycombe), not far from the Thames at Bourne End.

A few miles to the southeast of Wooburn, in the direction of Slough, is a large expanse of woodland, property of the Corporation of the City of London. In late October and early November, the visitor can see Burnham Beeches ablaze with colour, a wonderland of rich and varied hues, a sight which never tires the eye, a walker's and photographer's paradise.

Perhaps it is abundance of beechwoods in that part of the county, but there must be something in the air conducive to long life. That thought occurs to me every time I revisit Wooburn Green, and pay a call on Mary Hay, still hale and hearty in her 93rd year, and ready with a caustic remark about recent developments in the village. Daughter of a clergyman and widow of a bishop, Mary has strong feelings about some of the things that go on in church services these days. 'I don't like all this embracing. It's all too much. The vicar came to see me this morning, and he embraced me three times. You know, what we need is an epidemic: that would put a stop to all this embracing!' Laudably forthright sentiments from an outspoken lady!

Mary Hay used to live in a house that looks across the village green to where Douglas Young runs his newsagent's shop, just by the war memorial. The business name was S C Young and Son: Douglas, being the son in question, saw fit to carry on the family tradition. 'My father came here from Wycombe in 1914, when it was just a lock-up barber's shop. He used to cycle down, and there were flints in the roads in those days, so he would get a few punctures. He used to have a bed at the Old Western, the pub over the road — no, you wouldn't remember that.'

A casual visitor to the little shop would never guess the age of the man behind the counter, a spry character with a twinkle in his eye, always ready with a jest or a quick riposte. His appearance, his demeanour and his way of life belie his years. The surname, however, is singularly appropriate: Douglas Young was born in 1903, so you do not need a degree in higher mathematics to work out his present age. But it is still hard to credit, and just occasionally I wonder whether this is Douglas Young pulling his customers' legs yet again.

There cannot be many people in Wooburn Green who do not know Doug. For one thing, he always seems to be around: once or twice, perhaps, in a quarter of a century, have I opened the door of his shop and not found him behind the counter. A newsagent is on duty seven days a week; for him, days start early and often end quite late. Doug has never been particularly interested in holidays: the shop is the centre of his life, the place where it all happens. However, he has been known, just occasionally, to take an afternoon off to visit Ascot, and he confesses to having a bob or two on a horse now and again. Hardly a compulsive gambler! Then, of an evening, he is usually to be found having his meal in a local hostelry, or playing a game of dominoes. Where would he go, I wondered, if he really decided to take a holiday? 'Bourne End-on-Thames,' was his immediate reply, accompanied by a characteristic chuckle.

Although Doug has reached an age when most people would consider themselves entitled to an extra hour in bed in the mornings, such a thought does not even enter his head. 'This is what gets me up in the mornings!' he says, indicating the piles of newspapers on the counter. Their volume and variety have increased considerably over the years that Doug has been engaged in handling newsprint. 'In the old days, you could make up a morning delivery, and it would be no thicker than this.' And he holds up finger and thumb, an inch or two apart. 'But now it's magazines, colour supplements on Sundays — and on Saturdays, too!'

His mind goes back to former times. 'What about the *Daily Herald*, the *News Chronicle*, the *Sunday Dispatch*, and all the others?' He intones the roll of the departed like the chaplain at a memorial service.

Over the years, I have purchased all manner of items besides newspapers at Doug's miniature emporium: eggs, tomato plants, potatoes, torch batteries, fuses, birthday cards, wrapping paper, writing paper, fireworks, chocolates, sweets and, in the days before my reformation, tobacco. He may not stock everything, but he does his best to rise to an emergency.

Part of his secret, I believe, is that he really enjoys what he is doing. Ever happy to chat with a customer, he is eager to exchange local gossip. Then, if there is a question of loose change, Doug is ready with a suggestion: 'I'll toss you for the odd twopence — double or quits.' I have to report that he is almost invariably lucky, with me at any rate, for I have lost far more than ever I have won with this arrangement.

In former days, I used to have my hair cut there; one Christmas Eve, Doug saved me from social embarrassment by rapid shearing of my overgrown locks. But the hairdressing business ceased to operate some years ago. There is, after all, a limit to what even the most active man can crowd into the working day.

For more years than he cares to remember, there have been rumours of road plans which would have swept away his corner shop, the first trading-post encountered by travellers entering Wooburn Green from the south. After so long a time, Doug is unperturbed by such thoughts. He has much better things to occupy his mind. I can see him now, as he looks out for approaching customers, then leans across the counter confidentially with a mischievous gleam in his eye: 'Have you heard this one?' That, I suppose, is one of the things that keeps Douglas Young youthful, the ability to enjoy a joke and a chat with his customers, even in the midst of the busiest day.

Uphill from Wooburn Green, Whitepit Lane leads to the neighbouring village of Flackwell Heath, where dwells another old and dear friend of ours. Amelia Shirley-Quirk has a way with words. Although no longer in the first flush of youth, and despite rheumatic pains, she still displays a sturdy, determined independence. 'I've got all my facilities,' she insists, with a winning twinkle in her eyes indicating a lively sense of humour.

Mrs Shirley-Quirk, known as Granna to her family and friends, arrived in Flackwell Heath back in 1966; her origins and upbringing had been elsewhere. 'I come from the north, from Merseyside. I was born in Wallasey, but in my twenties I moved from there to Liverpool.' She retains clear and vivid memories of that distant time, near the beginning of the century. 'In my young days, the traffic was all on the Mersey, there was no tunnel. My father was assistant manager of the ferries, and he used to arrange the timetables of the boats. There was such a lot of river traffic then: the *Royal Daffodil* and the *Royal Iris* used to run as pleasure boats. All the luggage used to go over the water. It's got quite a history, that river. There was a book by Helen Forrester, called *Tuppence to Cross the Mersey* — it used to be twopence on the ferry boat. You'd get to know all about Liverpool and my younger days from that book, because it's just true to life.'

What brought her all the way to Buckinghamshire in the nineteen-sixties? Well, responsibility for that move really belongs to her son, John, today one of Britain's most distinguished singers, heard on concert platforms and in opera houses throughout the world, and on innumerable recordings. It was his idea, all those years ago, that his mother should come south with him and his young family. 'And that was what brought me down from the north, to look after the two grandchildren while he was abroad. I think it made his life a lot easier.' A photograph of John Shirley-Quirk is displayed prominently in the sitting-room of his mother's little bungalow on Straight Bit in Flackwell Heath; Amelia Shirley-Quirk does not attempt to disguise a mother's pride in her son's achievements over the years, and the reputation he has won for himself. 'I was very proud of him when he first started in the profession, and I still am.' For nearly a quarter of a century, Amelia Shirley-Quirk has been part of the community in Flackwell Heath. As a voluntary exile from the north of England, what are her feelings today? 'I do like living in the village, and I've made a lot of friends, friends who help me to keep going in my old age now.' Are there times still when she hankers to visit the north again, to see old haunts, and revive memories of her youth? Does she miss the life on Merseyside? 'I missed it at first, but I don't want to go back now. I wouldn't know Liverpool today, I think. If I had to go back, it would be to Wallasey, where my mother and father are buried. I don't think Wallasey has changed all that much; but there's nobody alive there I know, neither friend nor relation. There's nobody left: they're all dead. At my age, there aren't many of my contemporaries around; they're not thick on the ground! I used to want to go back, you know, but Flackwell Heath is my home now.'

Too often, people are inclined to view the past through rose-coloured spectacles. I asked Granna if she thought the quality of life really was better in the early days of the century. 'I don't really know whether it was or not. I think we were happier in our day. We were in ignorance of all the dangers around us, bombs and diseases and everything else. But it was hard work: you had to walk everywhere. There were horse-drawn buses, and then the trams started, and that was fine then. But that's a long while ago.' A slow smile spreads across her face at the recollection of times past. 'Mind you,' she continues, 'I do think people have an easier life today. Work is easier, everything is a lot easier for them. Housework is easier, isn't it?'

It would not be gallant of me to reveal the age of this admirable lady and very dear friend, but she has been heard to remark, with justifiable pride: 'I don't do too badly for an octogeranium!' As I said, Amelia Shirley-Quirk has a way with words.

Over the years, we have made many good friends in Buckinghamshire, some of them most distinguished figures in the public eye. Sir John Gielgud lives in impressive surroundings at Wotton Underwood; Dame Wendy Hiller has long been a resident of Beaconsfield; and Phyllis Calvert, a name engraved on the memories of post-war filmgoers, has a charming cottage at Waddesdon, almost within hailing distance of Waddesdon Manor, the 19th-century building of the Rothschilds, created in the style of a French renaissance chateau. All three, John Gielgud, Wendy Hiller and Phyllis Calvert, have graced our dinner table on more than one occasion in the good old days.

Literary and historical associations enrich the Thames Valley everywhere. In 1665, John Milton fled from the plague in London to Chalfont St Giles. There, Milton's Cottage is open between February and October on weekdays, except Tuesdays, and on Sunday afternoons; from November to January, weekends only. William Penn, founder of Pennsylvania, lies with his family in the grounds of the Friends' Meeting House at Jordans. Thomas Gray's 'Elegy' is said to have been inspired by the country churchyard at Stoke Poges. Jerome K. Jerome's *Three Men in a Boat*, published in 1889, records an ostentatious shopping expedition in Marlow. There is sport to be seen on the water here at Marlow Regatta, and just across the river, spanned by an attractive bridge, *The Compleat Angler* recalls in its name that famous treatise on fishing by Izaak Walton. Beaconsfield was the home of Edmund

Burke, of G K Chesterton, who wrote his Father Brown stories there, and of the poet Edmund Waller, who penned that lovely lyric, 'Go, lovely rose', and whose elaborate tomb stands in Beaconsfield churchyard. At Lacey Green is an inn with an odd name, 'The Pink and Lily', where Rupert Brooke used to spend weekends with his friends.

High Wycombe, in days gone by, a pleasant, country town, noted for furniture manufacture, is now a crowded, uncomfortable place, but escape from its urban oppression is swift and easy. To the north, in a pleasant stretch of valley, nestles Hughenden Manor, once the home of statesman and author Benjamin Disraeli. A few miles further on is the village of Speen, a relatively isolated rural retreat when, as an energetic youth-hosteller, I first came to know it forty years ago; it is now enlarged by clusters of neo-Georgian houses, signalling the affluent spread of commuter-land. In the grounds of the Baptist church an impressive stone marks the resting-place of Eric Gill. Stone-carver, engraver, typographer and author, Gill lived down the hill at Piggott's, now a centre for remarkable gatherings of amateur and professional musicians, attending music camp there. I was present at the opening and concluding performances of a memorable enterprise, spread over several years, presenting Wagner's *Ring* in its entirety, with performers easily outnumbering audience. This was music-making at its very best, I thought, as I listened to Siegfried's 'Funeral March' thundering out in the Buckinghamshire evening air.

Cliveden achieved a certain notoriety in the days of Stephen Ward, Christine Keeler and Mandy Rice-Davies. Today, Charles Barry's house is a luxury hotel, but in the grounds are reminders of earlier times: a small, grassy dell, once an open-air theatre where, on 1 August 1740, Thomas Arne's masque, *Alfred*, had its first performance, its finale introducing that patriotic number, 'Rule Britannia'. The extensive grounds, and a couple of rooms in the house, are open from March to October.

This enticing region is reasonably well served by bus and train services; the best way to enjoy the varied countryside is on foot, or bicycle. The walker will find a large network of public footpaths criss-crossing the woods and pasturelands. Ordnance Survey 'Landranger' sheets 165 and 175 together cover the area from Amersham to Henley-on-Thames and beyond.

Hotels and bed-and-breakfast accommodation are available in Beaconsfield, Amersham, Burnham, High Wycombe and Marlow, but for stays of a week and more it makes sense to rent a cottage or flat. An excellent booklet, giving full details of costs, facilities and locations, is published by the Thames and Chilterns Tourist Board, 8 Market Place, Abingdon, Oxfordshire OX14 3UD.

One of the advantages of self-catering holiday accommodation is that it provides a convenient retreat when the weather turns sour. Hotels and guesthouses tend, often with great show of politeness, to put guests out on the streets during the day, so that their staff can get on with the necessary business of cleaning and making beds. Reluctantly, we are forced to acknowledge that holidaymakers in Britain should be prepared for unseasonable conditions throughout the year.

Tours of the Thames Valley are organised by Mrs Ann Wheals, Dogwood, Marlow Road, Bourne End, Bucks SL8 5NL, telephone: 06285 23865. Her husband, Brian, is a local historian, and a mine of information about the area. Bourne End has a small, but fairly comprehensive, shopping-parade and there is a choice of restaurants and pubs, offering English, Chinese and Indian food. We have enjoyed meals at the Spade Oak, and at the Last Viceroy.

On the Berkshire side of the Thames, not far from Bourne End, is the self-consciously pretty village of Cookham. 'Bel and the Dragon', in the High Street, is a popular inn which has provided sustenance to many distinguished visitors, including Princess Margaret. They draw a good pint of Young's Special there. Just opposite, on a corner of the High Street, the Stanley Spencer Gallery is housed in a tiny building, formerly a chapel, where the artist attended Sunday school. There is a small, but immensely rewarding collection of Spencer's work, including the large, unfinished canvas, *Christ Preaching at Cookham Regatta*, and in the nearby church hangs a copy of his extraordinary and memorable painting of *The Last Supper*. Spencer was born in Cookham, and spent most of his working life there. Local worthies were not altogether flattered when readily-recognisable likenesses of them appeared in *Christ Comes to Cookham*. Spencer's grave is marked by a simple stone in the churchyard.

Which, rather grotesquely, reminds me of a story recently circulated in that part of the Thames Valley. It concerns a scheme, devised by two villages in the area, to pool their resources and establish jointly a crematorium serving the needs of both communities. Then arose the question of what it should be called: the obvious solution was to incorporate the names of both villages, but this idea was quickly abandoned when it was realised that the sign would read 'The Cookham and Burnham Crematorium'. (Try saying it aloud, if you have missed the point!)

I can promise any traveller to this part of the Thames Valley a range of pleasing distractions which will amply justify the journey. After all, it isn't far from London.

Shakespeare Country

Like Rome, Florence, Venice and Naples, Stratford-upon-Avon is somewhere not to be missed on any account. While it cannot compete with those Italian cities for sheer sumptuous wealth of artistic and architectural treasures, yet, in its own very special way, Stratford-upon-Avon symbolises something of the soul of England. Geographically at the heart of the country, historically the birthplace of the supreme English dramatist and poet, its credentials are impeccable. But it is not for such reasons alone that tourists swarm in large numbers each year to this Warwickshire town on the banks of the River Avon. There is a truly remarkable atmosphere which pervades Stratford and the surrounding countryside, dotted with inviting villages with names like Shottery (where, of course, Anne Hathaway's cottage is to be found), Wilmcote (home of Mary Arden), Charlecote (with its Tudor house and deer park), Hampton Lucy, Alveston (once home of the writer, J B Priestley), Pebworth (home of a famous actor), Aston Cantlow (home of another famous actor and his actress wife) and Tiddington (home of the National Farmers' Union, in a building of quite hideous aspect). Now and again, in idyllic surroundings, one is brought face to face with disillusionment and the 20th century. One day, driving out from Stratford with Shakespearean imagery singing in my head, I was jolted back to grim reality by the sight of a signpost pointing towards the Forest of Arden Industrial Estate. Not quite the same place as that in which Shakespeare's Duke Senior, in *As You Like It*,

> Finds tongues in trees, books in the running brooks,
> Sermons in stones, and good in everything.

When visiting Stratford, we usually contrive to avoid the buzzing, eager tourists by staying at the Charlecote Pheasant, a pleasing establishment just a few miles from Stratford, with a swimming-pool and tennis court, an excellent carvery restaurant and very comfortable beds. Telephone: 0789 840200.

The most famous building in Stratford is the house in Henley Street where, it is believed, William Shakespeare was born on 23 April, 1564. At that time, Stratford was a prosperous country town, with a population of about two thousand people. His father, John Shakespeare, was a glover by trade, and also dealt in timber, wool and barley. In 1556, eight years before the birth of William Shakespeare, his father had bought part of the house at Henley Street and established a business there. It became the home of the Shakespeare family, and in 1575 John Shakespeare acquired the rest of the property, with its two gardens and two orchards, and made it into a residence and shop combined. Today, carefully restored to its former state, the interior of the house, with its exposed beams and furnishings in the style of the period, probably appears very much as it would have done in Elizabethan times, more than four centuries ago.

38 ENGLAND

William Shakespeare was baptised at Holy Trinity Church, by the banks of the Avon. During that year, 1564, an outbreak of the plague, lasting for six months, killed almost a sixth of the town's population. In the parish register, three crosses mark the entry in Latin, registering his baptism as *Guglielmus filius Johannes Shakespeare*: William, son of John Shakespeare. The date of the entry, 26 April, 1564, supports the traditional theory that Shakespeare was born on St George's Day, April 23rd. Then was a time of high infant mortality, and children were baptised as soon as possible after birth, in this case, the Sunday following. William Shakespeare would have had two godmothers and a godfather, and the ceremony would have been performed at the same baptismal font which stands today in Holy Trinity Church.

John Shakespeare was a man of some standing in Stratford, and it is reasonable to assume that his son would have been educated at the town's Grammar School. Boys were usually admitted at the age of seven, and to gain admission a pupil had to demonstrate the ability to read and write in English, as well as the capacity to learn Latin. Hours were long for the boy of Shakespeare's day, 'creeping like snail unwillingly to school' at a quarter to six on summer mornings, and an hour later in the darker days of winter. With a break for lunch, school would continue until five in the afternoon, concentrating on the study of Latin rhetoric, some history and, of course, the Bible. One of the classrooms Shakespeare would have known is still in use today.

A mile outside Stratford is the village of Shottery, where stands a picturesque thatched cottage which belonged to the Hathaways, and remained in the possession of the family's descendants until 1892. Now it is known to everyone as Anne Hathaway's Cottage. Anne was married to William Shakespeare at Worcester on 28 November, 1582, when she was 26, and Shakespeare only 18. There were three children of the marriage: Susanna, born in May, 1583, and the twins, Hamnet and Judith, born in 1585. The twelve-roomed cottage contains much of the original furniture, and the garden at the front, and orchard to the side, make of the whole a delightful scene.

Four miles from Stratford, is the imposing Elizabethan house at Charlecote, which belonged to Sir Thomas Lucy. Queen Elizabeth is said to have visited Charlecote in 1566. For many years there persisted a legend, now thought to be without foundation, that William Shakespeare was caught poaching deer and rabbits in the park and, so the story goes, was whipped and imprisoned for the offence. There is no historical evidence to support this tale, but it is known that Shakespeare left Stratford to seek his fortune elsewhere.

By 1597, his work in the theatre had brought him an income sufficient to enable the purchase of one of the grandest houses in Stratford, New Place, and when Shakespeare returned to Stratford in about 1611, he took up residence there. New

Place had been built by Sir Hugh Clopton at the end of the 15th century, and it was demolished at some time around 1700. A later building now stands on the same site, just opposite the Gild Chapel, but some of the foundations of the old house can be seen in the garden.

Under the terms of his will, New Place and the other properties owned by Shakespeare in Stratford and in London went to his daughter, Susanna. His wife, Anne, was left the 'second-best bed' but, in fact, she was well provided for in other ways.

On April 23rd, 1616, William Shakespeare died, and was buried in the chancel of Holy Trinity Church. Nobody can identify the author of the lines which appear on his tombstone:

> Good friend, for Jesus sake forbear
> To dig the dust enclosed here.
> Blest be the man that spares these stones
> And curst be he that moves my bones.

Their purpose, however, is quite plain: to prevent a new grave being dug later in the same place, a not uncommon practice in those days.

> He was not of an age, but for all time!

Thus wrote his near-contemporary, Ben Jonson, author of *Volpone*, *The Alchemist*, *Bartholomew Fair* and many other plays and poems. Jonson it was who found an apt phrase by which to salute the greatest of English authors, when he addressed him as 'Sweet Swan of Avon'. Shakespeare's plays take in many localities, and touch different periods of history. He himself chose to spend his last years in his birthplace, the Warwickshire town of Stratford-upon-Avon, where he died at the age of 52. Here was his journey's end.

I first visited Stratford more than forty years ago, to see Godfrey Tearle as Othello and Macbeth, and I have been under its spell ever since. Hardly a year goes by without our spending at least a few days there, since we find quite irresistible that harmonious combination of an enchanting town (occasionally overrun by tourists), quiet rural retreats in the neighbourhood and theatrical fare of exceptional quality and range, provided by the Royal Shakespeare Company.

This last is perhaps the most compelling item on the agenda. There, in the best place in the world for attending performances of Shakespeare's works, I have seen, over the years, such celebrated performers as Laurence Olivier, Vivien Leigh, Ralph Richardson, John Gielgud, Peggy Ashcroft, Margaret Leighton, Michael Redgrave, Michael Hordern, Derek Jacobi, Jeremy Irons, Ben Kingsley, Donald Sinden, Judi Dench, Glenda Jackson and many more. In addition to the Royal Shakespeare Theatre, the main house, there is now a smaller building, the Swan, where plays by Shakespeare's contemporaries are presented in what can truthfully be described as the ideal setting. The Memorial Gallery at the Royal Shakespeare Theatre has an enthralling display of paintings on Shakespearean subjects: imaginative representations of scenes from the plays, and portraits of notable Shakespearean actors of many generations.

Within easy reach of Stratford, for a day's excursion, are many arresting sights: the castles at Warwick and Kenilworth; the cathedrals of Gloucester, Coventry and Worcester; the abbey at Tewkesbury; the University of Oxford, 'that sweet City with her dreaming spires'; the orchards around Evesham where, in their season, ripe fruits fall in profusion from the trees; the watershed between Severn and Thames at Edge Hill where, in 1642, was fought the first important battle of the Civil War; the haunting atmosphere of the ancient Rollright Stones, a great circle of seventy stones, a group known as the Whispering Knights, once a burial chamber, and the solitary King Stone; and Birmingham, where many roads meet, motorways from north, south, east and west. Birmingham, England's second city, has two notable art galleries: the Barber Institute of Fine Arts, which is part of the University of Birmingham, but normally open to the public; and the City Museum and Art Gallery in Chamberlain Square. Both are important and extensive collections.

Just recently, it was announced that plans are afoot to construct the world's tallest free-standing building near Dudley, in the West Midlands. The proposal is to erect a 2,000-foot tower, higher even than Toronto's CN Tower at 1,851 feet. The report goes on to say that this lofty edifice 'will house a nightclub, a prestigious revolving restaurant and an observation deck which will offer unmatched views across the heart of England'. There is a suggestion of jocularity in the proposed name, the Merry Hill Tower.

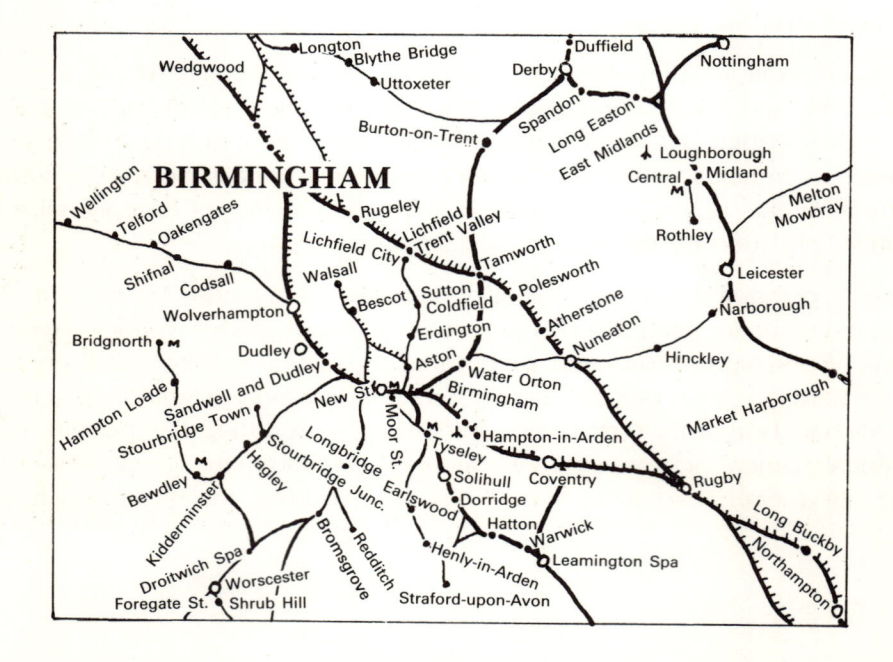

The white cliffs of Dover

Rochester Castle, Kent

The sea-front at Brighton

View from Devil's Dyke, Sussex

Morris dancers at Wooburn Green

Winter in Buckinghamshire

Burnham Beeches in autumn

Cookham, Berkshire

Thatched cottages near Stratford-upon-Avon

King's College, Cambridge

The North York Moors

Whitby Abbey, North Yorkshire

Wensleydale, North Yorkshire

Stonegrave, Yorkshire home of Sir Herbert Read

Dry-stone walls in the north of England

Windermere in the Lake District

The West Country

England's west country, which folk say begins somewhere in Oxfordshire, is a region of golden ripeness, a quality reflected in the honeyed stone of the buildings, the heady aroma of cider apples, the soft, slow speech of the inhabitants, and the appealingly lush countryside.

I spent almost two years of my life, during service with the Royal Air Force, at a place rejoicing in the name of Middle Wallop. Its near neighbours are Nether Wallop and Over Wallop, and a few miles to the south-east is Winchester, with the longest cathedral in England, while at a similar distance to the south-west lies Salisbury, its cathedral spire the tallest in England. Here, one is really well on the way to the west country.

> Clunton and Clunbury,
> Clungunford and Clun,
> Are the quietest places
> Under the sun.

So runs an old local saying, and the poet A E Housman borrowed the words to serve as an epigraph to one of his poems in *A Shropshire Lad*. These are among the most poignantly evocative verses, calling to mind the landscape and character of the border county of Shropshire. Years ago, the celebrated baritone John Shirley-Quirk and I made an arrangement of *A Shropshire Lad* which presented some of the poems in spoken form, others in musical settings by Butterworth, Ireland, Somervell and Moeran. It was something of a connoisseurs' programme, which we performed in various parts of the country. Best remembered is the performance we gave in Ludlow, at the very heart of the territory of which Housman wrote.

> Leave your home behind you,
> Your friends by field and town:
> Oh, town and field will mind you
> Till Ludlow tower is down.

The words had a very particular and potent poignancy when heard in Ludlow Church itself.

Cheltenham is an attractive town, noted for its racecourse, and centres of learning: Cheltenham College, founded in 1841, and Cheltenham Ladies' College, 1853. The encyclopedia records that it is 'favoured by retired civil servants and army officers', but omits mention of the annual festivals, one of music, the other of literature. It was at this latter that I had the rare privilege of sharing the platform with a writer who has been described as the greatest living English novelist, Sir William Golding, winner of the Nobel Prize for Literature in 1983.

Our recital of poetry and prose was due to take place on a Sunday evening, and that same morning Golding and I, in the company of our wives, drove to nearby Gloucester Cathedral, to view the tomb of King Edward II. Below the cathedral cloisters is the Undercroft Restaurant, where we decided to have lunch. On our way out, I drew my companion's attention to a poster, advertising the Cheltenham Festival of Literature, and giving a list of distinguished authors due to appear. The name at the head of the list was that of Sir William Golding.

'Fame at last!' he announced boisterously, to nobody in particular. A gentleman passing by came to a sudden halt.

'Surely, sir,' he said, 'you have been famous for centuries.'

Receiving no reply to this observation, the gentleman continued on his way. After a lengthy pause, Golding turned to me with an expression signifying mingled dismay and bewilderment: 'How old does he think I am?'

Between the Severn and the Wye, with Wales on its northern border, the Royal Forest of Dean offers a host of attractions, both natural and man-made. Walks include the Severn Way, part of Offa's Dyke Path and the Wye Valley Walk. Industrial activities of an earlier age, iron, steel and coal, have left their mark, and the Heritage Centre at Soudley, Cinderford, provides a useful introduction to the whole area.

At Winkleigh, in Devon, Sam Inch's establishment makes the best cider in Europe. I know this to be true because, on my first visit there, many years ago, old Mr Inch himself told me so. Mind you, I have to admit that this was after he had invited us to taste the various types of cider on offer: sweet, dry, medium, sweet scrumpy, dry scrumpy. And after we had worked our way though those, Mr Inch cunningly suggested that we should test them in different combinations: sweet with dry, medium with dry scrumpy, sweet and dry scrumpy mixed, sweet and medium mixed, then all mixed together. It was when we had exhausted every possible combination that Mr Inch claimed it to be the best cider in Europe; at that stage of the proceedings, we were unable and unwilling to disagree. Novices should be very wary of west-country cider!

From Okehampton, the main road runs into Cornwall, and the market town of Launceston, on the River Kensey. Here, I used to visit Charles Causley, the well-known Cornish poet, and local schoolmaster. Just before Launceston is the village of Lifton. Now, I know not if this small community has any real or substantial claim to fame, but it certainly remains fixed in our memories. Misfortunes, I suppose, are less easily forgettable than happier events; so it was at Lifton, anyway. We stayed there for one night, many years ago, in a hotel whose name need not be revealed here. The establishment had an appearance of modest grandeur, allied to a certain air of cosiness inside, and after a rather agreeable buffet lunch, we were of the opinion that we had chosen a good place to break our journey. However, the bathroom attached to our bedroom provided the opening chapter to an altogether different tale. To begin with, the lavatory seat (all right, toilet seat, if you prefer) became detached from its moorings without any warning, depositing the user on to the floor. The unfortunate victim, struggling to recover both balance and dignity, reached for the towel-rail, in the hope of support. The towel-rail immediately separated from the wall. A sense of insecurity began to assert itself. Later the same evening, returning to the hotel from a concert over the border in Cornwall, we thought that a nightcap would be in order, and made our way to the bar. A burly fellow looked at me rather disdainfully, and then announced that the bar was closed. Now, this was plainly untrue, since people were sitting there, drinking. My first thought was that the burly fellow had mistaken me for some wayfarer, who had just dropped in for refreshment on his way to somewhere else, so I set about disabusing him of this notion. 'No,' I said in the patient tone of voice I sometimes adopt in trying circumstances. 'You don't understand. We are guests at this hotel, and we should like a drink before we retire for the night.' I should, perhaps, explain that residents of a hotel are entitled to order drinks outside licensing hours, whereas non-resident visitors are obliged to 'sup up', as the phrase is, and make preparations for departure when the landlord calls 'Time'. However, in this instance, my residential qualifications availed me nothing. My announcement was greeted with a blank stare, reinforced by the words: 'We're still closed, whoever you are.' As I may have mentioned, the speaker was a burly fellow, otherwise I might well have taken matters into my own hands and drawn a glass of ale myself. On this occasion, I simply turned on my heel with a curt 'Very well', and stalked out in what I hope was a manner conveying both dignity and lofty reproach. All I can say is, that I shall not spend a night at that hotel again.

Cornwall can convey to the traveller from other parts of England the unaccountable sensation of being abroad, of finding oneself among people who speak the English language, with a distinctly regional burr, but who evince fierce pride in their own locality, and thereby give the impression that either they or we are foreigners. Perhaps the legends of Cornwall are in part responsible: some say that King Arthur was born at Tintagel, where Merlin's Cave can be found on the seashore. I have to admit that, on our first visit there, almost thirty years ago, my hopes of rediscovering the substance of the Arthurian legends were dashed by the unexpected sight of a banner across the street suggesting that we should come and have a cup of tea at King Arthur's Café. This is not the stuff of which myths are made, I mused sadly. Present-day Camelford, as its name implies, situated at the crossing of the River Camel, may be where once stood 'many-tower'd Camelot', though there are other towns which claim to have been the seat of Arthur's court, among them Caerleon and Winchester. But it does no harm to dream, and to recall the words of Sir Thomas Malory from *Le Morte d'Arthur*: 'Yet some men say in many parts of England that King Arthur is not dead, but had by the will of our Lord Jesu into another place; and men say that he shall come again, and he shall win the holy cross. I will not say it shall be so, but rather I will say, here in this world he changed his life. But many men say that there is written upon his tomb this verse: *Hic jacet Arthurus Rex quondam Rexque futurus.*' (Here lies Arthur, the once and future king.)

A local proverb proclaims there to be more saints in Cornwall than in heaven. St Endelienta, making her last journey, asked to be buried where her ox-cart came to rest. There, on a hilltop 133 metres above sea-level, St Endellion's church contains her shrine, and the carved letters, *Ora pro nobis Sancta Endelienta* (Pray for us, St Endelienta). It was a place much loved and often visited by John Betjeman, sometime Poet Laureate. A tablet in the church records his faithful attendances there, and Betjeman has said that 'there is something strange and exalting about this windy Cornish hill top looking over miles of distant cliffs, that cannot be put into words.'

Every Easter, in that remote part of North Cornwall, 65 miles from Land's End, a noteworthy musical event is held, for the last many years under the musical direction of Richard Hickox, the London Symphony Orchestra's Associate Conductor. Here you will discover an enthusiastic gathering of musicians both professional and amateur, and music-making of a very high standard in an atmosphere of informal sociability. For several years now, my wife and I have been privileged to take part in the Easter Festival. At lunchtime, singers, players and their families meet for pasties and beer at St Kew, which also has a lovely church. After evening programmes, everyone heads for the Cornish Arms, three miles away at Pendoggett.

At St Endellion one evening in 1988, there was a performance of Bach's *St Matthew Passion,* under Richard Hickox. My wife was singing in the chorus, I was merely one of a rapt and appreciative audience. Suddenly, some way into the first part, there came a very odd interruption. The rector, Hugh Fryer (a brave man in the circumstances), strode up the aisle and arrested the conductor's arm as it was about to give a downbeat. The Rector then turned to us and said: 'I'm sorry, but we have to stop. Something very serious has occurred.' My immediate reaction was that we were about to be told of the outbreak of World War Three: nothing less grave would appear to justify such an intervention. But he continued: 'A parked car has blocked the road, making it impossible for a coach to get past, and there is now a long tailback. Would people who have parked in the lane beside the church please move their cars at once?' There followed what, in musical terms, could be called a *lunga pausa*, but eventually a number of drivers returned rather sheepishly to their seats, having done what was required of them, and the performance continued. Needless to say, it was some little time before it was possible to recapture the atmosphere of intense concentration on the part of both performers and audience, but in time the power of music and words asserted themselves again.

On our visits there, we have rented a little flat from Kathy Alford at Penhill, Pendoggett, telephone: 0208 880278. There are numerous properties in the area available for holiday lettings, and lists are published by the Cornwall Tourist Board. This, for us, is quite the best sort of accommodation, since we are able to do our own cooking. Most mornings when we are there, I make my way to Port Isaac, there to espy what the fishing boats have brought in that day. Lobster, crab, sole, plaice and brill are but a few of the good things on sale at the harbour there.

There are fine walks in the district, too. One year, in the very best of spring weather, I took a circular route from New Polzeath and enjoyed stunning seaward views from Pentire and Rumps Point. On other occasions, I have scrambled up Rough Tor, strolled along the beach near Rock, taken the ferry across the Camel estuary to Padstow, and visited the Advent Chapel.

Cornwall has so much to offer, in terms of sea, scenery and history, and it also claims to have just about the mildest climate in mainland Britain. From Marazion, three miles east of Penzance, a causeway connects at low water with St Michael's Mount, once a place of pilgrimage. At Porth Navas, near Falmouth, there is an oyster farm, a regular part of my itinerary when I am there. A note of warning needs to be sounded: Cornwall can be very crowded in summer. Our first visit there was in August, many years ago, and we went to all the wrong places. The sight of so many people crammed into streets, hotels, beaches and open spaces was sufficient to put us off for some years. In fact, with careful planning, it is not hard to avoid the crowds; and, out of season, Cornwall is ready to assert its true magic.

East Anglia

The eastern part of England recalls its history in the name, East Anglia. It contains some of the best farming land in the country, and has a large number of popular seaside resorts. For the most part, it is fairly level terrain, while along its coastline land and sea merge so imperceptibly that sometimes it is impossible to discern any defined margin. There exists in the minds of many people the firm conviction that East Anglia is entirely flatlands, given over to corn, cows and bulbfields. This is a long way from the truth of the matter.

We may as well begin in the south, and work our way northwards. Southend has the longest pier in the world. Many years ago, I was invited to lunch by representatives of the Southend Council. The meal was served in a restaurant at the very end of the pier, which we reached by means of a jolly little miniature railway. Needless to say, we had that great English seaside dish, fish and chips. Afterwards, I was involved in recording a radio programme about the Punch and Judy Show which was going on there, part of the traditional entertainment at a typical seaside town, the closest of its kind to the capital, and consequently much beloved by Londoners of many generations. Nobody could describe Southend as beautiful, but it has a garish kind of attractiveness, rather like that of an amiable, blowzy barmaid, who is past her best, but still good for a few laughs. I have been to Southend but once; the experience was memorable, in its way, and I would not have missed it. Paradoxically, in its artificial way, Southend is entirely genuine: it is exactly what it pretends to be, no more and no less. Certainly, a visit there is a journey worth making — once. Having said that, I realise that it is highly unlikely that the Town Council will invite me to lunch there a second time.

Colchester was once famous for its oysters, and in days gone by I have returned home from there with suitable spoils of the chase. A few miles from Colchester, in the direction of Cambridge, is the East Anglian Railway Museum. Further to the west, the Nene Valley Railway, which has provided the scenery for a number of films, including *Octopussy*, runs steam trains on 7 miles of track from Wansford to Peterborough.

At the theatre on Clacton Pier, the comedians Will Hay, Stanley Holloway and Roy Hudd began their careers. Nearby, the largest container port in Britain is at Felixstowe, whence we have sailed by P & O European Ferries to Zeebrugge in Belgium; and from Harwich, its neighbour across the estuaries of the Stour and Orwell, Harwich, we have crossed by courtesy of Sealink to the Hook of Holland.

Aldeburgh, a windswept fishing town on the Suffolk coast, is now known throughout the world because of its most famous inhabitant, Benjamin Britten who, with his friend Peter Pears, made the Aldeburgh Festival one of the great musical events in the calendar. Even after the deaths of Britten and Pears, the festival continues, undiminished, in June of every year.

My own memories of East Anglia go back a very long way, to a recalling of Sunday school outings to the seaside at Skegness, sight of the bulbfields around Spalding and Wisbech on journeys from Yorkshire to Cambridge, rustic cricket matches on windswept pitches in Suffolk, appearances at the lovely Theatre Royal in Bury St Edmunds and the Guildhall in King's Lynn. But there is one region of East Anglia that I have come to know very well through repeated visits over some forty years.

Swinburne took rather a gloomy view of the Fen Country, which he saw as

> Miles and miles of desolation!
> Leagues on leagues on leagues without a change!

At the centre of the Fen Country is Cambridge, 'the nursery of all my good breeding', as Sir John Harington described it in a letter to Sir Robert Cecil in 1602. Two centuries later, William Wordsworth, newly-arrived from the Lake District, fell under its spell:

> I was the Dreamer, they the Dream; I roamed
> Delighted through the motley spectacle;
> Gowns, grave, or gaudy, doctors, students, streets,
> Courts, cloisters, flocks of churches, gateways, towers:
> Migration strange for a stripling of the hills,
> A northern villager ...

Wordsworth was at St John's College, next door to Trinity, in whose chapel stands a statue of Isaac Newton, the English mathematician, astronomer and philosopher, credited with discovering the law of gravity. Wordsworth saw in the statue

> The marble index of a mind for ever
> Voyaging through strange seas of Thought, alone.

The Cambridge I came to know in 1950 was still infected with post-war euphoria: there was a good deal of naive idealism around, and quite a bit of idle dreaming too, combining to create an atmosphere recognisably different from that which prevails today. It is the Cambridge of that era which I came to know when, in March, 1950 I won an exhibition in English at King's, and went up the following October, there to follow a course of studies under the guidance of such men as George Rylands, F L Lucas, L P Wilkinson, Noël Annan, John Saltmarsh and Christopher Morris, and to take part in amateur dramatics in the company of Peter Hall, John Barton and Peter Wood, names now well-known in the theatrical profession.

King's College was founded in 1441 by King Henry VI, Eton College being its sister-foundation. The chapel at King's is, quite simply, one of the most stupendous buildings in England. The Service of Nine Lessons and Carols, broadcast every Christmas Eve from King's since 1928, is now become an institution, a familiar part

48   ENGLAND

of the nation's festive celebrations. To attend the service is an unforgettable experience. In my time, candles illuminated the vast chapel, and from the shadows came a solo treble voice with the opening of 'Once in Royal David's City', followed by the choir, robed, moving in procession to their places in the carved stalls. To hear the well-known melodies, and the seasonal words of comfort and cheer, sung and spoken in such a place, resonant with history, is to be drawn into an atmosphere which seems scarcely to belong to this world. The fading day outside retains just sufficient light at the opening of the service to touch the rich colours of the windows. At the east end, attention is focussed on the sumptuous painting by Rubens, The Adoration of the Magi, an appropriate reminder of the occasion for such celebration. In this context, there may be some truth in Pope's charge that

> some to church repair,
> Not for the doctrine, but the music there ...

but even the most stony-hearted can hardly go away untouched by such ceremonial. Art, as a perceptive commentator remarked, partakes of religion, and man is, by nature, a sacramental animal.

Tourists from the United States have a formidable reputation in Europe. Having travelled all the way across the Atlantic they are seized, understandably, with a burning desire to see everything. Unfortunately, they do not have all the time in the world, so sightseeing usually has to be done in something of a hurry. A trio of those intrepid adventurers arrived one day at the gate of King's College. They stepped into the courtyard, and looked eagerly at what presented itself to their gaze. One of them took the initiative, and pointed to the right. 'I reckon that's the dining-hall, and that,' he said, now gesturing to his left, 'that is the chapel.' There was a pause while his companions regarded these two buildings. 'No,' said one of them, looking to his right. 'I'm of the opinion that that's the chapel, and that,' (turning to his left) 'that's the dining-hall.' The third member of the party, who had thus far remained mute, surveyed both of his comrades, then the two buildings in question, and finally announced tersely: 'Well, anyway, we've seen it. Let's go.' They had certainly seen it, whatever it was, and so they went.

The Provost of King's in my time was an extraordinary character, Sir John Sheppard. White-haired, benevolent of aspect, and seeming decades older than his true tally of years, he made his way around the college grounds, amiably blessing passers-by, regardless of whether or not they were members of the college. 'Bless you, my boy.' He would pronounce benediction, and then continue his progress before he could be engaged in conversation. His lectures, open to all, town and gown alike, were unforgettable performances. The subject was usually Greek classic drama, large parts of which he rendered impressively in his own translation while sitting on a desk before his audience, unceremoniously dangling his legs and kicking his heels against the woodwork to make a point. After one memorable address, he was approached by two ladies, who asked if they might possibly see his notes, just to refresh their memories on the detail of his talk, which they had so enjoyed. 'My notes,' said Provost Sheppard, slightly taken aback by this rather unusual request. 'Well, let me see ...' And from the pocket of his well-worn, dark suit, he produced an envelope. 'There!' he exclaimed, laying it before them. On the back was written: ZEUS — AGAMEMNON — ZEUS. And that was all.

John Saltmarsh, who did his best to guide my historical studies, used to offer memorable tours of the chapel, which involved some fairly energetic scrambling up stone stairways to gain access to the roof. John, who was Vice-Provost of King's for a time, told me one evening over port and dessert in the college wine room of how, in severe winters, he used to skate on the frozen river all the way from Grantchester to Cambridge. Grantchester: now there is a name to conjure with, for those to whom the name of Rupert Brooke, poet, and Kingsman, still means something. He it was who wrote in 'The Old Vicarage, Grantchester':

> Oh! there the chestnuts, summer through,
> Beside the river make for you
> A tunnel of green gloom, and sleep
> Deeply above ...

and asked those extraordinary questions:

> Stands the Church clock at ten to three?
> And is there honey still for tea?

For me, mere mention of Grantchester is enough to revive thoughts of afternoon teas and walks by the pollarded willows on the river banks with gorgeous girls in summer dresses, of arriving by punt for breakfast at The Orchard after a May Ball, of the unfailing sunshine which brightened those youthful days, brimming with promise of we knew not what, of the irresistible, evanescent charm of Cambridge at its best. It was my mentor at King's, George Rylands, who drew my attention in later years to a book by the American critic, Stark Young, in which he writes that 'memory is half of life, and more than half of all beauty'.

Spring is entrancing in Cambridge, when the Backs are bright with daffodils, the colleges are looking at their best, with well-kept lawns running down to the water's edge, and there is an atmosphere of lively expectancy which each spring brings as its benison to those who have endured the winter. But there is a certain magic in the dying year, too, when hours of daylight are few, lights start appearing early in the windows of colleges, mist begins to creep in from the river, and it is time for chapel.

The Fitzwilliam Museum on Trumpington Street is a place of exceptional interest, despite a monumentally forbidding exterior. Inside are some fine Italian paintings and drawings, including works by Titian, Tintoretto, Raphael, Leonardo and

Michelangelo. There is generous representation of Flemish, Dutch and English paintings, and a number of important French works. Less imposing, but of tremendous interest as an intimate, personal collection of twentieth-century art, is Kettle's Yard in Northampton Street, not far from Magdalene College. The gallery is the creation of Jim Ede, who gathered together a marvellous array of works by Ben Nicholson, David Jones (the luminous *Vexilla Regis* is one of his finest pieces), Miro, Henry Moore, Barbara Hepworth and Brancusi. In its modest, unassuming way, Kettle's Yard achieves something of the same effect as the Peggy Guggenheim collection in Venice.

The countryside around Cambridge, scenically less than dramatic, is yet worth investigation. Inviting villages beckon the curious traveller: places like Cherry Hinton, Grantchester, Waterbeach, Little and Great Wilbraham, Fen Ditton, and then the Gog Magog Hills, which do not rise to any great height, but are prominent amid surrounding flatlands.

Northwards lies Ely Cathedral, one of the loveliest pieces of ecclesiastical architecture in England. It is also just about the coldest place I have ever known. One winter's day, I was persuaded to drive my wife there, in order that she could take part in a performance of Bach's *St Matthew Passion*. At the rehearsal in the afternoon, the choir and orchestra, already numbed by the Arctic chill, agreed that their only hope was to don as many layers of clothing as could be accommodated beneath the decorous costumes which they were condemned to wear at the evening performance. Meanwhile, I pressed myself up against the iron ribs of one of the huge stoves that were supposed to impart some warmth to the interior of the cathedral. For all the good it did me, they might as well have been an illusion, the wintry equivalent of a mirage in the desert. In honesty, I have to say that I remember but little of the performance, except that it took place. A visit to Ely in midwinter is not recommended to the faint-hearted, though in fair weather it should certainly figure on every itinerary.

Norfolk is a county of secret villages and strangely remote seaside towns, like Cley-next-the-Sea (Cley pronounced to rhyme with high), where once I gave a lecture to enthusiastic members of the local literary society. Afterwards, we spent the night in a charming cottage, the property of Professor and Mrs Martin. Before dinner, he produced a quarter-bottle of whisky, which he offered to me with the words: 'I know you chaps like a little something after a performance.' I accepted with what I hope was proper gratitude.

Parts of the Norfolk coast present a bewildering sight: vast areas of salt marshes, so that the observer finds it hard to determine which is land and which is sea. Northwards is the Wash, a shallow bay which admits the North Sea to the coasts of Norfolk and Lincolnshire. Here, as in Belgium and Holland, there is constant battle between men and the water. If sea levels were to rise significantly, much of the land here (some of it reclaimed from the sea), would be permanently submerged. Many of those who live along the length of England's coastline are, understandably, nervous when they read about the 'greenhouse effect' on the global climate.

An entry in William Cobbett's *Rural Rides* for 23 April 1830, records a visit to Lincoln, whose 'cathedral is, I believe, the finest building in the whole world'. Lincolnshire, which Thomas Fuller thought might 'be termed the aviary of England, for the wild-fowl therein', properly belongs more to the north than to the south. Mostly flat-land, and largely fertile, it was once the second-largest county in England, after Yorkshire. My childhood memories of Lincolnshire are of Sunday school outings to the seaside town of Skegness, and a week at Butlin's Holiday Camp there, during that brief, innocent period of my life when I did not immediately recoil from enforced jollity. In later years, I found work as a rural postman in Lincolnshire, at Epworth, where the name of Wesley is revered still. The old rectory is worth a visit, as the place where Methodism may be said to have had its roots.

Grantham, an unremarkable town which I came to know, but hardly to love, during my service with the Royal Air Force, has certain claims to fame. The Angel Hotel, an inviting old inn where we whiled away many an evening in idle conversation, was where Richard III set his seal to the death warrant on the Duke of Buckingham. Isaac Newton was a pupil at the grammar school there, and Margaret Thatcher, Britain's long-serving Prime Minister, was born in Grantham. Every working day, around 240 commuters set out from the railway station at Grantham to travel to work in London, a distance of 107 miles, with a journey time of just over an hour. For these brave travellers, Grantham and Lincolnshire must appear as a distant suburb of the capital, a place within daily reach of a London office. In that sense, I suppose one could say that Grantham has been colonised by the south.

Northwards, beyond Scunthorpe, a bridge across the Humber has now opened a new trade route in that part of eastern England, making more accessible the university town of Hull, England's largest fishing port. For northerners, Hull is a convenient gateway to continental Europe, with nightly sailings in luxuriously-equipped vessels of North Sea Ferries to Rotterdam and to Zeebrugge. For several years now, this has been our favourite route to Holland, Belgium and France.

It was at Hull, in days gone by, that I enjoyed occasional and memorable lunches with the university librarian, a most congenial companion. His name was Philip Larkin, known to the civilised world as a poet of great distinction. I recall that, after one budget in which the Chancellor of the Exchequer raised simultaneously the prices of alcoholic drink and petrol, I received a letter from Hull which ended: 'Now I don't know whether to put petrol into my car, or drink into

Yours sincerely

Philip Larkin.'

A fine poet, and a good companion, his praises have been sung elsewhere by better men than I.

Hull was also the birthplace of Andrew Marvell and of Stevie Smith, making up a remarkable trio of poets to have associations with what is, essentially, an unpoetic sort of port on the banks of the Humber. But here we have, unwittingly, strayed into the north of England, which is the subject of the section that is to follow.

Ask Where's the North

    ... dark and true and tender is the North.

Tennyson had it right: darkness, truth and tenderness are essential characteristics of that part of England which lies north of a line drawn between the Mersey and the Wash. Here is an impressive panorama of contrasts: urban, industrial concentrations within hailing distance of some of the most dramatic, and least desecrated, countryside in Britain south of Hadrian's Wall. The Peak District, the Yorkshire Dales, the North York Moors, the Lake District, are all regions of particular beauties, each having its own special character. Here, one will find the great ruined abbeys of Fountains, Rievaulx, Bolton, Bylands, Kirkstall, Jervaulx, Whitby, and dazzling edifices like Durham Cathedral and the Minsters of York and Beverley, while down the middle of the land stride the Pennines, backbone of England. Here is room to breathe, space to enjoy the variegated wonders of creation.

Travellers from the south will notice a change as they journey northwards through Derbyshire, Nottinghamshire and South Yorkshire. Slag heaps on the horizon give notice of an important activity in this region, the mining of coal, and signs of industry manifest themselves insistently. These, we could say, constitute the darker side. Yet, reassuringly, it takes so little time to escape from the blackened tenements, the mill chimneys and factories of the industrial north, and to penetrate regions of astonishing beauty, places that inspired the writings of Wordsworth, Coleridge, the Brontë sisters, D H Lawrence, Sir Walter Scott and many other writers of distinction. They discovered, and recorded, the truth as they saw it.

As for the tenderness, each wayfarer through life must seek that for himself, in his own way. As one born and bred in the north, I must confess to a certain measure of bias in such matters, so the reader should not take my words on trust. As Tennyson notes

    ... that which we are, we are,

and it is not vouchsafed to everyone to perceive the depths of character residing in northern folk. As the saying goes, they do not wear their hearts upon their sleeves. But, as Tennyson reminds the truly intrepid explorer,

    'Tis not too late to seek a newer world.

It may be salutary to remind ourselves that many of the world's nations have been welded together, sometimes violently, out of disparate and often warring elements. Think of Germany, unified in the 19th century, divided again after the Second World War, and and now reunified; think of the United States, or of the Union of Soviet Socialist Republics, or of Vietnam; think of Ireland. Then Britain has endured successive invasions and occupations by the Romans, Angles, Saxons and Jutes, and Normans. England, 50,331 square miles in area, and the largest part of Great

Britain, was once divided into separate and rival kingdoms, prominent among them Wessex, Mercia and Northumbria. There has always existed a profusion of rivalries of various kinds and intensities, some finding harmless expression in sporting contests between Oxford and Cambridge, Eton and Harrow, Yorkshire and Lancashire, others, religious, social, economic, linguistic, proving more seriously divisive.

What history will recognise as the Thatcher years in Britain have brought many changes to the nation, inspired by the dynamism and energy of the first woman to achieve the highest elected office in the country. She has left her legacy to succeeding generations. 'In the eighties Britain became a more unequal country ... than it was 100 years ago during the reign of Victoria.' Such was the verdict delivered by the *Observer Magazine* in its issue of 17 December 1989. It went on to say that 'the latest official figures show a bigger gulf between top and bottom earners than at any time since records began.' The situation is highlighted by a brief note on the magazine's cover: 'Chris Wherton is a kitchen porter in a Wolverhampton hospital. He earns £4,524 a year. Christopher Heath is managing director of Baring Securities. He earns more than that in a day.'

Certainly, the division within Britain became clear to perceptive commentators during the nineteen-eighties, making it obvious that there were, perhaps, 'two nations, between whom there is no intercourse, and no sympathy; who are as ignorant of each other's habits, thoughts, and feelings, as if they were dwellers in different zones, or inhabitants of different planets; who are formed by a different breeding, are fed by a different food, are ordered by different manners, and are not governed by the same laws ... THE RICH AND THE POOR'. Strange to relate, those words were written almost 150 years ago, in a novel entitled *Sybil, or The Two Nations*, by a man who later became Queen Victoria's Prime Minister, Benjamin Disraeli.

South Yorkshire

My life began in the southern part of the county of Yorkshire, in a town of no particular distinction: Doncaster, centre of the South Yorkshire coalfield. A very long time ago, I paid sixpence in a secondhand bookshop for a nicely-bound copy of Scott's *Ivanhoe*. When I began to read it, the first paragraph engaged my attention immediately:

> In that pleasant district of merry England which is watered by the River Don, there extended in ancient times a large forest, covering the greater part of the beautiful hills and valleys which lie between Sheffield and the pleasant town of Doncaster. The remains of this extensive wood are still to be seen at the noble seats of Wentworth, of Wharncliffe Park, and around Rotherham. Here haunted of yore the fabulous Dragon of Wantley; here were fought many of the most desperate battles during the Civil Wars of the Roses, and here also flourished in ancient times those bands of gallant outlaws whose deeds have been rendered so popular in English song.

Those words of Sir Walter Scott's set me thinking: yes, I knew about the bands of outlaws all right, because I had been taken to see the film *Robin Hood*; I had been to Rotherham, and to Sheffield, and I had been born in Doncaster, and still lived there at the time when Scott's novel of knights and tournaments and battles came into my possession. But I knew nothing then of the noble seats of Wentworth and Wharncliffe Park: Cusworth Hall was about the grandest place I had seen in that locality. Of the Dragon of Wantley and the Wars of the Roses I was quite ignorant, except that I had a suspicion that the Wars of the Roses had some connection with a cricket match I had seen taking place at Sheffield between Yorkshire and Lancashire.

But the bit that really surprised me was the mention of beautiful hills and valleys between Sheffield and Doncaster. In my youthful journeys by bus from Glasgow Paddocks in Doncaster to Pond Street in Sheffield (fare, three shillings return), all I had seen were stretches of rather dirty water, houses crammed together, back to back, rolling mills and factories — but beautiful hills and valleys, no! Mind you, there are more interesting sights than you might at first think along that eighteen-mile run from Doncaster to Sheffield: just two miles outside Doncaster, neatly perched beside the river, is Sprotbrough, where Scott stayed when he was writing *Ivanhoe*. Not so long ago, I revisited the village for the first time in many years. It had changed, of course: new housing estates where once there were fields, but that is a common tale throughout the land. The old village church still stands, and the building where Scott lodged has been rescued from its derelict state and is now once more an inn, where we have enjoyed excellent lunches in recent years. Not far away, above the towpath which runs alongside the Don, there is a nature reserve, with hides from which keen observers can survey expanses of water populated by many kinds of wildfowl.

From the bus, we used to enjoy a good view of Conisbrough Castle, with its massive keep. That is still *Ivanhoe* territory, but from there onwards buildings begin to close in on you, through Rotherham and Tinsley into Sheffield. I must explain that for a Doncaster lad, Sheffield held an extraordinary attraction: it was a big city. There were theatres, and first-class cricket was played in those days at Bramall Lane, where I first saw Len Hutton bat. I recall being taken to see *Peter Pan* at the Lyceum Theatre, the day after there had been a particularly heavy air-raid on the city centre. On our way to the theatre, we had to pass through an area still smoking and littered with rubble, all that was left of Fitzalan Square. I had not previously been as close as that to the aftermath of bombing, and it left a deep impression on a young mind.

If you walk along Thorne Road in Doncaster today, starting from its junction with Hallgate and South Parade, very soon you will come to the gates of Hall Cross Comprehensive School. The fabric is that of Doncaster Grammar School, an educational foundation dating back several hundred years, but occupying the present site only since the last century. The name has vanished, in the interests of progress, no doubt; but, during the war years, when I was a pupil there, it was still the town's grammar school, with a staff including a number of notable eccentrics. There was Michael Lenihan, who was seen in his orchard one evening when the weather forecasters had predicted a severe frost, carrying a shovel full of hot coals, which he was waving vaguely and optimistically around the trees in a vain attempt to raise the air temperature. Then there was the Reverend F T Barton, who held a living at West Stockwith, in Lincolnshire, and who, during that time of shortages, used to sell communion wine to his colleagues on the staff. The senior English master, one Michael Towers, believed in exposing his pupils quite early to the facts of life. He abhorred bowdlerised texts, and insisted that we write in the margins of the books all the rude bits, which had been carefully removed by editors to avoid offending our delicate sensibilities. It may have been in one of his classes that we came across the delicious emendation of that outraged exclamation by a cuckolded husband: 'My wife has played the trumpet in your bed!'

Student unrest was not the commonplace then as it became in more recent years, but we did have our moments of rebellion. In my penultimate year at Doncaster Grammar School, I was involved in a series of hoaxes inspired by the presence of a most unpopular headmaster. I have kept the press cuttings to this day. 'FIVE EMPTY DESKS IN THE SIXTH FORM' was the headline in the *Daily Express*. The *Sheffield Telegraph* described the unexpected arrival at the school of furniture vans, piano-tuners, ice-cream salesmen, taxicab drivers. The *Daily Mail*, in an uncharitable mood, was the only paper to name all the 'boy jokers', among them David Parker, later to become Professor of Law at Liverpool University! 'PREFECTS THREATEN TO RESIGN', read another headline; the *Yorkshire Evening News* carried, rather incongruously, a photograph of the headmaster in a running-vest, and one paper even included mention of the incident in its 'Stop Press' column of late news. As an end-of-term escapade, it turned out to be quite a storm in a teacup, and provided briefly a good deal of amusement in some quarters. Such was one aspect of the character of schooldays in a South Yorkshire town some forty years ago.

At that time, there lived a pawnbroker in Doncaster by the name of G C Barton, a well-known character in the town, no relation to F T Barton of the Grammar School. It was no secret among his friends and acquaintances, who were numerous, that Mr Barton enjoyed a drink. After imbibing freely, he was apt to indulge in extravagant gestures. On one such occasion, a companion offered to sell him some rabbits he had caught in traps: rabbit pie, in those days, in the north, was a popular dish. Mr Barton responded in prodigal style, saying that he would take all the rabbits the man could supply. Next day, about a hundred furry corpses were delivered to the Barton residence in The Grove, Wheatley Hills. I can vouch for this, because I called there the same evening to escort one of his two daughters to the cinema, and found the household in some disarray. On another occasion, Mr Barton called for a taxi to take him home after a convivial evening down town. The night was foggy, and the driver had not travelled far from Silver Street before he halted the vehicle, explaining to his fare that he was unable to continue in such poor visibility. At this Mr Barton leapt from the taxi, saying to the driver: 'It's all right, just follow me.' He then walked slowly and carefully along the road, with the taxi following: up Nether Hall Road, following the bus route, on to Highfield Road, a right turn into King's Road, left into Thorne Road, and the long haul, past the hospital and the Green Tree public house, right up Thornhill Road, and left into The Grove, this strange convoy made its way. Arrived at the gate of number 43, Mr Barton thanked the taxi-driver, paid the fare, and said good-night. History does not relate how the driver found his way back to town.

The Peak District

In little more than two hours' driving time from London, at Junction 28 of the M1 motorway, a turning presents itself which, if taken, conducts the traveller into a very different world. For here, just beyond Matlock, begins the Peak District, Britain's first national park. The River Wye cuts through limestone of the White Peak, and the county abounds in water-mills, now mostly forsaken and derelict, although we were lucky enough to find one which had been carefully restored, and converted into flats. We shall come to that later.

In the gentle countryside around Bakewell stand two great houses, each notable in its own way, Chatsworth and Haddon Hall. Chatsworth, seat of the dukes of Devonshire, is an imposing pile, with a remarkable art collection and extensive gardens, designed by Joseph Paxton, who was also responsible for the Crystal Palace. Haddon Hall is a magnificent medieval manor house. Both make an ideal start for the visitor from the south, who may like to pause between the two for a bar lunch at the Devonshire Arms in Beeley, where a little stream runs alongside the village street. Then, for children of all ages, there is the pleasureland of Alton Towers.

White Peak and Dark Peak, limestone and gritstone, form a landscape amiable and smiling in the south, fierce and forbidding in the north, which I, born some thirty miles distant, have known and loved almost all my life. The Peak District lies between the great cities of Manchester and Sheffield, Yorkshire on the one hand, Lancashire on the other. From either place, a short journey by car, train, bus or even bicycle, brings you easily into spectacular surroundings: moorland punctuated by dry-stone walls, river valleys, and rock-faces which challenge the ardent climber.

Vivid memories linger from childhood when, as soon as winter had finished its worst, my father would take us to Grindleford or Hathersage, to stroll by the banks of the River Derwent, or to trek over the high moors, where it was not uncommon to stumble on the stiffened carcass of a sheep which had strayed from the flock and now remained as a frozen legacy of winter. A friendly, as well as a wild place, the Peak district offers peaceful recreation to those of leisurely disposition, and strenuous exercise to those of more energetic persuasion. Monsal Head and Longstone Ridge, between Bakewell and Tideswell, are easily accessible by car, and promise immense views on clear days, as well as rewarding walks. The Monsal Trail follows the course of a former railway line. Footpaths are clearly marked and bicycles are available for hire at many centres in the region. Those who do not suffer from claustrophobia will enjoy exploring the underground chambers of the Peak, Speedwell and Blue John Caverns, close to Castleton, crowded in season, but otherwise a pleasant village of narrow, steep streets, waterside walks, and numerous teashops, all overlooked by the ruins of Peveril

Castle. Since my enthusiasm does not extend to subterranean adventures, I can fervently endorse some of the comments which I came across in the visitors' book of Edale Mill. One young contributor noted of Treak Cavern that 'it is well worth seeing, but the ceiling drips a lot'. Just as I thought! Another remarked that Bagshawe Cavern at Bradwell is 'recommended for those who don't mind going half a mile underground'. As it happens, I do mind, so we stayed above ground and consoled ourselves with generous portions of Bradwell's excellent ice-cream. We went nowhere near Thor's Cave, which was said by another contributor to be 'not for the faint-hearted'. In such circumstances, I have no hesitation in admitting to cowardice.

Westwards, one comes to Buxton, a town of real architectural distinction, with its fine houses, and recently-restored opera house, which presents entertainment of all kinds, including, of course, opera. We once enjoyed a nostalgic evening there of Victorian music-hall. Buxton boasts the world's only Micrarium, a truly astonishing place where, at the touch of a button, the visitor can project on large screens wondrously-detailed microscopic images of the tiniest objects, magnified many times: a minute embryo, larvae, the wing of a moth, coloured crystals, a snowflake in resin. We stayed at the Lee Wood Hotel, an excellent establishment close to the centre of the town, with comfortable rooms and an imaginative and resourceful chef. Buxton is a spa, famous for its waters, in whose therapeutic properties sufferers from rheumatism and gout profess much faith. It is also the highest town of its size in England, and it is not unknown, in severe winters, for all roads in and out of Buxton to be impassable.

Eyam (pronounced Eem), is one of the strangest, most intriguing, places in Britain, a haunted village in a beautiful setting, 800 feet above sea-level. Its Saxon name indicates a dwelling-place by the water. I first went there as an eager youth-hosteller, thirty years ago, and have been lured back frequently ever since. Eyam lies in the heart of Derbyshire's Peak District, a dozen miles or so from Sheffield, a quiet, pleasant village with attractive stone houses and a fine parish church. All around, large stretches of gorgeous countryside promise splendid walks, among the best in England. A lovely area, offering just about every kind of outdoor pursuit from hang-gliding to potholing: yet Eyam, in the midst of this rural wonderland, confronts the traveller with a tragic tale. In 1665, an itinerant tailor, George Viccars, was staying there. He received from London a parcel of cloth, which was infected by bubonic plague, then raging in the south. Viccars was the first to die, and the infection swept through the village. Its Rector, William Mompesson, and a nonconformist preacher, Thomas Stanley, prevailed upon the inhabitants to put themselves into voluntary quarantine, in the hope of preventing spread of the plague throughout Derbyshire. Supplies of food were delivered to several points on the outskirts of Eyam and, in return, money was left to be cleansed in running water. The church was closed, and services were held a little way off, in the open air, at a cave which bears the name of Cucklet Church.

The death toll was heavy: five out of every six inhabitants perished in a year, 260 in all. Today, Eyam is a village containing almost a thousand souls, who have learnt to live with memories of the past. For some of them, the writing is, quite literally, on the wall: to the brickwork of the 'Plague Cottages', near the church, are affixed boards listing the names of those who lived and died there in that time of pestilence. Eastwards from the village, near Riley Farm, are the Riley Graves, where most of the Hancock family were buried. Over the tomb of John Hancock, who died on August 7, 1666, is written this sombre verse:

> Remember man
> As thou gost by
> As thou art now
> Even so was I.
> As I doe now
> So must thou lye
> Remember man
> That thou shalt die.

At the parish church, Norman in origin, built on a Saxon foundation, the curious visitor will find a copy of the parish register with a grim record of that dreadful year. Both church and churchyard are worth a visit: inside, there is a fine Jacobean pulpit, with a 'squint' behind, intended to afford a view from the south aisle to the altar, and a chair belonging to William Mompesson; outside, an 18th-century sundial and a magnificent Celtic cross, thought to be a wayside preaching cross of the 8th century, and the tomb of Catherine Mompesson, William's wife and herself a plague victim.

Well-dressing (the decoration of wells with colourful and elaborate designs in a frame made up of leaves and flowers pressed into a base of wet clay) is a tradition peculiar to Derbyshire. Originally a pagan custom, it acquired Christian connotations as a thanksgiving for pure water in communities through the region. The observance has particular poignancy in Eyam, taking place in late August or early September, the last of the season. When I spent a night at the Miners' Arms in Eyam, I was quite unprepared for the generous portions served up at dinner; indeed, I had to dismiss part of the procession of waitresses bearing dishes of vegetables. Telephone: 0433 30853 for reservations.

Edale is, for me, the choicest of spots: easy of access by road, only sixteen miles from Sheffield, and four miles from the village of Hope on the A625, it has its own railway station, at about the halfway mark on the line connecting Manchester with Sheffield. Its situation, conveniently close to two large cities, makes it a focus of attention for walkers, climbers and campers, so that on high days and holidays the village and the hills around are swarming with young and old, sensibly shod, many with back-packs. Indeed, some of the more popular and heavily-used paths in the area are now reinforced with wooden or stone steps, in an attempt to arrest further erosion of the soil. But it is quite easy to escape the crowds.

Two pubs, a post office, general stores, a church and an information centre cater for the needs of visitors and local inhabitants. On our latest visit to the area, we rented a charming flat on the second floor of Edale Mill, admirably restored by the Landmark Trust. There again, we were reminded of times past, as we read the regulations for mill-workers in the last century: 'If two persons are known to be in one Necessary together they shall be fined 3d each; and if any Man or Boy go into the Women's Necessary he shall be instantly dismissed.' Various scales of fines are set out for unpunctuality, smoking, swearing and other offences. In those days, of course, cleanliness was next to godliness, as is confirmed by a notice which reads, 'The Masters would recommend that all their workpeople wash themselves every morning.'

Furnished in a style reminiscent of that period when it was a working cotton-mill, the rooms have rough stone walls, exposed beams, and capital views of hills. There is the atmosphere of a bygone age at the mill, in its peaceful setting by a swiftly-running river. Each evening, I would take my seat on a high stool at the sort of desk which would have been familiar to Tim Linkinwater and other Dickensian clerks. On a night of full moon, I wandered to the river's edge for a glimpse of silvery light gleaming on the water and girdling hills silhouetted against a star-laden sky: sheer magic, the sort of enchantment that could easily hold you to a place for the rest of your days.

Edale nestles comfortably at the centre of some of Britain's best walking country. Here, for instance, is the start of the Pennine Way, a scramble by Grindsbrook Clough to the top of Kinder Scout, a flattish, boggy plateau, with stones weathered into extraordinary shapes. From there, a hard slog of 270 miles leads to Kirk Yetholm, on the other side of the Scottish border. This famous walk is not one to be undertaken lightly, especially in inclement weather. In mid-November, with more modest aims in view, I made my way up to Hollins Cross, along the windy ridge to Mam Tor ('The Shivering Mountain'), where hang-gliders hovered almost motionless above my head, then down through Harden Clough to Edale. From there, the Pennine Way is clearly waymarked. I took a right turn from the main path, up to the Nab and the base of Ringing Roger (said to be so named from the French *rocher*, rock or crag). Thus, in a single morning, I was privileged to enjoy grand vistas across the broad valley of the Noe from both sides without undue exertion.

The Peak District is not all natural beauty, untouched and unspoilt; there is plentiful evidence of man's industrial activities through the ages: lead mines, limestone quarries, cement works, mills, copper and iron mines, limekilns. That notable pioneer of spinning and weaving machinery, Sir Richard Arkwright, set up his water-powered spinning frame at the village of Cromford. The National Tramway Museum at Crich has a number of working trams to stimulate nostalgic reminiscence among older visitors: we had a grand day out there.

More melancholy symbols of past days are the submerged villages of Derwent and Ashopton, covered by the waters of the Derwent and Ladybower reservoirs. The Ladybower Dam was opened in 1945 by King George VI, marking the completion of a scheme to meet increasing demands for water, a project which, sadly but necessarily, involved evacuation of two communities before their homes were destroyed and flooded. In a dry season, such as the long, hot summer of 1989, their ghostly remains are seen again above the waters, mute indicators to later ages of the cost of what we call progress.

Not far distant from the national park's boundary is Sherwood Forest, where Robin Hood and his band of merry men are said to have hidden from the Sheriff of Nottingham. In the churchyard of St Michael's, a 14th-century building set on a hill above the comfortable settlement of Hathersage, you can see the grave of Little John, most renowned of Robin Hood's outlaws. In the church itself are the brasses of the Eyre family. Charlotte Brontë visited there in 1845, and took the name for the heroine of her novel *Jane Eyre*, published in 1845. Hathersage is a place so at one with its tranquil environment that it is hard to believe that Sheffield lies only ten miles away. In the main street, several pleasant shops cater for the needs of tourists, with ample stocks of walking, camping and climbing gear, maps and guidebooks, food and drink. We have often stayed at the George Inn, a solid-looking establishment whither diners from Sheffield often make their way for an evening out in the countryside.

There are many surprises, so much to discover, in this fascinating corner of England, described by a 17th-century traveller as a 'strange, mountainous, misty, moorish, rocky, wild country'.

Here, between the north of England and the Midlands, is a place for recreation, for renewal, for relaxation. I have known it for half a century, ever since childhood days, and today it still has the power to summon me back to its moors, rivers and hills, by virtue of its astonishing variety and endless fascination, back to

   ... where Derwent rolls his dusky floods
   Through vaulted mountains, and a night of woods.

Details of properties for rent are available from the Landmark Trust, Shottesbrooke, Maidenhead, Berkshire SL6 3SW, telephone: 062 882 5925. Maps, guides and helpful advice are readily available from information centres in Edale, Hope and many other centres throughout the Peak District National Park.

North Yorkshire and Cleveland

For almost twenty years, we have owned a tiny house in the pleasantly solid market town of Guisborough, ancient capital of Cleveland, on the main road which runs between Middlesbrough and Whitby. As backcloth to the scene, heavily-wooded slopes rise to Highcliffe Nab and the expanse of Guisborough Moor beyond. When we first came to Guisborough, it was possible to look out of our living-room window across an expanse of open fields, affording an uninterrupted view towards the hills. The march of time has changed all that, and now we stare at the facades of other houses, mirror-images of our own. Those with longer memories will hark back to the days when the railway ran along the tracks now used by cyclists and walkers.

Guisborough offers constant reminders of the past. Around here, there are records of alum manufacture in the 17th century, and ironstone was mined in the Eston Hills in the nineteenth century, but many of the mines were closed before the dawn of the 20th century. Disused shafts are now fenced off, but one winter, when the snow lay heavily, I was walking on Guisborough Moor and wondering what those little pieces of wood were, just poking through the snow. Of a sudden, I realised that they were the tops of fencing posts, and that sudden descent into one of the old shafts was a real possibility. In which eventuality, I should have been heard of no more until the following spring and you, dear reader, would have been spared these rambling observations. In the circumstances, I decided that prudence dictated a hasty retreat down the hill.

Some changes have been for the better, some for the worse. Guisborough's cinema is now a health club, to the improvement, one hopes, of well-being and fitness among its customers. New houses have brought more people into the town. Hunter's Hill Estate, to the south, with wooded slopes for a backcloth, has a great open space, a clearing of grass with swings and a see-saw for children. Sadly, in these days, it has become a repository for discarded cans and bottles of drinks, chip bags, toffee papers and the offerings of numerous dogs, all equally unwelcome.

Stand on the windblown top of Highcliffe Nab, and the pattern of old and new unfolds beneath you. The old centre of town is clear enough to see, surrounded and hemmed in by new estates, and pubs like The Voyager and the Huntsman. Separated from Guisborough by some acres of grazing and farming land is Hutton Village, which has a real feel of rural seclusion. From there, broad paths lead through woodland in one direction to Roseberry Topping, the region's most prominent landmark, and in another to Highcliffe Nab. Station House at Hutton Gate furnishes a reminder that trains used to run that way, but the tracks have long since gone, and overgrown platforms bear mute witness to the fact that many years have passed since trains or passengers were seen there. Today, you can cycle along the route of the old railway, eastwards over the bridge which crosses Belmangate. The route affords a view across the cricket ground, which has such a slope that only half-size sightscreens are needed at one end. That arena has seen mighty deeds over the years. A few years ago, Guisborough's professional was none other than West Indian Test opener, Desmond Haynes, who really used to crack the ball around the ground and into the nearby car-park. More recently, that same arena has witnessed some remarkable performances by another West Indian, Phil Simmons.

Eating out has become increasingly popular in recent years. If you intend to have dinner, or Sunday lunch, at the Fox in Bow Street, it's a good idea to book a table well in advance. Their weekday lunch is extraordinarily good value, and their lamb cutlets a constant temptation. For something rather grander, in an opulent country-house setting, Grinkle Park Hotel, a mile or so off the Moors road to Whitby, makes an agreeable change. The restaurant has a good choice of menus, and bar meals are served in a pleasant conservatory looking out across the tree-fringed croquet lawn to the duckpond.

Not so long ago, through the kind offices of a friend, I was introduced to another side of life in the area, a nocturnal view of local activity. It was half-past three in the morning, and dawn still some way off, when we set out for Middlesbrough in pale grey light. To be out and about at such an hour was something of a novelty for me, but for Robert Cook, greengrocer of Guisborough, it is a way of life, summer and winter alike. Robert, born in Kildale, one of eight children of farming stock, was for a time driver for a firm of fruit and vegetable merchants. Five years ago, he set up as a greengrocer, with a shop at Enfield Chase, on the Hunter's Hill Estate.

Passing a few all-night cafës, with a handful of customers at their tables, we reached the wholesale market in Middlesbrough before four. Already there were signs of resolute activity: huge lorries, from various parts of Britain, and from continental Europe, were discharging loads of fruit and vegetables. 'Morning, Robert.' 'Morning, Paul.' Obviously, everybody knew everybody else, and there followed spirited exchange of banter, most of which passed over my head. It was still what some people would consider the middle of the night, and I began to wonder what on earth had persuaded me to undertake such an excursion. 'These are nice; try one.' Robert was holding out a plump, shiny, good-looking strawberry. It tasted good, too. Then he was opening a bag of carrots, checking them for size and colour. Breaking off a piece, he munched it thoughtfully, before going on to smell broccoli and turn over cauliflowers.

'You've got to get here early, when the stuff's fresh and nobody's touched it. Drop a cauli, you've bruised it, it's no good. Here, mind your back.' A fork-lift truck was making its way with astonishing dexterity around the piles of crates. Robert picked up a head of celery, felt it carefully, wrinkled his face in disapproval, and returned it to the box. 'Too wobbly,' he pronounced. I nodded sagely as we moved on. If Robert makes a mistake, he can find himself landed with a load of unsaleable merchandise. 'It's a very chancy business, but if you buy good stuff, it keeps fresh. These are nice eating,' he said, handing me a couple of pegs from a satsuma. 'And what about those cherries?' I said, popping one into my mouth. I was beginning to enjoy myself.

Robert had come armed with a shopping list of formidable dimensions, and turned his attention to tomatoes. After squeezing a few, he took a bite out of a particularly attractive specimen. Then we moved over to the more exotic items, which Robert is keen to introduce to his customers: paw-paws, kumquats, lychees, pineapples, aubergines, bright yellow courgettes, and peppers in a startling range of colours — green, red, orange, purple, white and black. 'They're a challenge, more exciting than ordinary cabbage and cauliflower. Years ago, there wasn't such a thing as nectarine; there were peaches, and that was it. Most people are curious, and in the shop we give them a sample to taste. I enjoy different things; we always take them home, and try them first.'

We had been there an hour or more, and already Robert's white van was filling up rapidly. 'I always load the stuff myself, so it isn't thrown in, doesn't get damaged.' The sun was peeping over the horizon by now, and the bustle intensified as more and more white vans drew up. It was obvious that white is the colour most favoured by greengrocers. To my surprise, the market turns out not to be an exclusively male preserve. Many of the buyers are ladies, hefting sacks of potatoes and bags of onions with the best. 'You know, those women have got more stamina than us,' Robert remarked wryly.

So it came round to half-past six, with everything in full swing, and time for us to go home with our cargo. 'It's not really been a hard morning,' Robert observed. 'The produce has been available for us to get hold of. Some days it's rough, there isn't enough to go round, and everybody's fighting for what they can get.'

Robert was looking forward to a hearty breakfast on his return. The hard part was still to come, unloading the boxes from the van and putting the goods on display before opening-time. Then, of course, he is serving customers throughout the day, helped by his wife and a small team of assistants. Robert is in bed by nine every night, and no longer has spare time to enjoy playing football and cricket. 'It certainly puts a lot of strain on your family,' he said. 'You get tired, very tired!' I asked him what had tempted him to become a greengrocer, rather than settling for a more mundane job with regular hours. 'Insanity, I think!' he replied, with a chuckle. For me, the whole thing had been, quite literally, an eye-opener, and now I can say that I really do understand what is meant by that phrase, a hard day's night.

Not so very long ago, Stockton was the very heartland of the industrial north. Who has not heard of Britain's first passenger railway line, opened in 1825 between Stockton and Darlington? And it was at Stockton in 1751 that Thomas Sheraton was born, he who became famous for his furniture. In 1924, the constituency returned as Unionist Member of Parliament one Harold Macmillan, who later took the title of Lord Stockton. The River Tees still runs softly by the town which, since 1968, has been part of the conurbation known as Teesside.

Time has not dealt altogether gently with Stockton. Today, signs of dereliction loom conspicuously alongside more cheering indications of new and vital growth: the famous racecourse, now a desolate prospect, suffers the pangs of redevelopment, and the broad High Street, with its fine 18th-century parish church and Town House, reveals the familiar complement of motley shop-fronts, unlovely emblems of an age of change. But there is still civic pride in the town's history, and its rise to eminence in the 19th century. Stockton Borough Council Museum Service has exercised proper diligence in keeping the past alive: on the outskirts of Stockton, in a bend of the Tees, and amid rolling parkland, the curious visitor may look again at Stockton's past, and be reminded of its character in former days.

Preston Hall, dating from 1825, was modernised and enlarged when Sir Robert Ropner, a local shipbuilder, bought it in 1882. Converted to offices in 1937, it continued to be used for that purpose until after the Second World War. Then, threatened with demolition, it was rescued by the enterprise of Stockton Corporation, who bought the Hall and Park, and opened a museum there in 1953.

A remarkable recreation of times past is the period street, a paved way with shops, pub, bank, working smithy, a courtyard with public water-pump and ice-cream cart, and advertisements on the walls for Sunlight Soap, BSA motor bicycles, Spratt's Patent Dog Cakes and other wonders of the age.

The draper's offers velvets from one shilling and three-farthings a yard (old money), 'mantles and dresses made to order with care and expedition', 'French hand-made underclothing kept in stock', a hint of things to come with 'new Japanese imports' and the promise of 'funerals conducted in a most careful manner'.

The ironmonger opposite presses the claims of W B Robinson's Patent Erimus Damp Proof Paint ('patent' was the buzz-word of those days), while the tailor advertises trousers to measure from 10/6d. I spent some time gazing at a window crammed with colourful china: a Crown Derby tureen for 4/10d, a sumptuously-decorated Doulton punchbowl for 6/3d, and fine specimens of Wedgwood, 'Willow' pattern and Staffordshire figurines. The establishment of E. Winpenny (an appropriate name for a 'smart, up-to-date hatter') displays folding opera hats for twelve shillings and (again, a sign of times ahead), Japanese straw boaters at 3/6d.

Laid out in the police station are instruments of restraint, chains and handcuffs, and on the walls, notices provide good reading. One announces the loss of a half-guinea with a hole in it, and promises that any person bringing the same to the police officers will be handsomely rewarded. A reward of £2 is offered for the return of a black pocket-book containing a cheque 'which has already been stopped', and a police notice encourages the apprehension of two young apprentices who have deserted from a fishing smack (shades of poor Smike in *Nicholas Nickleby*!), and of an embezzler who, it is thought, 'will endeavour to emigrate'.

The grocer sets out dried peas at 1d a pound, lentils at 2d, Rington's tea, varieties of biscuits in decorative tins and Hillaby's Best Pontefract Cakes, while the chemist's, with its shelves of bottles containing exotically-coloured fluids, provides for people of a certain generation an instant return to childhood days. Of course, all these are museum pieces, but the street also contains a little shop where excellent sepia photographs of old Stockton are on sale, together with the usual stocks of picture postcards, guidebooks and souvenirs.

For me, the most intriguing part of the whole complex lies in the period rooms on the first floor, presenting detailed recreation of a nineteenth-century kitchen, cosy and crowded with ingenious culinary apparatus; a bathroom equipped with what must have been quite a novelty, an all-round needle shower, suggesting to modern eyes something devised by Heath Robinson; a bedroom, with warming-pan ready, rocking cradle by the open fire, and an *escritoire* with conveniently tilting surface for writing and reading; and a sparsely-furnished maid's room in contrast to the music-room and parlour. Amid all these trappings of a departed era my companion, a lady of goodly years, gave vent to delighted affirmations of recognition.

A treasure-trove for the social historian, the rooms remind us of the Victorian quest for comfort and convenience, allied where possible to boldly decorative design and a sense of spaciousness. Those ideas are carried on elsewhere in the museum: in the winter garden, with its cacti, orchids and potted palms; in the rooms themselves, with their lofty ceilings and ornate plasterwork; and in the glass cases, housing such varied exhibits as a fascinating store of snuff-boxes, Valentine cards of most intricate design, some showing hearts embedded with shells, and a parade of wedding gifts, among them a stone hot-water bottle, a model of the Taj Mahal, brass candlesticks, sugar tongs and salt cellars.

Downstairs, there is a small costume gallery, and a room given over to the history of Preston Hall, with portraits of various worthies. General Sir Fowler Burton, KCB, JP, looks exactly as you would imagine him, while Sarah Burton, seated demurely at the keyboard, seems much more approachable.

The most notable exhibit at Preston Hall is a striking picture by the seventeenth-century French artist, Georges de la Tour. A study in concentration, *The Dice Players* shows five figures around a table, four of them intent on the game, eyes down, while a fifth, slightly more remote, enjoys a contemplative pipe. What makes the work so compelling is the dramatic use of light and shadow in its composition: the light source, a single candle, remains almost completely hidden from view by an outstretched arm, but its reflection on the table-top, and in the armoured breastplates of the players, forms vivid splashes of illumination. Colours are rich, varying shades of a single tonality, from lightish pink through warm russets and orange to darker areas of shadow. The picture hangs by itself in a small gallery, with subdued lighting to focus attention. It is the highlight of a most absorbing place which, for an hour or two, or even an entire day, offers a tantalising escape from the twentieth century, and a nostalgic excursion into the recent past. Let me assure readers that there is not a whiff of any musty odour of municipal museums as we used to know them; rather it is a centre of excellence, a place of delight for time-travellers of all ages.

Preston Hall Museum, Yarm Road, is situated 3 miles south of Stockton on the A135, and just south of the Stockton West intersection on the A66: open Monday to Saturday, 9.30 am to 5.30 pm, Sunday 2.00 to 5.30 pm; closed Christmas Day, Boxing Day, New Year's Day, Good Friday.

So many English seaside towns these days have the air of being permanently out of season. The crowds that used to gather in former days have gone elsewhere; the grand hotels are largely bereft of custom, and the seaside amusements stand forlorn and almost deserted. Across the sands stride a few hardy locals, exercising their dogs. The rest is silence. Such is the picture in many resorts which once enjoyed enormous popularity.

Saltburn is a funny, dear old place, where echoes of the past sound everywhere. More years ago than most of us remember, it was a flourishing seaside resort, with fine hotels and guest-houses. But times change, and holidaymakers began to desert this little town on the north-east coast with its sandy beach and towering cliffs, and yielded instead to the siren-call of more seductive locations. No longer does the train run into a special platform behind the Zetland Hotel to discharge its load of prosperous guests. The pier is shorter than it was, but the tramlift still runs up and down the cliff, when it is not closed for repairs, and every year Saltburn erupts into a recreation of its past with an exuberant Victorian carnival. The town is still at the end of a railway line, although the imposing station buildings now house smart little shops like Crumbs Bakery.

Happily, Saltburn does not live in the past. There is ample evidence of a new, vital spirit in the town. Down by the seashore, The Ship continues to attract customers, while higher up, the Zetland Hotel has been converted to luxury apartments. What was once a Methodist chapel is now Saltburn's Community Theatre, with a seating capacity of 160. Recently, I dropped in on a most enjoyable production of Alan Ayckbourn's play, *Absent Friends*, presented by the Saltburn '53 Society, an amateur dramatic group founded, as its name implies, in 1953, the year of the Coronation.

Today, there are about fifty members, putting on four main productions a year. The secretary, Liz Macdonald, a vivacious and energetic lady from Edinburgh, has lived in Saltburn for the past twenty years. She is able to recall times when things were rather harder than they are now. 'In its early days as a theatre, the audience actually sat in wooden pews, which were very, very uncomfortable. Knowing persons brought along their own cushions! And then the local rotary club got some seats from an old cinema, and fitted them for us. A lot of work has been done, to construct an apron to make the stage bigger. We managed to get money to provide curtains, and we've now got quite a lot of lighting.'

We talked about the changing face of Saltburn over the years: 'My daughter Fiona has just done a project entitled "The Decline and Rise of Saltburn as a Seaside Resort", or words to that effect, which was very interesting. She found that the population hasn't increased very much, there have been very few houses built. When we first came here, there was a more elderly population; now, though there's still an elderly population, there appear to be more young people as well.'

Saltburn, like Guisborough, finds itself in the county of Cleveland, a comparatively recent creation. When we first moved to this part of England, it was called Yorkshire, and many people still regard it as part of that proud county of the white rose. It is a good centre from which to explore the North York Moors, traversed by pedestrian routes along the Cleveland Way and the famous Lyke-Wake Walk, or along the changing coastline from Redcar to the town of Whitby. A more peaceful base can be found in a charming little village just ten miles inland from Whitby, Goathland, where grass verges are cropped by docile sheep, where there is a fine waterfall, the Mallyan Spout, and a station on the North Yorkshire Moors Railway. In season, from Grosmont (literally, 'big hill'), passengers are carried on rolling stock once used by the London and North-Eastern Railway, hauled by steam or diesel, southwards to Pickering in the vale. The compartments on these trains are adorned by framed sepia prints of English watering-places to remind travellers of a more gracious age, and they are treated on the journey to a succession of delightful views, including a spectacular glimpse of the huge, white golf-balls of Fylingdales Early Warning System, with their strangely-compelling, if rather sinister, beauty. On summer weekends, dinner is served on the journey, in luxurious Pullman cars.

It is only right that railways should continue to flourish in this area, since so much of the history of the iron way was forged here or hereabouts. From Middlesbrough, in Teesside's industrial heartland, a train will transport you gently along the course of the Esk Valley and, in about an hour and a half, bring you to the North Sea at Whitby. The journey itself is a succession of rare delights, since the Esk Valley railway is among Britain's most picturesque routes. Once clear of Middlesbrough itself, factories, warehouses and all the emblems of the northern industrial scene quickly fall behind and are forgotten; houses continue to fill the scene until past

Nunthorpe, but then unfolds a succession of beguiling sights: hills, moorland, isolated farmsteads and upland pastures nourishing sheep and cattle, who stare placidly at passing carriages. On through dales goes the iron road: Kildale and Commondale, then Danby and the North York Moors Centre, with its nature trails. Further eastwards still, the traveller reaches Grosmont, northern terminal of the North Yorkshire Moors Railway.

The railway crosses and recrosses the meandering River Esk, stopping along the way at what look almost like toy stations. After Sleights (pronounced Slates), the whole character of the journey begins to change: a faint whiff of ozone in the air, the river becoming broader and deep enough to float small craft; mobile homes glimpsed near the banks, a cluster of eager ducks at Ruswarp, and then houses becoming more numerous again as, with brakes screeching on a curving line, the train passes under a huge, gaunt, brick viaduct. Then, quite suddenly, there is Whitby on the right, the masts of sailing vessels in the harbour like a miniature forest and, higher up, rows of respectable terraced dwellings. A chandlery shop slides by the window before the terminus is reached: Whitby Station, its facade reminding travellers of grander days but, standing rather pretentiously as it does today, a mere shadow of its former self. Now, most people come to the town by car.

A short walk away, the town's real and serious business reveals itself at the water's edge, for Whitby is a busy port: the bridge swivels to admit larger vessels to the inner harbour, bringing a temporary halt to the town's traffic along Bridge Street. Hard by, a placard outside the offices of the *Whitby Gazette* demonstrates a proper concern for local matters: WHITBY ACCIDENT MAN DIES, it reads. On the corner, a signpost points towards the house where James Cook lodged when serving his apprenticeship to a Quaker shipowner, James Walker. A visit to the museum there completes the cycle of a journey which begins and ends with reminders of that famous explorer, born in 1728 at Marton, now a suburb of Middlesbrough. Recently opened there is the birthplace museum; then his memorial, a simple obelisk on a high hill, can be seen from the train on its way past Great Ayton.

But back to Whitby, a place of great charm and character, compact enough to allow thorough exploration on foot, although gradients are often steep. At the centre of town, fish and chip shops are on almost every corner; a sign of the times, perhaps, that next to Hadley's Fish Restaurant stands the Good Luck Chinese Restaurant. Whitby claims two entries in *The Good Food Guide* for 1989: the Magpie Café in Pier Road, and Trenchers on New Quay Road. Then, there are antique shops, jewellers selling Whitby jet, bookshops, and a small, attractive, market place with lettering prominent on the face of the market hall to remind passers-by that the fine structure was built by Nathaniel Cholmley Esq., MDCCLXXXVIII, Jonth Pickernall, Arch.

NORTH YORKSHIRE AND CLEVELAND

A curious aspect of the town's other role, that of holiday resort, is an establishment announcing itself as The Dracula Experience. As you may remember from Bram Stoker's horrific tale of vampires, Count Dracula came to Whitby with his boxes of Transylvanian earth, and it was there that poor Lucy Westenra became one of his victims. But, of course, that is all fiction, and there really are no vampires in Whitby! Yet, as the gatekeeper at the abbey remarked to me, 'It's good for the tourist trade.' So, indeed, it would seem. I even came across a shop with Dracula erasers on show in the window; presumably, for rubbing out your enemies!

Gulls wing around the harbour constantly, swooping and screaming as fishing boats return with their catch. On winter days, the wind comes bitingly off the sea. From the town centre, a roughly-cobbled street, with parallel stairway, winds steeply upwards, past the youth hostel and St Mary's Parish Church, to the abbey, which dominates the town from on high. Whitby has long occupied an important place in ecclesiastical history, mentioned by the Venerable Bede (whose bones lie in Durham Cathedral) as Streonaeshalch. The first abbey on the site was founded by King Oswy of Northumbria in 657, and a stained-glass window in Oxford's Christ Church Cathedral commemorates its abbess, St Hilda. Hilda took in the indigent herdsman, Caedmon, whose Hymn became recognised as one of the great jewels of early English literature. In 867, the monastery was destroyed by the Vikings; still standing today, and well worth inspecting, are the remains of a reconstruction which began in 1220. Whitby Abbey was closed in 1539, by order of Henry VIII, that formidable despoiler of monastic institutions throughout the land. The buildings fell into ruin and, in more recent history, were further damaged by shells from a German warship in 1914.

Beyond the abbey, the Cleveland Way, here sensibly reinforced by duckboards, runs past the coastguard station and along the cliff edge, affording on a clear day magnificent prospects, with sightings of large tankers far out at sea, small fishing boats closer to shore, and at the base of the cliffs, dangerous shallows, threatening the unwary mariner. Beyond Saltwick Nab, a huge rock stands above the surface, shaped like the dark fin of some massive creature, continually battered by successive lines of breakers.

North-eastwards from Whitby, the road leads to Runswick Bay, where an assortment of quaint houses clusters precariously on steep slopes running down to the half-moon curve of the shore, and strolling visitors feel like intruders into the privacy of neat back-gardens. Further on is Staithes, an attractive fishing village where James Cook, the famous explorer, was briefly apprenticed to a shopkeeper. A mile or so further on rise the dizzy heights of Boulby Cliffs. A long stretch of firm sand begins in Saltburn, and continues through Marske to Redcar, where the industrial belt takes over, but it must be one of the few towns where one can walk out of a large department store, cross the road to the promenade, and purchase from the boats there freshly-landed crab, plaice, haddock and cod.

72   ENGLAND

Inland, the uncompromising sternness of place-names reflects the character of the area, known in earlier days for its mining of iron ore and minerals from the Cleveland Hills, and later for its chemical industries and oil refineries: Brotton, Loftus, Skelton, South Bank, Eston give way, as the traveller leaves the urban sprawl, to more evocative names, like Upleatham, which claims to have the smallest church in England, Newton-under-Roseberry, nestling cosily beneath the broken peak of Roseberry Topping, a famous viewpoint, Ingleby Greenhow, Westerdale and Rosedale Abbey, all in healthy walking terrain, where high moors purple with abundant heather in late summer, and soft, green dales laugh with bright acres of daffodils in spring.

At Kirkleatham, the Old Hall Museum affords a fascinating insight into one of the enchanted areas of Britain. To the casual eye, Kirkleatham may present something of an enigma. Only a couple of miles from Redcar, its appearance of tranquil, rural seclusion is immediately contradicted by the blatant proximity of steel towers and belching chimneys which make up the huge ICI complex at Wilton. Yet things were not always thus: closer investigation and exercise of the imagination uncover a fascinating pattern of history which has shaped the village over successive centuries. Architecturally arresting, this tidy little settlement represents a powerful link with bygone ages, manifested by St Cuthbert's Church and its mausoleum, Kirkleatham Old Hall, now an important museum, and Sir William Turner's Hospital, a graceful courtyard of almshouses with a chapel in the midst.

One of the first things to meet the gaze of curious visitors to Turner's Hospital is a tablet, noting that the institution was 'Founded and endowed 1676 by Sr Wm TURNER, Knight, Lord Mayor of ye City of London'. The chapel and two school houses were erected in 1742 by Cholmley Turner, Sir William's great-nephew, who was largely responsible for the substance of the foundation that has survived to the present day, and whose original purpose is observed still.

Sheila Simpson was born in Guisborough, and has known the place since childhood; now she is warden at the Turner Hospital, constantly on call to respond to emergencies which occur from time to time among the inhabitants of this friendly establishment. 'We have twenty people living in the cottages,' Sheila told me. 'Each cottage has its own small front entrance, a living-room with a bed space, a kitchen and back lobby, and it has a toilet and shower unit with seating arrangement. Then they all have their own little garden.' Captivatingly charming and neat was the prospect which greeted me on a recent visit. A most agreeable place to live, I mused, and enquired what were the qualifications for admission: '63 or over, widow, widower or single, because it's only single accommodation, and member of the Church of England. They each pay £11 a week. That's for the cottages; there are flats, but they're run on a commercial basis. They get meals on wheels, there's a mobile library, and a hairdresser. There's a service in the chapel on the first and third Wednesdays of every month, and the Vicar of Kirkleatham, David Purdy, presides. Attendance used to be compulsory: they used to have the mace, and they would all line up, walk round the square and into the chapel. Then, of course, there was the school here, with the children. Originally, it was designated for ten poor men, ten poor women, ten poor boys and ten poor girls.'

The chapel, thought to be the work of James Gibbs, is the real gem of the whole complex, and well worth inspecting. The tower has a remarkable feature, in the shape of a single-handed clock. Behind the altar is a fine window, creation of an Italian artist, Sebastiano Ricci. A magnificent chandelier and two eighteenth-century chairs also merit attention. Alfred Baldwin, Kirkleatham's most knowledgeable resident, and former curator of the chapel, comments on their present-day value: 'There are two gilt chairs in the chancel; those were bought, I think, for two guineas each. The chandelier in the centre cost three guineas. Well, when I was clerk in the nineteen-seventies, I asked Christies to value them: they said that if they were put on the market, they thought the chairs would bring at least two thousand pounds each, and the chandelier at least ten thousand pounds.'

A fine place, Kirkleatham, deserving an afternoon of anyone's time: fitting memorial to many generations of the Turner family, and a stylish segment of our history preserved more or less intact.

Men of the Northlands

Herbert Read, poet, critic and co-founder of the Institute of Contemporary Arts, was born on 4 December, 1893, near Kirkbymoorside in Yorkshire. The scenes of his childhood, where he had his early schooling, are vividly depicted in *The Innocent Eye*; and the poems which make up his *Eclogues* preserve the impressions of that time.

> 'If only I can recover the sense and uncertainty of those innocent years,' he wrote, 'years in which we seemed not so much to live as to be lived by forces outside us, by the wind and trees and moving clouds and all the mobile engines of our expanding world — then I am convinced I shall possess a key to much that has happened to me in this other world of conscious living.'

Read's autobiographies, collected together in *The Contrary Experience*, carry an epigraph from Wordsworth:

> ... fostered alike by beauty and by fear.

His book, *Wordsworth*, is a perceptive study of the life and work of a poet to whom he felt drawn by temperament and conditioning — they were both northerners — and much of his autobiographical writing has a Wordsworthian ring to it. 'All life,' Read asserts, 'is an echo of our first sensations ...'

The early poems use an adult vocabulary with mature assurance, yet at the same time they possess the clarity and quick perception of a child's vision. There are intimations of a world beyond the fields and the high-road:

> A rising fish ripples the still waters
> And disturbs my soul.

Already, the patterns of life are forming, in a firm and steady mould, so that half a century later, when the matrix has hardened, the same sense of wonder persists in the lines of a sonnet:

> And a rook if it should swerve in the sky
> Will move the whole world momentously.

Herbert Read went to Halifax to continue his schooling, and from there to Leeds University. During those years of his adolescence and early manhood, war was gathering in Europe, soon to break out into an accumulation of horrors. Read saw the innocent eye of childhood as a kind of defence against such things. 'The child even has a natural craving for horrors,' he explained. 'He survives just because he is without sentiment, for only in this way can his green heart harden sufficiently to withstand the wounds that wait for it.'

In January, 1915, he was commissioned to the Green Howards, a Yorkshire regiment and, with many others of his generation, was sent to the front, where he won the Military Cross in 1917 and the Distinguished Service Order in 1918. His reactions to the scenes of war are recorded in the *War Diaries*: 'The young man we meet at the opening of the *Diary*, in January 1915, had recently attained the age of twenty-one ... he had just joined his battalion, then under canvas in a hastily improvised camp in the south of England (a country strange to him, for hitherto he had not left his native county in the north of England). He had lost both his parents and was now homeless ... Sympathy is needed for such an Innocent, cast into the frenzy of war with no better covering than the philosophy of Nietzsche.'

After the war, Herbert Read left the army, and in 1919 went to the Treasury. But, like the army, this was not a world he wished to inhabit for long, and he became Assistant Keeper at the Victoria and Albert Museum in London. In 1931, he was appointed Professor of Fine Art at the University of Edinburgh. Much of his life was devoted to writing and lecturing on art, literature and education but, as Kathleen Raine said, 'it will after all be as a poet that he will be longest remembered.'

When the Second World War came in 1939, he was living at a thatched house set in an acre of beechwood, at Seer Green in Buckinghamshire. Three years earlier, he had married my mother's sister, and we spent the first Christmas of the war there, with snow thick on the lawns and woodlands. The conflict was one that Herbert Read viewed from a distance, but his feelings were much the same as they had been a quarter of a century earlier, feelings he expressed in a poem addressed 'To a Conscript of 1940', in which one generation speaks to the next:

> We went where you are going, into the rain and the mud;
> We fought as you will fight
> With death and darkness and despair;
> We gave what you will give — our brains and our blood.

All through his years spent in the south of England, Read felt himself to be an exile. Indeed, one of his poems is entitled 'Exile's Lament', and closes with the prayer:

> God grant I may return to die
> Between the Riccall and the Rye.

That prayer was granted. In September, 1949, Herbert Read returned to Yorkshire, to Ryedale and the landscape of his youth, which was to fortify his later years. This was where he knew his roots to be, this was where he belonged, though his horizons now stretched far beyond the girding hills. It was in the tiny northern village of Stonegrave that he settled, and made his home for the remainder of his life. 'The house,' he wrote, 'is built of honey-coloured stone and roofed with the warm crimson pantiles characteristic of all the old houses in Ryedale.'

His autobiographies contain much that evokes the character and history of this region of England, and his sole excursion into the dramatic form, *Moon's Farm*, a dialogue for three voices conceived for radio, was written as an elegy for the silent and deserted farmsteads that cluster the moorlands of Bransdale.

Herbert Read died at Stonegrave on 12 June, 1968, in his 75th year. The funeral service was in the little church a few yards from his house, and the interment at Kirkdale, where his father was buried. As we drove through the narrow lanes leading to St Gregory's Minster at Kirkdale, there ran insistently through my mind the opening lines of his sonnet:

> One day you will intuitively come
> Home again driving westward
> Into the burning sun: memory
> a dusty screen that blinds the vision ...

In the serenity of a summer's afternoon, there was the sure knowledge that Herbert Read had come home again to rest 'in a wild valley, near a running beck'.

His autobiographies, *The Contrary Experience*, carry a simple inscription, the initials of his four sons and one daughter, *filiis meis sodalibusque*. The *Collected Poems* are dedicated to his wife, Margaret.

The north is famous for its characters, often rough and tough, because they have been brought up the hard way. To a southern eye, northerners may often appear undemonstrative, taciturn, blunt and outspoken. They can take some getting to know, as can be seen from the true stories I am about to relate of two sturdy northcountrymen of my acquaintance. One story has a happy ending, the other does not.

Cock and hen, buck and doe, donkey, upright, tilted, Mendip top, through-style. What, you may wonder, is this all about? Double Dutch to many readers, I suspect, but part of the everyday vocabulary of Middlesbrough-born Eddie Rowney. This is the story of an ancient craft, that of dry-stone walling. Eddie is a walling tutor for Specialised Technical Services in Dormanstown, working in Employment Training on the North York Moors. For the past twelve years he has lived in an appropriately-named dwelling, Stonehouse Cottage, at Fangdale Beck, Chop Gate.

'I live, breathe and dream walls, I'm very fortunate that I get paid to pursue my hobby. Besides being an instructor, I'm a master craftsman, I'm chairman of the North Yorkshire Branch of the Dry-Stone Walling Association, British Trust for Conservation volunteer, instructor for the Duke of Edinburgh Award Scheme.' There is the authentic voice of the dedicated enthusiast. Indeed, after talking to Eddie, you go away with the feeling that here is someone who has found his proper niche in life, who is entirely contented with his lot.

What exactly is involved in the business of dry-stone walling, I asked him? How does it differ from modern methods of building. 'A dry-stone wall is a wall built of stone without the aid of sand or cement. You might see one or two with the tops cemented on, but that's purely to deter people from stealing the stones, nothing else. You build a house, the mortar will crumble, it needs pointing, but a dry-stone wall will last indefinitely; its own weight keeps it together. But there's more to walling than just putting stones on top of one another. I could sit and talk to you for three weeks about the different sorts of walling. If you go along the A66 across Bowes Moor and through Durham and Cumbria, you'll see about thirty different types of walling, just in that road alone.'

Years ago, dry-stone walling was a flourishing activity all over the country; but times change, and now there remain only the walls to remind passers-by of the labour of many hands. 'At one time, it was a real industry: every estate had two or three wallers. At the turn of the century, I should think in North Yorkshire alone there would have been fifty or sixty wallers. Now, we have one professional waller. There's a vast amount of work to be done. You can see the walls are crumbling. There was a survey which found that the industry could take 47,000 men to restore all the walls in England and Scotland. The walls may be crumbling, but you need the same expertise as was needed a thousand years ago. It's a long-standing craft.'

Now, Eddie is concerned to remedy the present situation, to encourage young men to take up this time-honoured occupation. 'There's a shortage in North Yorkshire: plenty of walls to do, but no wallers. When you're a waller, you've got to like your own company, because you're stuck on the moors, miles from anywhere. Unfortunately, a lot of young lads today won't work in a lonely situation like that: they like company. And that is one of the problems. I'm a walling tutor: one of two in England, probably in the world. I'm teaching walling because I realised that there were people wanting to wall, and they couldn't, because there was nobody to teach them. So this is why I've taken the road I'm taking now: I teach it, instead of earning money as a professional working waller. It's a highly-paid profession: go to any walling shows, and you'll see that the professionals don't just drive up in any old bangers; they all have really good cars, because there are very few wallers, and they get good money.'

Eddie has an interesting cross-section of society in his group currently undergoing instruction: 'I've got some good lads, some good up-and-coming wallers. I have among them a textile designer, an ex-security officer, a machinist, an electrical engineer.'

But it is not a job for everybody, as Eddie is quick to point out: 'It's quite hard work, physically, but anyone who is reasonably fit can do it. But you've got to have a certain aptitude: you need your hands to pick the stones up with, but you must have a brain to build the wall. If you work on the moors, people think you're a thicky; but if you haven't got the intelligence, you'll never be a dry stone waller. And you've got to like it. If you come to work in the morning and you don't like doing it, then you're wasting your time.'

Is there a secret to the whole business, a special knack? 'The art of dry stone walling is stone selection. Until you've mastered the art of stone selection, you won't get your speed up. The stones we get in North Yorkshire are bigger than those in Derbyshire, but if you grade them, you don't have to lift the large ones. You dig a trench for the foundations, and you put your biggest, most awkward stones in there, at the bottom. And a good foundation is the key to the wall's strength. You need very few tools, just what the wallers of years ago used: a walling-hammer and a walling-pick, a line and a frame; and you wear gloves. You build within the frame, and then take the frame away; so you can go for thousands of miles, and still get the same width. You don't use a spirit-level, you judge it by eye. It's like brickwork: one and two, and two and one, one lapping another one so you have no running joints. Gravity, and careful selection of stones will keep it together. You shouldn't break any stones; just use them as they are. There are two sides to a wall, so you put your good ones on the face side, and the not-so-good on the other side. It's two layers thick, and the middle has packing of small stones, adding to the strength. Then halfway up the wall, you'll have every yard one that spreads right through, and that's called the trough: the same principle as ties used in houses. A standard wall is four-foot-six high, and you should be putting up an average of six yards a day. You only get this through practice. Some wallers in West Yorkshire do eight to ten yards a day.'

Eddie Rowney has no hesitation in recommending dry-stone walling as a trade, even as a way of life. As he says, it brings so many rewards: 'Job satisfaction: you're building things that are going to last for thousands of years. It's good money, it's a chance to work for yourself and it's a healthy life.' There is no doubt in Eddie's mind that this is the only career for him; nothing in life would bring greater fulfilment. 'I sleep well, and I can't wait to get to the job in the morning. I'm content; if you work near the soil, then you're content.' Who could ask for anything more?

Eddie Rowney is a fortunate man: that much is obvious. In fact, most of us don't realise how lucky we are. The thought struck me after talking to Ernie Newby and his wife, Sylvia, of Guisborough. Not that Ernie is the sort of person who goes around feeling sorry for himself: far from it, even though he has had more than his fair share of life's burdens. An accident on New Year's Eve 1961, when a snowball came through the window, eventually led to Ernie's losing the sight of his left eye. But that incident, sadly, was only the prelude to his misfortunes: in his own words, 'Nothing has ever gone right since.'

Born in Grangetown, Ernie saw something of the world as a young man. 'I spent a couple of years in the merchant navy, went to Australia twice, and to South Africa. I was in the steelworks for a bit, then the next thing, I was in the army.

22302771 Guardsman Newby, 2nd Battalion Coldstream Guards.' Ernie recalls with military precision the details of his 3-year term of service in the army, and his demobilisation on 7 August, 1955. After that, it was the steelworks again, where he learnt to operate cranes and other machinery; then the shipyards for a while and, most important of all, marriage to Sylvia. Ernie takes up the story.

'We had two boys and two girls. When the elder boy, Stephen, was ten or eleven years old, we found out he had muscular dystrophy. Then his younger brother, Paul, had to go to the specialist, and they discovered he was suffering from it as well. When we first found out, I just went to pieces. As time went on, they became more and more helpless, and somebody had to be with them all the while. It's a progressive ailment — well, it's a terminal ailment: they got weaker and weaker, and we had to do literally everything for them. The main burden fell on the wife.' He exchanged a glance with Sylvia. 'We had to get up in the middle of the night to turn the lads over; we used to take turns in doing it. We went for years without a proper night's sleep. We've had two holidays on our own since it started. Then, from 1980, I had to pack in work to care for the lads.'

For a while, Sylvia had a job, but Ernie has not been as fortunate. 'Apart from six months on "Ring and Ride", I haven't done any paid work since 1980. Now, I've only got ten years of work left in me before retirement age. In the last few months, I've written 165 letters, and had about 30 replies. I'd like to do something in the way of helping disabled people, like "Ring and Ride", which is a great thing, a service for those who can't get out by themselves. For the likes of me, it's an ideal job, but with only one eye, I'm disqualified from any driving job. But I'd like a job in community service, particularly with the disabled, because I understand their needs.'

Ernie is not the sort of person to dwell on past sadness, but he cannot forget, and some memories are particularly painful. 'My youngest lad, Paul, if he could have stood, he'd have been about six-foot-four, and I would love to have seen him in the Guards. He knew what I wanted for him: just before he died, we were watching the trooping of the colour on the telly, and he said, "I'm sorry, dad." There was a pause, while Ernie quietly composed himself: 'It still hurts, you know, but it helps to sit and talk about it with people who understand your problem.'

I asked Ernie about those years he spent caring for his two disabled sons, watching their steady deterioration. 'We just tried to treat them as normal lads. They used to get around; they had electric wheelchairs to go about in, and we could let them go about on their own. We liked to go to Bridlington, because it was nice and flat. And I used to take them down to The Fox for a pint — well, they weren't strong enough to lift a pint mug, so it had to be halves. And they made friends down there, who would keep an eye on them, so that we could go home and leave them to their own devices, knowing that they were well looked after.

Guisborough being a small town, everybody knew them. They needed their independence, they didn't want parents with them all the time, when they were in their twenties: they were perfectly normal lads, they had normal feelings.' 'Yes, and I was the one who was sent out to borrow the saucy videos for them!' chipped in Sylvia. Ernie chuckled at that recollection before continuing.

'They'd go to parties, they'd go to dances in a wheelchair, and the lasses would dance with them. They were intelligent, too: Stephen had a diploma in art, in textile design. Then they went to Majorca several times, on holidays organised for the disabled, while we stayed at home. Paul died when he was 21; Stephen was 28 when he died in January last year. Even though you know what's going to happen, you know it's inevitable, it's still a heck of a kick in the guts when it comes.'

'We had so much support,' Sylvia added. 'The social services did everything they possibly could, and our doctors, and particularly the people in Guisborough — they were marvellous.'

There is no false sentimentality about Ernie and Sylvia. One thing emerged quite clearly from our conversation, that they had done the best that was possible for their boys in the circumstances, without any thought for themselves. 'You try to treat them as normal people, you try to keep them on their feet as long as possible. Life has to go on, no matter what. You mustn't feel sorry for them. Sympathise with them, yes, but you mustn't feel sorry for them: that's the worst thing you could do. Don't pamper them. What they can do for themselves, you must make them do. Let them get on with it. Another thing that's upsetting: you're pushing them in a wheelchair, and people stop and ask you how they are, instead of asking them. I'd say to them, "Ask him!" There are folk that think, if they see a person in a wheelchair, that they must be mentally defective!'

A tragic period in the life of Sylvia and Ernie Newby, but not a time of unrelieved sadness. There was still the closeness of family life, with its rewards. 'It wasn't all gloom, you know: we had some great times, there were lots of laughs, lots of happy memories. Of course, it put a strain on both of us. One day, when we were having a disagreement, Paul said, "Don't argue over me!" They were a happy pair of lads, though they knew what the score was. And you don't need remembrance notices in papers, and memorials and that kind of thing: it's all here.' Ernie tapped his heart, and then his head. 'You cannot plan ahead. You must take life as it comes.' Simple words from a brave man.

The North-west

One of the finest train journeys in England is on the line which runs from Settle to Carlisle, a memorable excursion through wild and lonely countryside. I had forgotten, until we travelled by that route recently, that such wilderness still existed south of the Scottish border. From the train, we surveyed huge tracts of land almost untouched, or so it seemed, by human influence. Now and then a deserted farmstead came into view, but beyond were the endless vistas of rolling moors, and the snow-flecked heights of Penyghent, Ingleborough, Whernside, Wild Boar Fell and Mallerstang Edge. We rattled over the impressive span of Ribblehead Viaduct, a wonder of railway engineering, through tunnels up to the summit of Ais Gill, 1169 feet above sea level. The line has been threatened with closure on more than one occasion, and its future is by no means assured. Fortunately, public support for its retention has been stimulated by a most praiseworthy band of enthusiastic volunteers, Friends of the Carlisle-Setlle Line, whose members include the Bishop of Carlisle, Sir Harry Secombe and no fewer than five Members of Parliament. The secretariat is at 33 Temple Rhydding Drive, Baildon, Shipley, West Yorkshire BD17 5PX. Long may they flourish, and long may passengers continue to enjoy one of the best train rides anywhere.

We stopped for lunch in Appleby, once the county town of Westmorland. There is a castle, with a Norman keep, and several pleasant inns. In all a delightful place to linger, except in June, when large numbers of gypsies converge on Appleby for the annual horse fair. That is the time to be out of town. At the northern end of the line, Carlisle, Luguvallum to the Romans, Caer Luel to the British, is worth a visit, for its 11th-century castle which held Mary, Queen of Scots, prisoner; the 12th-century cathedral; and the Carlisle Museum and Art Gallery, which presents the work of a number of 19th- and 20th-century artists.

The large towns and cities of north-western England have an aggressive air of stern purpose about them. For generations, their business has been cotton, shipping and manufacture, and folk here are known to be as hard-headed, in their way, as their counterparts on the other side of the Pennines, eastwards.

Liverpool enjoyed for a term the reputation of the liveliest city in Britain. It was there, on 9 October 1940, that John Lennon was born, he who was later to achieve worldwide fame as one of the Beatles, and to meet an early death. Liverpool is still a rewarding city to visit. The Walker Art Gallery is a marvellously satisfying collection, full of good things. The city has its own Tate Gallery, in Albert Dock, with exhibitions of modern works; then, the Anglican cathedral, designed by Sir Giles Gilbert Scott, and the Roman Catholic cathedral, the work of Sir Edwin Lutyens, are both outstanding examples of 20th-century British architecture. Liverpool is a busy port, with seven miles of docks along the River Mersey. It was from here, during my service with the Royal Air Force, that I sailed for the Isle of Man,

Carlisle to Leeds (Settle–Carlisle Line)

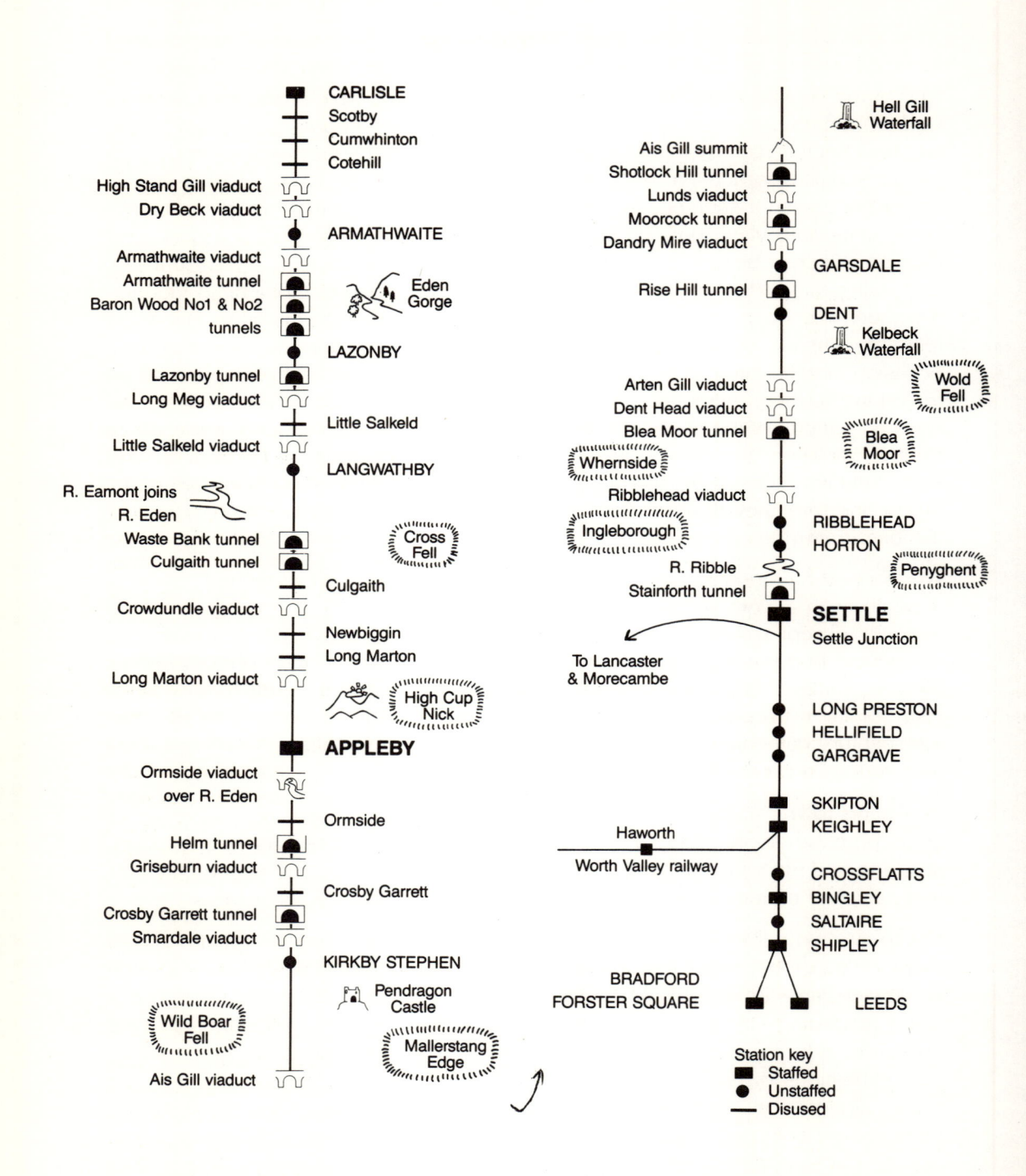

Carlisle
- Scotby
- Cumwhinton
- Cotehill

High Stand Gill viaduct
Dry Beck viaduct

ARMATHWAITE

Armathwaite viaduct
Armathwaite tunnel
Baron Wood No1 & No2 tunnels

Eden Gorge

LAZONBY

Lazonby tunnel
Long Meg viaduct

Little Salkeld

Little Salkeld viaduct

LANGWATHBY

R. Eamont joins R. Eden

Waste Bank tunnel
Culgaith tunnel

Culgaith

Cross Fell

Crowdundle viaduct

Newbiggin
Long Marton

Long Marton viaduct

High Cup Nick

APPLEBY

Ormside viaduct over R. Eden

Ormside

Helm tunnel
Griseburn viaduct

Crosby Garrett

Crosby Garrett tunnel
Smardale viaduct

KIRKBY STEPHEN

Pendragon Castle

Wild Boar Fell

Mallerstang Edge

Ais Gill viaduct

Ais Gill summit
Shotlock Hill tunnel
Lunds viaduct
Moorcock tunnel
Dandry Mire viaduct

Hell Gill Waterfall

GARSDALE

Rise Hill tunnel

DENT

Kelbeck Waterfall

Arten Gill viaduct
Dent Head viaduct
Blea Moor tunnel

Wold Fell

Whernside

Ribblehead viaduct

Blea Moor

Ingleborough

RIBBLEHEAD
HORTON

R. Ribble
Stainforth tunnel

Penyghent

SETTLE
Settle Junction

To Lancaster & Morecambe

- LONG PRESTON
- HELLIFIELD
- GARGRAVE

SKIPTON
KEIGHLEY

Haworth
Worth Valley railway

- CROSSFLATTS
- BINGLEY
- SALTAIRE
- SHIPLEY

BRADFORD FORSTER SQUARE   **LEEDS**

Station key
■ Staffed
● Unstaffed
— Disused

an utterly delightful spot, even in the depths of winter. More recently, we returned to Liverpool on the ferry from Belfast, along one of the traditional sea-routes between Ireland and England.

Thirty miles to the east of Liverpool, inland but connected to the Mersey and the sea by canal, is Manchester, at the heart of the Lancashire cotton industry. Manchester, one of England's major cities, has its Opera House, and the Museum of Transport. It is also renowned, if that is the right word, for its frequent rain. Granada Television provides a kind of nostalgic fiction: tours of their studios have included Coronation Street, location for the long-running television series, and Baker Street, where Sherlock Holmes and Dr Watson were to be found in the pages of Conan Doyle's stories.

On tour with a group of professional actors, I have played in Wigan before an audience of thirteen. Nobody in Wigan seemed to know where the theatre was, and we had the greatest difficulty in finding it ourselves. There are jokes about Wigan: George Orwell encapsulated their flavour in the title of his book, *The Road to Wigan Pier*. Wigan is an inland town. We packed our bags and left it without any lingering regrets; but the following evening saw us little better served in nearby Southport where we had an audience of twenty-five. Lord Street has been described as the finest shopping street in Britain. Apart from shops, and a number of elegant buildings, it contains the Atkinson Art Gallery, with paintings by Sickert, Steer, Augustus John and Roger Fry, and sculptures by Epstein and Henry Moore.

However, after our performance, we felt the need of other kinds of consolation, and we enjoyed one of the best Chinese meals I have eaten in Britain, at a place called the Peking Garden. I am told by my cousin, who lives at nearby Formby, that this establishment still functions. We ordered the banquet, a sumptuous meal with many courses, of which the duck was most memorable. After eating steadily for about an hour and a half, and starting to feel more than satisfied, we naturally assumed that we were near the end of the menu, and that perhaps coffee would be the next thing to appear. One of our number sought confirmation from a waiter. 'Oh, no! Now we bring main course!' I am ashamed to admit that our party found itself quite unable to do full justice to the main course, delicious though it undoubtedly was. The recollection of what we had left behind haunted us all next day, as we drove southwards down the motorway with little chance of further gastronomic delights along the way.

On April 22 1912, at the village of Higher Walton, near Preston, in Lancashire, a daughter was born to the headmaster of the local school, William Ferrier. She was Kathleen Mary Ferrier, a name that remains clear in the memory of those who heard her sing, and in the memory of many, many more, who did not have that singular good fortune, and know her voice only through recordings. Kathleen Ferrier, in her brief career, was someone very special, someone much loved by all who knew her. In a way, she symbolised the character of the north, and its well-known talent for making music.

While still quite young, she married Albert Wilson, and went to live in Silloth, a town of around two and a half thousand inhabitants on the Cumberland coast. Her husband, Bert, worked in a bank there, and today, on the wall of that same bank in Silloth, there is a plaque recording the fact that the contralto Kathleen Ferrier lived there from 1936 to 1941, and that in 1937 she won the Silver Rose Bowl as the best singer in the Carlisle Festival. She made many friends at Silloth, but they knew her simply as Kath Wilson, a charming and attractive housewife eager to join in all the local activities — sporting, theatrical, social and musical. Today, as I discovered when I went to gather material for a BBC radio programme, there are still people in Silloth with clear recollections of Kath Wilson, a lovely girl who swam, played tennis, golf, cracked practical jokes, and sang with the local choir. Her subsequent career was meteoric, in its brightness and its brevity: London, Glyndebourne, the Edinburgh Festival, New York, Chicago, San Francisco, Montreal, Toronto, Paris, Rome, Vienna and Salzburg. In her spare time, such as it was in such a demanding career, she took up painting, always signing her pictures KK. The initials stood for Klever Kaff, a decoration bestowed on her in earlier days by an admiring three-year-old boy in Silloth. And Klever Kaff she remained, to her family and friends. I was fortunate enough to hear her in person twice, both times in Cambridge: in 1950 and in May of 1952, after she had fought off the first serious assault of cancer. At the first of these concerts, she sang Schumann's song-cycle, *Frauenliebe und Leben*, A Woman's Love and Life. I shall not forget the tears that ran unchecked down the face of an elderly lady sitting near me, as we listened to that voice, with its youthful bloom and beauty allied to a rare and wonderful depth of poignant expression. Hers was a remarkable personality: sublime and majestic on stage, in private life bubbling with merriment. Kenneth Wilkinson, one of Decca's supreme wizards in the business of sound recording, remembers a toast she gave to the crew at a celebration after the successful completion of a day's work in the studio. At the dinner table, Kathleen Ferrier rose to her feet:

> Here's to the girl who lives on the hill.
> If she won't, her sister will.
> Here's to her sister!

Nineteen fifty-three, the year of the coronation of Queen Elizabeth I, and the conquest of Everest, was also the year of what many would call Kathleen Ferrier's greatest triumph: her triumph as an artist, and as an extraordinarily courageous and determined human being. For some time, she had been battling against cancer. In the early part of 1953, four performances of Gluck's opera, *Orfeo*, were scheduled to be given at the Royal Opera House, Covent Garden, with Kathleen Ferrier in the title role, and conducted by her dear friend, Sir John Barbirolli. In the event, there came about a combination of triumph and tragedy. At the second performance, she was attacked by the disease that was soon to prove fatal. Somehow, she continued, concealing the pain and distress, but after the last enthusiastic guests had left her dressing-room, her sister Winifred asked if there was anything she could do to help. 'Yes,' replied Kathleen. 'Get me a stretcher.' On 8 October, 1953, Kathleen Ferrier died at the age of 41. A close friend of hers, the distinguished accompanist Gerald Moore, wrote of her passing thus: 'In the early summer of her glorious course, she left us. She left us for ever in her debt, for ever grateful for her example of nobility and humility, for her shining beauty and grace, for her goodness and her truth.'

So many years after her death, memories are still clear and radiant. Into a career that lasted little more than ten years, she had been able to compress so much. One of those rare birds that just occasionally come into view to brighten our humdrum existence, Kathleen Ferrier will be long remembered, especially by friends she made half a century ago in the town of Silloth, in the north-west corner of England.

An old friend of ours, once Chairman of the English Department at Durham University, lives at Grasmere, where we have stayed on several occasions. Built of local stone, the grey house stands on a hill overlooking the village; a stream tumbles down the sloping garden, and there are green hills all around. In December of 1799, William Wordsworth and his sister, Dorothy, came to live in Grasmere, in what is now known as Dove Cottage. Despite the inevitable floods of summer visitors, Grasmere still retains something of that air of tranquillity recorded by Dorothy almost two centuries ago: 'Grasmere was very solemn in the last glimpse of twilight; it calls home the heart to quietness.' In 1813, the Wordsworths moved to a larger house a short distance away, Rydal Mount, and it was there that Wordsworth died in 1850. He is buried in the churchyard at Grasmere, close to his sister and his wife, Mary. Now, thanks to the labours of many enthusiasts, among whom our friend Ted Dorsch is numbered, Dove Cottage is open to visitors, with an exhibition of *memorabilia* relating to Wordsworth and his life in the Lake District.

For an understanding of the Lake District, past and present, and all its complex beauties, read the poems of Norman Nicholson. He has spent all his life in Millom, a small town in the south-west of Cumbria, looking out across the Duddon Sands to the iron and steel works of Barrow-in-Furness. Nicholson has captured in his poetry the essence of that strange contradiction which repeats itself in many parts of England, the juxtaposition of the most unattractive features of industrial society and the most spectacularly beautiful countryside. A short drive from many a muddy and enervating city leads to unspoilt acres of peaceful landscape. England is, truly, a land of contrasts both startling and pleasing.

Towards the Border

'History is now and England', wrote T S Eliot in 'Little Gidding', the last of his *Four Quartets*. It is an odd sort of statement, even for a poet, and I have often wondered how much truth it contains. Yet, when you come to think of it, the north of England is a marvellous repository of the past, containing solid and visible reminders of the Vikings, the Romans, the Saxons — our ancestors, you might say. Here, I thought, is as good a place as any to pick up the trail of history. So, on a bright spring morning, we set out on a tour of three of the north's most famous Saxon churches. It turned out to be a day on which history suddenly came alive, and we found ourselves almost, as it were, face to face with the past.

Jarrow, part of the sprawling Tyneside conurbation, is a place resonant with memories: there are people around today who talk still of Jarrow in the days of the depression. Drab streets of tightly-packed houses recall those days, while other, more recent structures belong to our new age of technological advances. But we were there to dig deeper, to search further back still. St Paul's Church, Jarrow, was dedicated in 685 AD, in the fifteenth year of the reign of King Ecgfrith, on April 23rd which, coincidentally, happens to be St George's Day, and the birthday of William Shakespeare. Though their bones now rest in Durham Cathedral, memories of the Venerable Bede and St Cuthbert linger potently here. Both of them, along with Benedict Biscop who, in the year 681, founded the monastery at Jarrow, are significant figures in the early history of Christianity in these islands. Bede, who became Prior of Jarrow, is probably best remembered for his famous history of the English church and people, a work written in Latin, but readily available today in modern English translation. Cuthbert, originally a shepherd, became Bishop of Lindisfarne in 685, just two years before his death. The church itself, a Saxon foundation, was restored in 1866 by Gilbert Scott. A short walk from the church, the Bede Monastery Museum has some excellent displays, and regular showings of an audio-visual programme about the site and its significance in our chronicles. Then just to remind visitors that they have not escaped completely from the twentieth century, a road sign points towards the Bede Industrial Estate. We ignored the invitation, and turned southwards towards Sunderland.

St Peter's, Monkwearmouth, was built in 674 AD, by Benedict Biscop. There, some six years later, came Bede, to enter the monastery, where he became a brother. Nowadays, the background is composed of views of Sunderland's industrial activity, with cranes and derricks rising against the skyline. Inside, an arch, the original of which dates from Norman times, separates the nave from the chancel. The chancel roof is a remarkable piece of Victorian artistry, aiming at a representation of heaven. After a fire in 1984, the roof was painstakingly restored to its original condition, a process which called for some four thousand sheets of gold leaf. Through a transparent panel, let into the floor, can be seen parts of the Saxon foundations. Indeed, there is plenty to see at St Peter's: a notable porch, with a few surviving carved decorations, a modern mosaic on the chancel floor, and a number of interesting memorials, in stone and in glass.

On, then, to our last port of call and, for me, the pick of the collection. Escomb is a pleasant village, a few miles west of Bishop Auckland. The road descends steeply to St John's Church, whose records go back to the 7th century, and whose walls are made with stones taken from the Roman fort at Binchester. Set upside down into the outside of the north wall can be seen a curious stone, bearing the inscription of the sixth legion (LEG VI). To the east of the porch, there is a fascinating Anglo-Saxon sundial, surmounted by a carved snake.

'You're not looking at a fossil,' observed the vicar, Nicholas Beddow. 'This is a church which has been used continuously through the centuries, in good times and bad times, by ordinary people.' Then, in case we should think that he was being too solemn, he added: 'The best view of the church is from the pub over the road.' And so we repaired to the appropriately-named Saxon Inn, to enjoy the best view of St John's Church, and to mull over the events of a memorable day out, a journey into the past which is, after all, not so very remote.

Almost four centuries ago, the historian William Camden wrote of Northumberland: 'The ground itself for the most part rough, and hard to be manured, seems to have hardened the inhabitants, whom the Scots their neighbours also made more fierce and hardy, so that they are a most warlike nation, and there is not a man amongst them of the better sort, that has not his little tower or pile.' There, in essence, is the character of that northern kingdom, as it once was, bordering on Scotland. The Romans left their mark implacably on this terrain. Here it was, in the seventh century, that King Edwin, or Eadwine, of Northumbria was converted to Christianity by a priest from Rome, Paulinus. In later times, the Percys were proud lords of this land. Hexham Abbey, Lindisfarne, or Holy Island, Dunstanburgh Castle, the Roman Wall — these are but a few from many impressive reminders of the history of these lands north of the Humber.

To the traveller journeying northwards, the landscape assumes, outwardly, a less hospitable appearance. Houses and farmsteads become infrequent landmarks along the way, and bare expanses of high moorland are punctuated but occasionally by lonely clumps of trees, bent to an angle imposed by prevailing winds. Only in the green plantations of the Forestry Commission does more profuse vegetation appear, and the total effect is of grand and austere landscape, offering little by way of encouragement to the faint-hearted. Due compensation is offered, in the form of expansive views, on clear days extending many miles in every direction from fine points of vantage in the county. Distant sightings are an encouragement to the artillery-men whose practice ranges lie near Otterburn, scene of a famous battle in August 1388. In earlier times, such extensive views were of advantage to Roman garrisons keeping watch on Hadrian's Wall, that great line of defence stretching across the neck of northern England, from the Solway Firth and Carlisle in the west to Wallsend and the mouth of the Tyne in the east, a distance of 72 miles.

Nearly two thousand years later, much yet remains of that mighty construction. A good starting-place for exploration of these fascinating remains is Corbridge, a most pleasant town at a crossing of the Tyne, astride the A68 trunk road which runs northwards to the Scottish border at Carter Bar, and on through Jedburgh to Edinburgh. The Roman station, Corstopitum, stood on high ground about half a mile beyond present-day Corbridge, occupying a vital strategic position at the crossing of two main routes, Dere Street and Stanegate. Here was established a fort, manned, it is thought, by Roman legionaries and Gallic cavalry. There are fairly extensive remains on the site, and also an admirable museum, containing armour and weapons, inscribed and sculptured stones, pottery and glass, fragments from a frieze and sculptures, including the Corbridge Lion, an emblem of ferocity as it devours its prey, a stag.

Corbridge itself is a restful place, with several pleasant inns, and any number of hospitable establishments offering bed and breakfast. Indeed, our frequent visits there have persuaded us that there is a league of ladies in Corbridge providing for the comfort of travellers. If you call at a house where the accommodation has already been let, then its owner will pass you on to one of her colleagues in the town: such has been our happy experience on so many occasions in times past. So often, on journeys north, have we spent a night at Corbridge in one of the many welcoming homes offering bed and breakfast, and set forth the following morning fortified by an enormous repast of porridge, eggs, bacon, mushrooms, tomatoes, sausages, fried bread, toast, marmalade and coffee. A few miles away is Hexham Abbey, with its majestic 'midnight stair', a flight of steps down which clergy and choristers descend in procession for the first Mass of Christmas Day, and its reminders of Saxon times.

A short distance north of Corbridge, the main road crosses the line of Hadrian's Wall; you will even find a village called Wall here. There are forts at intervals along the length of the wall, where defending garrisons were stationed. On a cloudy afternoon of late autumn, we spent an instructive afternoon at Chesters, where a small museum, surviving fortifications, the dormitories and the bath-house down by the river, all prompted the imagination to people the site again with visions of armed soldiery manning the wall, with those detailed for watch peering through mist and rain, across the broad spaces of this bleak landscape, for invaders from the north.

Northwards runs the route to the border and on into Scotland, once a kingdom on its own. A few miles to the south-east of Coldstream is Flodden, scene of a fierce battle on 9 September 1513, when James IV, King of Scotland was killed, and his forces suffered defeat at the hands of the English. Sir Walter Scott has written

> Of the stern strife, and carnage drear,
> Of Flodden's fatal field,
> Where shivered was fair Scotland's spear
> And broken was her shield.

These last outposts of England before the border have a melancholy, sometimes savage, grandeur, set amid immense tracts of lonely moorland, through which the road winds inexorably on towards Scotland.

Part Two
Scotland

SCOTLAND

Fair Caledonia

Scotland is famed throughout the world for a goodly number of things: Scotch whisky, tartan, shortbread, haggis, Robert Burns, Bonnie Prince Charlie, Mary Queen of Scots, the Edinburgh Festival, bagpipes, and jokes about the supposed meanness of Scotsmen, and what they actually wear beneath their kilts.

In Scotland, despite the influx of oil, and periodic crises in the herring-fishing industry, there remains still the sublime consolation of vast, lonely tracts of terrain virtually untrodden by human feet. For more than half a century, I have been able to retrieve from the Scottish landscape a secure sense of refuge and reassurance, and even a kind of renewal. However, I have to admit that there is something of my own ancestry working most potently here, along with tantalising backward glances towards childhood days long gone, and those simple but irresistible delights which are never entirely wiped from the bank of memory: soggy picnics in steady rain by the banks of the River Dee; compulsory walks taken on the instructions of fierce aunts who could not tolerate children hanging around the house; solid high-teas, made even more disagreeable by the constraints of food rationing; seemingly interminable overnight journeys to Aberdeen in dirty, brown carriages of the London and North-Eastern Railway (LNER), overcharged with travelling companions both civilian and military. It was Vita Sackville-West who put her finger on that particular aspect of our lives in 1945, when she wrote to her husband, Harold Nicolson: 'Why people have this passion for moving about passes my understanding ...'

Well, the passion for moving about has certainly intensified in the later years of the twentieth century, and one may be tempted to ask how the naive, youthful, Wordsworthian visions of 'splendour in the grass' stand up in comparison with such truly adult pleasures as Loch Fyne lobster served at a table in the window of the Four Seasons Hotel at St Fillan's, where the view down the length of Loch Earn is itself worth a fiver of anybody's money. Then, what about the stunning drive through the most lovely scenery of Wester Ross to the port of Ullapool, or sailing on a summer's evening on MacBrayne's ferry out of Oban into the setting sun towards the magical island of Colonsay, or moorland walks taken at one's own sweet will or even the more sophisticated delights of the Edinburgh Festival?

There are some finer points of address, which I mention in passing. You may call a Scotsman Jock, if you will, but you do so at your own peril. If in doubt, Mac is usually safer. An inhabitant of Scotland is usually known as a Scot or a Scotsman. There is a breed of small, black dog known as Scottie. What a Scotsman will probably do, after he has taken his Scotties for walkies, is to pour himself a glass of Scotch whisky. If you accept an invitation to a haggis shoot, then you are yet another victim of a very old practical joke. I once heard a game-dealer explaining the facts of the haggis to a customer: 'They are not alive! You do not shoot them!'

The Outer Hebrides, where Gaelic is spoken, are farther from London than are any other parts of the United Kingdom. Access to such distant places is not always easy. It is not unknown for Colonsay, an island of the Inner Hebrides, to be cut off from the mainland for weeks when particularly heavy weather has prevented the regular ship from making its berth. In dire emergency, helicopters and other forms of airlift come to the rescue.

For many visitors, the very remoteness of these islands adds to their charm. Here is another world, of mists and mystery, of strange enchantment and exciting discoveries.

Southern Scotland

The transition from England to Scotland is gradual, but quite definite and readily perceptible. The best place to cross the border is at Carter Bar, where the traveller may pause to enjoy the immense views northwards and southwards, and luxuriate in the feeling that he has passed from one country into another, over a great divide. Much less interesting is the western route through flatlands, although it does pass by Gretna Green, a place with romantic associations for eloping couples in days gone by. Northwards from Carter Bar, you enter the territory about which Robert Burns and Sir Walter Scott have written so eloquently. The region is too often neglected by holidaymakers intent on reaching other destinations: in winter, the ski-slopes of the Cairngorms, in summer the seductive beauties of highlands and islands. But it is worth tarrying awhile in the border country, for there is much to see in this region where the River Tweed forms, for part of its 97-mile length, the boundary between England and Scotland: the pleasingly-rounded contours of the Cheviot Hills; abbeys, such as Melrose, Dryburgh, Kelso and Jedburgh; the tributaries of the Tweed — Teviot, Till and Ettrick Water; historic sites like the battlefields of Flodden, where in 1513 the English defeated the Scots. History was shaped in these parts.

The shortest sea crossings to Northern Ireland are from south-western Scotland: Stranraer and Cairnryan to Larne. On our last visit there, we stayed at the enchanting little fishing village of Portpatrick, just 8 miles from Stranraer, with narrow streets, a clean, scrubbed appearance, a marvellous prospect of the sea as we looked into the fiery glare of the setting sun, and a most friendly hotel, the Downshire Arms, telephone: 077681 300. Dinner was in pleasantly convivial surroundings, nothing at all grand, at the Crown Hotel, telephone: 077681 261. At Portpatrick is the start of one of Scotland's long-distance paths.

Then the Ayrshire coast is not without interest, especially for golfers, who will respond immediately to mention of Turnberry and Troon, two of Scotland's most famous courses. Inland is Prestwick, a major international airport.

There is considerable rivalry in matters artistic between the cities of Edinburgh and Glasgow. Edinburgh has its world-famous festival, but Glasgow has several major art collections, including those at the Glasgow Art Gallery and Museum in Kelvingrove, the Burrell Collection in Pollok Park, opened by the Queen in 1983, the Hunterian Art Gallery in the University of Glasgow, the Stirling Maxwell Collection in Pollok House, and the People's Palace, Glasgow Green, opened in 1898, and intended as a museum and art gallery for the working-class inhabitants of eastern Glasgow. Glasgow, Scotland's largest city, has its aspirations, many of them fulfilled. In 1990, it assumed the title of European City of Culture. One in the eye for Edinburgh, Glaswegians were saying smugly to each other.

Edinburgh is not a city through which I should choose to make a daily journey by motor car. Traffic can be fierce, especially at the time of the annual festival, although things have improved recently with the opening of a ring road. In days gone by, I used to be in Edinburgh quite often, on my way north to the highlands, visiting family or recording Scottish poets for the British Council and for Harvard. This last occupation was not without its perils. The Scots, as is well known, are not averse to drinking. All too often, this means the consumption of large quantities of that beverage which is distilled and bottled within their own borders, to wit, Scotch whisky. A sage once remarked that if a man could determine exactly the right amount of Scotch whisky to drink every day — not too much, not too little, just the right amount — then he would live for ever. There is no means of establishing the truth of this claim, since its originator has now gone to his reward, as the saying is. But many Scots have shown sufficient interest in the notion to test its validity. There is also a custom, perhaps more honoured nowadays in the breach than the observance, that when two or three Scots come together with cause for celebration, they open a bottle of whisky and immediately throw away the cork.

Sydney Goodsir Smith (oddly enough, born in New Zealand), was a poet who wrote most exquisite Scottish lyrics, the best of them not unworthy to be compared with those of Robert Burns. My first encounter with him was in Milne's Bar in Edinburgh; he had asked that we meet for a quick drink before the recording, just to loosen him up a little, as he was inclined to be nervous on such occasions. Just a quick drink, he said. Well, it turned into the sort of occasion which I suspect is fairly typical of life in Edinburgh. We had a drink, fairly quickly, and then it was suggested that perhaps it would be advisable to have another drink. At some stage we were joined by an amiable gentleman, who claimed to be one of the Queen's Pipers, a noble occupation, without doubt. He insisted on buying drinks for us, and then, of course, we were obliged to return the compliment. He had many a good story to tell, though I am ashamed to confess that I cannot now recall any of them. But then it was twenty-five years ago. What I do remember is that about two hours later I decided to take a firm grip on the day's events, and insisted that it was time we got on with the recording. So it came about that we left the cosiness of Milne's Bar and made our way, rather slowly, towards Sydney's flat, where we were to make the recording. I forgot to mention that we had been joined by a lady who seemed to be on very good terms with Sydney. She, being in rather better shape than either of us, was sent on ahead to a licensed grocer, there to obtain further supplies of whisky to see us through the ordeal of the recording. I am glad to say that the results of this session can still be heard on an Argo spoken word recording called *The Poet Speaks*, and that Sydney Goodsir Smith's reading of some of his most appealing pieces, such as 'The Winter o' the Hert' and 'Simmer Nichtsang', sounds the true note of lyric poetry, and continues to give pleasure long after the poet has departed this life.

Unfortunately, completion of the recording did not conclude my tribulations for that day. Unwisely, perhaps, I had made a second appointment for later that same afternoon, with another notable Scottish poet, Norman MacCaig, on the far side of Edinburgh. It was rush-hour in the streets of the city when I set out for this second engagement, and every route was choked with vehicles, making their way homewards bumper to bumper and nose to tail. Somehow I got through, and the second part of the day's business was accomplished. I know everything must have gone as it should have done, because the recording is still available, as proof positive of the deed. But the adventure planted in me a long-lasting dread of Edinburgh traffic.

On the outskirts of Edinburgh, at the water's edge, is what used to be a small fishing village in years gone by. Even today, it has an inviting air of seclusion, a retreat from the hurly-burly of Edinburgh. We have enjoyed many a meal of delicious fish at the Cramond Inn, and then wandered down to look across the Firth of Forth, the prospect opening across Cramond Island to Burntisland on the northern side. The Forth Bridge, that great steel structure carrying the railway line across the Firth of Forth, was opened on 4 March 1890. 8,296 feet in length (more than a mile and a half), it took seven years to complete, at a cost of more than three million pounds. For us, as children travelling overnight to Aberdeen for our annual summer holidays, the crossing of the Forth Bridge was the highlight of the journey. If we were lucky, we found seats in the dining-car, there to enjoy porridge and kippers as the train rattled along between the huge girders. We were happy. We were heading north, our destination Aberdeen, the place of my baptism many years ago.

The Trossachs and Beyond

North of a line drawn between Scotland's two largest cities, Edinburgh and Glasgow, the traveller becomes conscious of transition: he is entering a wilder part of Scotland now, advancing towards the Grampians, the highlands and the islands, and the most colourful and arresting Scottish scenery.

The approach by road is dramatic enough, along the motorway, M9, passing close to Bannockburn, where on 24 June 1314, Robert Bruce won a decisive battle against the English army under Edward II, and secured independence for Scotland. Then comes Stirling, a royal burgh since 1100, its castle standing proud on the hill that dominates the town, its modern university in an attractive waterside setting. North-eastwards lies Auchterarder, and nearby the famous Gleneagles Hotel and golf courses. North to Crieff, the mountains loom larger in the camera's viewfinder, for this is the passage to the highlands. Westwards are glens, lochs, forests, the Trossachs and mountains rising above three thousand feet.

How often we have sat at a table in the window of the Four Seasons Hotel at St Fillan's, dazzled by the setting sun reflected in the waters of Loch Earn. A narrow road follows the southern shores of the loch, opening splendid vistas, once it is past the caravan park. I like to call in at the Drummond Fish Farm to obtain supplies of local trout, both fresh and smoked. With adequate stocks of delectably soft baps, crunchy oatcakes, haggis and malt whisky, one can live like a prince in these parts. A little further afield, but still within easy reach, Loch Katrine, Loch Voil, Loch Lubnaig, Loch Ard and Loch Chon are some of the aqueous gems in this glistening collation, while westward is the grand stretch of Loch Lomond. Here, in this supremely beautiful and romantic locality, only forty miles or so from Glasgow, is where the traveller sets foot on the route to the highlands, or the road to the isles.

Along the Braes of Balquhidder (pronounced Balwhidder), you come to Balquhidder Church. The present building was opened in 1855: 'many experiments have been tried to cure its damp walls', the brochure notes gloomily. A 17th-century bell, from an earlier church on the site, stands on top of an old Session Chest, said to have belonged to 'Black Duncan' Campbell of Glenorchy. In the churchyard are the ruins of an earlier building, and the grave of Scotland's equivalent of Robin Hood, Rob Roy, otherwise known as Robert Campbell or MacGregor. Here we repair in an act of pilgrimage, since my wife is a Campbell and I, as an Orr, salute the MacGregor as head and founder of our clan.

On my most recent visit, I contrived an unscheduled diversion, and took a narrow, unfenced road southwards, along the course of the Calair Burn to Ballimore. Sheep strayed across my path and, at one point, the way was blocked by a herd of obstinate cows, reluctant to move. This, I was forcibly reminded, is not a land for someone in a hurry. Clouds, scudding low, made cotton-wool wreaths on the peaks; there were shaggy ponies in a field, variegated shades of green and brown as bracken turned colour on the hillsides, and the sight of occasional, isolated farmsteads. Winters can be severe here, and communities have learned to engineer their own measure of self-sufficiency. On a gate was affixed the bold sign, PRIVATE DANGER. In these parts, the inhabitants are determined to keep even their dangers to themselves! Torrential rain descended as I reached the end of the road, encouraging a speedy retreat to more cosy surroundings.

It was at the Munro Arms at Strathyre (which, with Callander, provided the scenery for the television series, *Dr Finlay's Casebook*), that I encountered a splendid old shepherd called Archie. Like many of his kind, Archie liked a wee dram or two of an evening, and sometimes the drams became larger, with more frequent administration. One evening, after an exhilarating ascent of Beinn an t-Sithein (pronounced Ben Sheen), I joined Archie, the owner of the hotel and his wife in the bar. Suddenly, in the midst of our conversation, Archie toppled from his bar-stool, and crashed to the floor. Alarmed, I made to assist him, but was deterred from the attempt by my other companions. 'He always does this,' they explained. 'Just leave him alone. He's perfectly all right, and he'll recover in his own time.' So, indeed, he did, and some little while later, Archie was seen to take his precarious position once again on the bar-stool, to resume the conversation where he had left off, just as if there had been no interruption to the proceedings. This took a bit of getting used to, I must say, particularly since the happening was re-enacted several times during the course of the evening, and it was with some misgivings that eventually I watched Archie set off in the pitch dark to walk home, a trek of several miles over the hills. 'Och, he'll be fine,' I was assured. 'He's been doing this for years.'

Recently we returned to that area of Scotland, which we have come to know so well after many visits. This time, it was November, and autumn colours were ablaze on the hills, along river banks and in neat beech-hedges at the roadsides, while there were distant glimpses of snow on the high peaks. Never have I seen Scotland looking quite so ravishingly lovely. We made our base at Comrie: the name means a confluence of the waters. There, through the good offices of the Landmark Trust, we were able to rent a flat in the Mackintosh Building, dating from 1903 and a typical creation of the distinguished Scottish architect, Charles Rennie Mackintosh. It had a bay window, formed by the extrusion of a turret, a steep, slate roof, its line broken by a tall, tapering, slender chimney and, inside, high ceilings and dark-stained, wooden floors. In the evenings, rummaging among well-filled bookshelves, I took the opportunity to renew acquaintance with Lewis Grassic Gibbon's *A Scots Quair*, a famous trilogy comprising *Sunset Song*, *Cloud Howe* and *Grey Granite*. Gibbon, whose real name was James Leslie Mitchell, distilled into his writings something of the essential character of Scotland between the Grampians and the sea, in the days when a ploughman earned 'no more than thirteen shillings a week and he'd had thirteen of a family ...' The privations, the harshness of institutionalised religion, and the feel of Scottish life are captured in rich and full narrative which, incidentally, recalls 'the days of William the Lyon, when gryphons and suchlike beasts still roamed the Scots countryside and folk would waken in their beds to hear the children screaming, with a great wolf-beast, come through the hide window, tearing at their throats.' Those familiar with Scottish towns will recognise the authentic touch when Gibbon observes that 'the street walls were dripping with fog'.

There is a remarkable passage of exact delineation when the central female character, Chris Colquhoun (pronounced Ca-hoon), is seated on the summit of the Barmekin, with night closing in fast.

> Over in the Hill of Fare, new-timbered, a little belt of rain was falling, a thin screen that blinded the going of the light; behind, as she turned, she saw Skene Loch glimmer and glow a burnished minute; then the rain caught it and swept it from sight and a little wind soughed up the Barmekin. And now behind wind and rain came the darkness.

> Lights had sprung up far in the hills, in little towns for a sunset minute while the folks stirred and went off to their beds, miles away, thin peeks in the summer dark.

> Time she went home herself.

> But she still sat on as one by one the lights went out and the rain came beating the stones about her, and falling all that night while she still sat there, presently feeling no longer the touch of the rain or hearing the sound of the lapwings going by.

Eastwards from Comrie is the town of Crieff, its respectable granite dwellings conveying a certain sternness of purpose, the vast, Victorian mass of Crieff Hydro an open invitation to good, clean, healthy living. I imagine that they must serve excellent porridge there. Behind the town rises a hill, the Knock, which offers, on fine days, panoramic views of that area where the highlands begin. On my last ascent, every prospect was concealed by thick mist, but nevertheless I enjoyed the walk. The Glenturret Distillery is close at hand, for those eager to conduct researches into the business of making whisky.

To the west, through Crianlarich, lies the way to the port of Oban and thence to the isles; and a very beautiful route it is, too, along Glen Lochy, by the Falls of Cruachan, and through the Pass of Brander, where lochs divide the land into long strips. Even on a day of mist and drizzle, the journey is sheer enchantment; in sunshine, it is quite ravishing. More than twenty years ago, my father and I arrived late one evening at a hotel in Arrochar, on the edge of Loch Long. It was dark, there was heavy rain, we were tired and hungry; but, in the inexorable fashion of those days, the hotel's dining-room had closed, and there was no food to be had. We were directed to a small establishment down the road where, we were assured, a meal would be readily available. When we got there, it turned out to be a rather shabby roadside tavern, filled with locals drinking beer and playing darts. On entering, we were immediately made to feel like intruders. It transpired that the total store of food on those premises amounted to one steak pie and two sausage rolls. (I am not making this up! The memory is vivid still.) We bolted down these unappetising items, and hastened back to the hotel, resolved that an early night was the only solution in such circumstances. However, I am glad to report that the delectable view which greeted us on rising the next morning was more than enough to compensate for the hardships of the previous evening: heavy rains had swollen the water courses, which tumbled effervescently down the steep slopes of hills enclosing the loch, while the sun glinted and made patterns on the rippling surface of the waters. It was, quite literally, a sight for sore eyes. Happily, I can declare that catering arrangements there and, indeed, over the whole of Scotland, have improved almost out of recognition in the years since that episode.

In the opposite direction, eastwards from Crieff, the A85 runs into the pleasant city of Perth where, at the Isle of Skye Hotel, we first ate *scampi pernod*. Thence, northwards, the A93 passes Scone and its castle, where the ancient kings of Scotland were crowned, and whence came the Coronation Stone, the Stone of Destiny, which in 1297 was taken to Westminster by Edward I. There it has remained, although in 1950 Scottish nationalists succeeded in achieving its brief removal from that English resting-place. The road runs on, rising and falling, through Blairgowrie and Rattray, by the River Ericht, in an area famous for raspberries, on through the green length of Glen Shee to the Devil's Elbow and the Cairngorms. Along this route, familiar to us now after countless expeditions, there grows a beech-hedge of prodigious length and height. It is a notable landmark on our progress, indicating that our destination is not far distant. Invariably, sight of this formidable boscage summons to mind that passage in Book Four of Milton's *Paradise Lost*, when Satan reaches the border of the Garden of Eden, and beholds a prospect of 'delicious Paradise', where

> overhead up-grew
> Insuperable highth of loftiest shade,
> Cedar, and pine, and fir, and branching palm,
> A sylvan scene, and, as the ranks ascend
> Shade above shade, a woody theatre
> Of stateliest view. Yet higher than their tops
> The verdurous wall of Paradise up-sprung ...

Aberdeen and Royal Deeside

Memories die hard, but the parts of Scotland I came to know in early childhood have changed less than other landscapes through which I have moved in the past fifty years. True, there is running water and electricity now where they did not exist before; no longer does one have to drink milk still disagreeably warm straight from the cow, or use the wooden privy with its pair of seats placed sensibly over the midden. In such matters, one can only register gratitude for present-day improvements. But there is regret, too, for the disappearance of the admirable and convenient steam train which ran westwards along the valley of the Dee from Aberdeen, through Cults (pronounced as you would expect), Culter (pronounced Cooter), Drum, Park, Crathes, Glassel, Torphins, Lumphanan, Dess. Aboyne, Dinnet, Cambus o'May and Ballater. The line would have gone further, as far as Braemar, but for the intervention of Queen Victoria. Venturing forth one day from her stronghold at Balmoral, and strolling by the bubbling Dee, Her Majesty observed some workings on the opposite bank of the river. 'What, pray, is that?' Her Majesty is said to have enquired. The answer came back: 'That, ma'am, is the extension of the railway line from Ballater to Braemar.' Queen Victoria was quite obviously not amused, and such was the power of monarchs in those days that she was able to issue the royal command: 'Go back into Ballater and stop it!'

So the tracks terminated in Ballater, and many generations of royals have been greeted in the square as they alighted from the train, bound for their holiday home at Balmoral. The pomp and circumstance of those visits are now committed to memory, but tourists still flock to the little church at Crathie on summer Sundays, when the Royal Family can be seen on their way to and from morning service, while Grampian Council make a healthy income by utilising a nearby field for parking.

Ballater, 44 miles east of Aberdeen, has hardly altered in the fifty years and more that I have known it: the railway station is gone, as too is the cinema where we used to seek refuge on rainy days, while a large time-share complex has appeared just off the Braemar road, but life goes on much as it did, under the shadows of Craig Coillich and the pudding-shaped hill of the oaks, Craigendarroch. Our friend Jack Sweeney one weekend drank the Craigendarroch Hotel dry of vodka, causing us to recall Dylan Thomas's story of a Welsh outing, when they drank the 'Mountain Goat' dry.

Ballater is a place of small shops, some overflowing with tartan, others offering sensible garments and stout footwear. We go there almost every year to remind ourselves of simple delights. An old-fashioned concert party in the Albert Hall and the horticultural show in the Victoria Hall revive memories of bygone days. The burbling Dee, with its salmon pools, rushes beneath the solid stone bridge linking North and South Deeside routes, and a few yards downstream the piers of a previous structure still stand above the waters, decorated with tangled weeds. The area round about boasts a wonderfully evocative roll-call of place-names, which spring to the mind unbidden as reminders of childhood days: Logie Coldstone, its densely-packed pines and firs carpeting the woodland ways with fallen needles; Braehead of Tullich and Bridge of Gairn; Craig of the Knock and Burn o' the Vat where, so the legend goes, my ancestor, Rob Roy, hid from his pursuers behind the waterfall; Glen Muick, where the road passes close to foaming falls, then on to the deep, dark loch, and the daunting sight of that massive mountain, Lochnagar, towering at 3789 feet. On 12 September 1933, my uncle Charles Ludwig wrote his name in the annals of mountaineering by conquering the Gibson Gully with 'an extraordinary solo ascent after 33 years of attempts on the route'. One summer's day, on the lower hill slopes by Loch Muick, we counted more than a hundred red deer.

I have known Aberdeen from my earliest days, long before it achieved a somewhat transient fame as the oil city of the north. In fact, this was the place of my baptism, so I can lay valid claim to have roots in that part of the world. The proud tower of Marischal College once dominated everything else in Aberdeen, the granite city. One night, my uncle Charles Ludwig, who was given to practical jokes with a hint of danger in them, scaled the dizzying heights and placed a skeleton on the highest pinnacle. I should add that he was a medical student, and thus had easier access to skeletons than is afforded to most of us.

Two rivers run eastward from their sources in the high hills into Aberdeen, the Dee and the Don, and around them lies some of the most gorgeous countryside to be found anywhere. Heather-covered moors with clumps of silver birch around Dinnet give way to bleaker and sterner vistas as the A93 turns southward at Braemar and runs for a while alongside Clunie Water towards Devil's Elbow (now straightened and no longer a terror to motorists), and to the chair-lift that rises to the summit of Cairnwell. To the north-west of Ballater, the Lecht Road offers spectacular views of the Cairngorms as it leads to the highest village of the Highlands, Tomintoul, with its souvenir shops, tartans, haggis and malt whisky.

Fortunate holidaymakers, such as we were, may catch a glimpse of Prince Philip steering a horse-drawn conveyance along twisting roads by the Dee or find, as we did one magical Christmas, a real sense of occasion in attending service at Crathie Church, where the Queen worships when staying at Balmoral. This is countryside for the walker, who can choose anything from a gentle stroll through woods to a strenuous hike across rough and often boggy moorland, with only the cries of grouse and lapwing to disturb the immense peace of the scene.

When the sun shines on Deeside, it is easy to fall into rhapsodic mood: everything seems to be in the right place for the fisherman, the walker, the climber, the golfer or the contemplative idler; the texture of the landscape, ablaze in days of late

August with the purple of heather, lightened by silver birch whose leaves glisten in the sun and reflect in the waters of Lochs Davan and Kinord — all these things bring something like intoxication to the soul. But when it rains (as it often does in these parts), and when the porridge at breakfast is lumpy (which is not unknown), or the sprouts and cabbage at dinner are overcooked, grey and sodden (as happens frequently), then there can come a sinking of the spirits. Nevertheless, in half a century of wandering around Deeside, despite damp picnics, swarms of midges and overbearing aunts, I have not known discontent endure for long in such idyllic surroundings.

It is not hard to see why Queen Victoria took such pride and pleasure in the highland retreat at Balmoral, her 'dear paradise'. The majority of today's visitors will not be guests at a castle, but there are castles to visit at Craigievar, Crathes and Drum, where my cousin, Charles Foster, and his merry minstrels from Aberdeen, the Kincorth Waits, have often provided musical entertainment appropriate to the period. There is a whisky distillery at Old Meldrum, a tannery at Lumphanan, a pottery at Kincardine O'Neill, and luscious raspberries in Glen Tanar, all worth investigation. And when the weather improves, as it always does, bicycles can be hired from the Huntley Arms Hotel at Aboyne, water skiing arranged on Aboyne Loch, grouse-shooting in season on the moors, salmon-fishing on the Dee, or gliding just beside the A93 North Deeside Road near Dinnet.

The standard of cooking, and the choice of food, have improved out of all recognition over the past few years, though it is still possible to eat 'traditional Scottish fare' at its very best and also at its almost unbelievable worst. As I say, things have changed less in these parts than elsewhere, and not a few hotels preserve an atmosphere of baronial grandeur suiting well with the atmosphere of Royal Deeside, although the thrifty holidaymaker may think the baronial prices more like those demanded in London. Tullich Lodge Hotel, at the eastern entrance to the Pass of Ballater, manages to combine something of grandeur with a feeling of cosiness. In Ballater, the Invercauld Arms, hard by the bridge across the Dee, has long been a favourite of ours, through successive managements.

The Invercauld Arms, in the days when we first came to know it, was a rambling place, the entrance hall invariably festooned with fishing tackle and muddy waders. It was a hotel of distinctly eccentric charms, and whether or not visitors enjoyed their stay depended on their attitude towards vague and erratic service, and also on whether the proprietor, Andrew Logan, took a liking to them. Andrew, or Paddy, as he was known to his intimates, was a delightful man in his way, who liked a wee dram now and again, and perhaps again. Fortunately, we remained in his good books, perhaps because my father-in-law, who often accompanied us there, had a title; in Ballater, my father-in-law, Sir Charles Campbell, was thought (quite erroneously) to be the Governor-General of Jamaica, whose name was Sir Clifford Campbell. I am still not sure whether we fostered this legend to gain

Loch Earn, Perthshire

Glenshee, south of Braemar

Linn o' Dee, near Braemar

The harbour at Aberdeen

Sunset over the Isle of Skye, Hebrides

Dame Flora MacLeod of MacLeod, Isle of Skye

Colonsay House, Isle of Colonsay, Hebrides

View from the Isle of Mull

privileges for ourselves.

Paddy Logan was not what you would call an energetic hotelier. He would spend a good deal of time dozing behind the reception desk, his reverie occasionally interrupted cruelly by the telephone. Once, I happened to be nearby when he was answering a call. 'No,' he was saying into the mouthpiece. 'No, we do not have any vacancies. The hotel is full. I'm sorry we can't help you. Good night.' I thought this rather strange, since my wife and I, and another couple, were the only guests in that quite large establishment. However, Paddy just could not be bothered to face any more people that night, so he rang off and closed his eyes again contentedly.

Of course, it could not last, and he was succeeded by a military gentleman, who insisted on doing most of the plumbing himself, sometimes with curious results. It was said at that time there were rooms on the uppermost floor with holes in the roof through which pigeons made entry, but I cannot vouch for the truth of such an accusation. Anyway, it must have been basically all right, because we continued to go there, year after year.

Then came a change of management, and a kilted Scot took over. We arrived one summer to find that he had done strange things to the inside of the hotel, none of which could honestly be described as improvements. Then, he made desperate attempts to inject new life into the place by organising dinner-dances. Somehow, they did not seem to catch on in Ballater, and eventually he gave up.

My own view is that the Invercauld Arms has a character, a personality of its own, and will not readily tolerate unseemly goings-on within its precincts. Anyway, kilts and ceilidhs came to nothing, and another era in the hotel's chequered fortunes opened. So far as I know, it is still going strong under the new management; every year, I receive details of activities organised, encouraged or sponsored by the hotel, so perhaps after all the years of struggle someone has found the right formula for the Invercauld Arms, so marvellously sited on the banks of the River Dee, in one of the most attractive villages in Scotland.

Probably the best vista in the area is from the old inn at Pannanich, on the South Deeside Road near Ballater, looking north across the river towards Culblean. Westwards, at Braemar, there is a famous highland gathering every summer, where can be seen such unashamed demonstrations of brute strength as tossing the caber, as well as elaborate demonstrations of Scottish dancing. Braemar has two imposing hotels, the Invercauld Arms and the Fife Arms, where we have frequently eaten substantial and satisfying lunches. All along Deeside are inns and guesthouses to suit every taste and, for the sturdily independent, there is abundance of caravan and camping parks.

Not so long ago, we took a large flat in the grounds of a hotel in Ballater: comfortable and warm, with spacious rooms, generously furnished, it had a long, narrow kitchen more like a ship's galley, where we prepared such delicacies as haggis and bashed neeps. Available April to October, contact Mr C D Franks, Darroch Learg Hotel, Braemar Road, Ballater, Aberdeenshire AB3 5UX, telephone: 0338 55443. Behind the hotel, a footpath leads upwards, to the summit of Craigendarroch, 1300 feet above sea level, achieved by an energetic scramble through woodland, heather and bracken, opening up a panoramic view: to the north, the Pass of Ballater; immediately below, neat lines of granite houses and gentle contours of Ballater's golf course at the river's edge; to left and right, the valley of the Dee; across the water, Craig Coillich, bristling with conifers and, eastwards, Pannanich Wells, its long, stone inn set high on the green hillside. Our visit was a family affair: my mother and sister stayed in a two-bedroom flat just across the road, with a gloriously colourful garden and an electricity meter which apparently consumed coins at an alarming rate. Details from Mrs R Menzies, Tangley House, Braemar Road, Ballater, Aberdeenshire AB3 5RQ, telephone: 0338 55624. Again, April to October availability. Also on the Braemar Road, we liked the look of the cottage and bungalow in the grounds of a typical Ballater guest house: bookings all year round through Mr and Mrs Nimmo, Morvada Guest House, Ballater, telephone: 0338 55501.

Ordnance Survey 'Landranger' series, Sheet 44, includes Ballater; more detail, of course, in the 'Pathfinder' maps, at a scale of 1:25000. Sheet number No. 29/39 takes in Ballater and Balmoral Castle.

The Western Isles

Tales, marvellous tales
Of ships and stars and isles where good men rest.

James Elroy Flecker was not writing of Scotland, but the sentiment fits. After many visits, over two decades, the islands off Scotland's west coast still draw us back to magical calm and glorious scenery, enhanced by indelible memories from former days. However, Samuel Johnson thought the Hebrides appealed only to lovers of 'naked nature'. There are about 500 Hebridean islands, perhaps 100 of them inhabited, of every shape, size and character. They were under Norwegian rule until the mid-thirteenth century, hence some surviving Norse names like Uig (bay), Carbost (bost, a settlement), Trotternish (ness or nish, point or headland), Skigersta, Islivig. Caledonian MacBrayne's shipping services operate throughout the region, with vessels of all kinds, from modern ferries to venerable boats impregnated with lingering odours of fried fish. For some early-morning departures, berths are available overnight. Car rover tickets offer the best bargain for island-hopping. Access to the smaller islands, not touched by Caledonian MacBrayne, can best be described as 'problematical'; the recommended procedure is to contact local operators. Single-track roads with passing-places are common, and call for courtesy and care from drivers. Some islands, mercifully and sensibly, ban caravans completely. Train services run to the ports of Oban, Mallaig, Kyle of Lochalsh, Largs, Ardrossan and Wemyss Bay, and there are air services to several islands. Weather is distinctly unpredictable, frequently very wet, and there are often midges in summer. On days when the heavens smile, seas twinkle and heather glows on hillsides, I can think of no better place to be. My top five islands, in purely alphabetical order, are Arran, Colonsay, Gigha, Islay and Skye. But I certainly do not ignore the rest!

There is welcome evidence of regeneration in catering and accommodation throughout the isles: slowly, and late, comes recognition that not everyone craves overcooked vegetables reduced to the consistency of porridge, food straight from the freezer, or lumpy beds at night. Two islands, at least — Colonsay and Gigha — have eponymous hotels offering fresh produce and imaginative menus. But dismal fare can still be found, too.

As good a way as any to begin the voyage of discovery is to travel to the islands of the Clyde. Great Cumbrae proposes a most persuasive introduction to the whole adventure. Actually, its name is misleading, since the island is hardly great in size: 4 miles by 1, making a 10-mile circuit by a good road, with bicycles for hire in Millport. Easily accessible from the cheerful port of Largs, Cumbrae is composed largely of old red sandstone, marls and basalt outcrops. From Glaid Stone, the highest point at 417 feet, long and lovely views take in Arran, the mainland of Kintyre, the urban coastal spread of Ardrossan and Fairlie, and a distant, misty

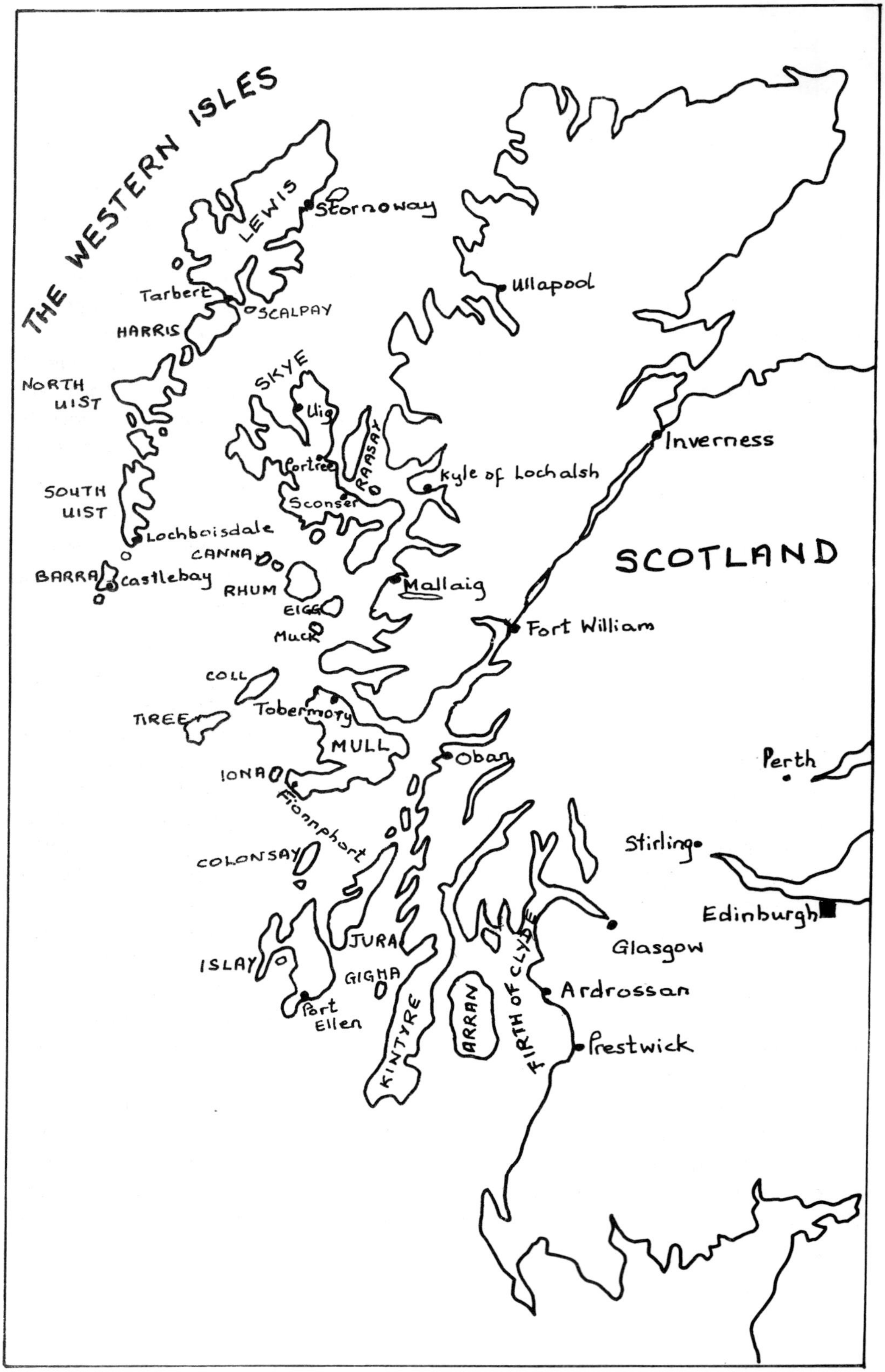

THE WESTERN ISLES
LEWIS
Stornoway
Ullapool
Tarbert
SCALPAY
HARRIS
NORTH UIST
SKYE
Uig
RAASAY
Inverness
Portree
Kyle of Lochalsh
SOUTH UIST
Sconser
Lochboisdale
CANNA
SCOTLAND
BARRA
Castlebay
RHUM
Mallaig
EIGG
Muck
Fort William
COLL
Tobermory
TIREE
MULL
Perth
Oban
IONA
Fionnphort
Stirling
COLONSAY
Edinburgh
JURA
Glasgow
FIRTH OF CLYDE
ISLAY
GIGHA
Ardrossan
Port Ellen
ARRAN
KINTYRE
Prestwick

sighting of the Ailsa Craig rock. We two made up half of the congregation for evensong in Europe's smallest cathedral, the Cathedral of the Isles. Simple accommodation there is available in adjoining college buildings, for adults and children over 9, telephone: 0475 530353.

Glasgow University maintains a resident marine biology centre here, and within it, the Robertson Museum is open to the public, an extraordinary aquarium displaying submarine wonders such as vividly-coloured starfish, sea anemones, spider crab, octopus; instructive, entertaining, and not to be missed, it prompts investigation of plant and animal life on the seashore. Millport has an 18-hole golf course and bowling greens to occupy hours of leisure. The Royal George Hotel on the quayside was due for refurbishment when we were there: Peter and Nicola Marston promise en-suite facilities throughout. We occupied a small room, and cricked our necks watching television on a set positioned precariously atop the wardrobe. The hotel has the virtue of being quite inexpensive: telephone: 0475 530 301.

All Millport menus seem virtually identical: scampi and chips, haddock and chips, sausage and chips; the easiest solution may be to take a day trip to Great Cumbrae with your own picnic. From Largs, only 31 miles from Glasgow, the crossing to Cumbrae Slip takes 10 minutes, and there is a frequent service.

Bute only just qualifies as an island: only 400 yards at the narrowest crossing from the mainland, it measures 16 miles top to bottom, 5 miles across at its widest. A cheerful sort of place it is, with sandy beaches, easy walks, smallish hills, good roads, gentle landscape, and a golf course. The long, curving promenade at Rothesay is embellished by neat gardens and a fountain. We stayed at the Palmyra Private Hotel, a little way outside town, telephone: 0700 2929. There, we had a clean, large room looking seaward, and the amiable Mrs Cowie invited me into her kitchen to taste from mounds of giant prawns just brought in by her husband, a fisherman. Rothesay's former popularity has obviously faded: architecturally, the town presents an unhappy jumble, though steep roads and steps lead quickly into agreeable countryside. Distinctly grand, the Glenburn Hotel overlooks town and harbour; coach parties were in occupation when I called, and I could hear bagpipes warming up for the evening *ceilidh*. Telephone 0700 2500 for reservations and information. At the Victoria Hotel, Len Griffiths offered me a drink on the house, and promised en-suite facilities soon (where had I heard that before?) The hotel is bang in the centre of town, telephone: 0700 3553 or 2226. The crossing to Wemyss Bay affords grand vistas all round, with Arran's peaks dominating the skyline. Sight of a submarine off our starboard beam reminded us that the base at Holy Loch was nearby. The ferry takes 20 minutes to cross from Wemyss Bay to Rothesay; there is a frequent service on that route, and also on the 5-minute crossing from Colintraive to Rhubodach. Landranger sheet 63 covers Bute and Cumbrae.

110   *SCOTLAND*

Approaching Colintraive from the north, we discovered the Loch Fyne Oyster Bar at Cairndow, at the head of the loch on the A83. There was a tempting range of seafood, venison, and local cheeses, served in an agreeably informal atmosphere. We had a super and quite inexpensive meal for two with house wine. Worth a detour, but wise to book: telephone: 04996 264, open every day in season, 9 to 9.

Arran, which means in Gaelic a kidney, has a population of under 5,000. Less than 20 miles north to south, 10 miles across, it is one of the most beautiful islands anywhere, with ravishing variety of scenery: mountains, beaches, wild moorland, lochs, rivers, footpaths, all within that small space, and Glasgow only 30 miles distant as the gull flies. Navigation is simplicity itself: one road runs round the island, the 'string' road cuts across the middle. There is ostentatious profusion of teashops, craft centres and wayside inns around the coast, but it is quite easy to escape the crowds. Arran has several golf courses: I found an interesting one at Blackwaterfoot, with 12 holes, most greens invisible from the tees, and elaborate warning systems for players putting. It turned out to be great fun, even though my opening drive ended in the sea. Rhododendrons at Brodick Castle are quite spectacular in season; in the grounds, cheeky chaffinches boldly approach visitors. The National Trust for Scotland lets holiday flats in the castle. The summit of Goat Fell at 2868 feet, still heavily-decorated with snow when we saw it in mid-April, offers challenging climbs and walks. The Tourist Information Centre in Brodick has leaflets on fishing, riding, walks, golf and pony-trekking. We enjoyed a friendly welcome from Dorothy Forgie at Invercloy Hotel, Brodick, more guesthouse than hotel, telephone: 0770 2225. The Douglas Hotel is more substantial, but new management was still settling down when we dropped in for a nightcap. I was slightly disappointed by the small selection of malt whiskies, but things may have improved. Telephone: 0770 2155. Ardrossan is 29 miles from Glasgow, and from there the crossing to Brodick takes 55 minutes. Claonaig, 106 miles from Glasgow, offers a seasonal service to Lochranza, with a crossing-time of 30 minutes. This route provides a good stepping-stone to more distant islands. Landranger sheet 69 covers Arran.

Now we turn to the Hebrides. Gigha (pronounced Ghee'a), our newest discovery, is a narrow strip of island, six miles top to toe, nowhere wider than one-and-a-half miles, seen from the approaching ferry as a series of humps, with the mainland of Kintyre eastwards, Islay and Jura westwards. Although it is easy of access, yet a serene sense of remoteness prevails here, in gentle contrast to the wildness of Arran. As we approached, an aerodynamically-designed gannet dived gracefully; an age passed before the long, probing beak broke the surface.

A car is really unnecessary on Gigha, as nowhere is more than 3 miles from the ferry, and the hotel will arrange to collect guests from the pier. Extensive, delightful gardens at Achamore House, with rhododendrons and azaleas, lead to well-marked walks from 1½ hours to 2 hours in duration. A 9-hole golf course has been laid out by local enthusiasts, and other attractions include the ruins of 13th-century Kilchattan Chapel, fishing in the loch, an abundance of wild flowers and birdlife, all blessedly relaxing. James and Margaret McSporran (what a marvellous Scottish name!) run the Post Office Guest House, offering dinner, bed and breakfast, telephone: 05835 251. We stayed at the Gigha Hotel, a whitewashed building near the ferry, light and airy inside. Prawns in puff pastry, and delicious baked salmon for dinner can be enthusiastically recommended. The hotel, telephone: 05835 254, also offers self-catering at Achamore House. No caravans are allowed on Gigha. From Tayinloan, 115 miles from Glasgow, there are upwards of four crossings daily, taking just 20 minutes. At the Macdonald Arms in Tayinloan, awaiting the next ferry, we sat by an open fire, enjoying home-made soup, herrings in oatmeal, pork escalopes and pudding. Landranger sheet 62 includes Gigha.

Islay (pronounced Eye'la), with a population of around 4,000, is a charming, largish island, with fuchsia hedges at the roadside reminiscent of Ireland, an extremely fine cross at Kildalton, a good golf course, and scope for extensive explorations. Bowmore is a pleasant 18th-century settlement overlooking the loch, celebrated for its malt whisky, the peaty-brown waters imparting a distinctive flavour. On a visit to Bowmore Distillery, we were invited to 'taste the product'; the measures were exceedingly generous, and afterwards I was unable to find my car keys, which was probably just as well! Fortunately, our hotel was close by: the Lochside, Shore Street, telephone: 049 681 244. Crossings are from Kennacraig to Port Ellen or Port Askaig, taking two hours or a little more, with two or three sailings daily. There is also an air service to Glasgow.

Jura has a population of just over two hundred souls. George Orwell lived here while writing *Nineteen Eighty-Four*, which was published in 1949. The Paps of Jura are a prominent feature of the skyline; deer and goats here heavily outnumber human inhabitants. There are frequent crossings, taking just five minutes, from Port Askaig in Islay to Feolin. Accommodation is available at the Craighouse Hotel, on the south-east coast, telephone: 049 682 243, closed Christmas and New Year.

Colonsay, 2 hours from Oban, or by seasonal service from Kennacraig via Islay, is one of our very favourite places, remote, uncrowded, with fine, sandy beaches, gentle walking, marvellous opportunities for bird-watching, a rough golf course and possible sightings of grey seals off the coast. A recent visit confirmed the continuing excellence of the Isle of Colonsay Hotel (the only one on the island), run by Kevin and Christa Byrne; self-catering chalets are also available, telephone: 09512 316 for information or a pleasant, informative chat with the proprietor. Kevin compiles the island's trade telephone directory ('not the yellow pages'), including suppliers of lobsters, oysters, prawns, and a list of services such as 'Insemination (artificial)'. No caravans are allowed on Colonsay.

Mull (the name probably means 'bare summit'), is a larger island, reached by a short crossing from Oban. James Boswell found '... a hilly country, diversified with heath and grass, and many rivulets'. His distinguished companion, Dr Johnson, was less enamoured: '... a most dolorous country!' We have made frequent visits here, ridden on the miniature railway, viewed the gardens of Torosay Castle, enjoyed good venison, rather ordinary pork and stunning views at the spacious Isle of Mull Hotel, Craignure, open mid-April to mid-October, telephone: 06802 351. At a small pub somewhere in the north of Mull, I found two flies in my soup. 'One may be misfortune, two looks like carelessness!' I exclaimed, echoing Lady Bracknell, to no effect: the barmaid was unapologetic, even surly.

Iona, a small island off the south-westerly tip of Mull, is one of the world's magical places, historically associated with St Columba. George Macleod inspired the restoration of the Abbey, which provides the best reason for visiting Iona. Despite many day-trippers, it is still a tranquil, atmospheric site. Here is the most ancient of Christian burial grounds in Scotland, where many Scottish kings were interred. The 5-minute crossing is from Fionphort (no cars), and there are also excursions from Oban. Skye, the 'winged island', has more than 8,000 inhabitants, is a magnet for visitors, and can be wildly busy in season, but it remains among the most attractive of the Hebridean islands. The famous Jacobite heroine, Flora Macdonald, died in Skye on 5 March 1790. 'A native of this isle requires treble the dose of physic that will serve one living in the south of Scotland for a purge.' Thus wrote M. Martin in 1703. Very true, as we discovered on our first visit, many years ago: prominent in the hotel's bathroom was an enormous bottle of liquid paraffin! At Dunvegan Castle, we admired a dazzling display of azaleas, saw the 'fairy flag', and were entertained to tea by Dame Flora Macleod of Macleod, a most gracious lady. On one journey across Skye, our overloaded mini failed to manage a fierce gradient, and my passengers were obliged to get out and walk. Despite such minor hardships, we have loved every minute of our time there.

It is now proposed that a bridge should be built across the waters of Loch Alsh, to join Skye to the mainland. Framed with an eye to the tourist trade, no doubt, such a notion represents yet another step in the wrong direction, part of the remorseless campaign to tame the wildernesses and make remotest parts more easily accessible. Long may Skye remain an island!

Barra, St Barr's Island, has some fine beaches; overlooking one of the very best of them is the Isle of Barra Hotel, where we hired bicycles or, on rainy days, borrowed one of their many Monopoly sets, thoughtfully provided for indoor recreation. Telephone: 087 14 383 for reservations. The crossing from Oban to Castlebay takes 5 hours.

We have vivid memories of Lewis and Harris, of driving across the causeways that link North Uist, Benbecula and South Uist; of pleasant beaches on low-lying Coll, and of leaning on the rail of the ship to watch sheep being loaded at Tiree, the

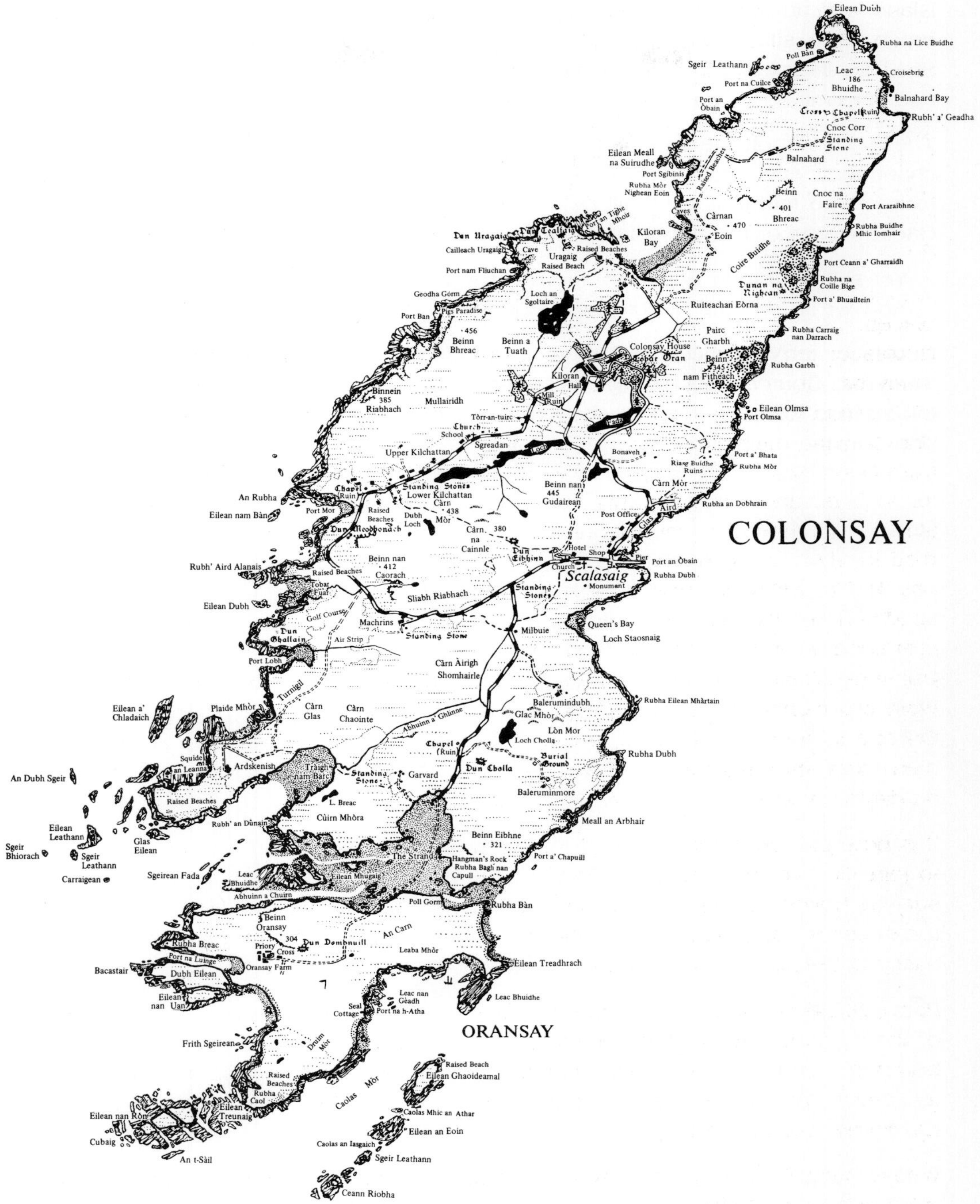
COLONSAY
ORANSAY
Eilean Dubh
Rubha na Lice Buidhe
Poll Bàn
Sgeir Leathann
Port na Cuilce
Leac 186 Bhuidhe
Croisebrig
Balnahard Bay
Port an Òbain
Cross
Chapel (Ruin)
Rubh' a' Geadha
Cnoc Corr
Standing Stone
Eilean Meall na Suirudhe
Balnahard
Port Sgibinis
Raised Beaches
Rubha Mòr Nighean Eoin
Beinn 401 Bhreac
Cnoc na Faire
Port Araraibhne
Caves
Càrnan 470 Eoin
Port an Tighe Mhòir
Dun Uragaig
Dun Tealtaig
Kiloran Bay
Rubha Buidhe Mhic Iomhair
Cailleach Uragaig
Cave
Raised Beaches
Uragaig Raised Beach
Coire Buidhe
Port Ceann a' Gharraidh
Port nam Fliuchan
Rubha na Coille Bige
Loch an Sgoltaire
Dunan na Nighean
Geodha Gòrm
Port a' Bhuailtein
Port Ban
Pigs Paradise
Ruiteachan Eòrna
456 Beinn Bhreac
Beinn a Tuath
Pairc Gharbh
Rubha Carraig nan Darrach
Colonsay House
Tobar Oran
Beinn 345 nam Fitheach
Rubha Garbh
Kiloran Hall
Binnein 385 Riabhach
Mullairidh
Mill (Ruin)
Eilean Olmsa
Port Olmsa
Tòrr-an-tuirc
Fada
Church
School
Sgreadan
Loch
Upper Kilchattan
Bonaveh
Port a' Bhata
Rubha Mòr
Riasg Buidhe Ruins
Chapel (Ruin)
Standing Stones
Lower Kilchattan
Beinn nan 445 Gudairean
Càrn Mòr
An Rubha
Raised Beaches
Càrn 438 Mòr
Aird
Rubha an Dobhrain
Eilean nam Bàn
Port Mor
Dubh Loch
380
Post Office
Glas
Dun Meadhonach
Càrn na Cainnle
Dun Eibhinn
Hotel
Shop
Pier
Church
Port an Òbain
Rubh' Aird Alanais
Beinn nan 412 Caorach
Scalasaig
Rubha Dubh
Raised Beaches
Tobar Fuar
Monument
Standing Stones
Eilean Dubh
Sliabh Riabhach
Golf Course
Machrins
Queen's Bay
Dun Ghallain
Air Strip
Standing Stone
Milbuie
Loch Staosnaig
Port Lobh
Càrn Àirigh Shomhairle
Turnigil
Eilean a' Chladaich
Plaide Mhòr
Càrn Glas
Càrn Chaointe
Rubha Eilean Mhàrtain
Balerumindubh
Abhuinn a' Ghlinne
Glac Mhòr
Lòn Mor
Loch Cholla
Squide
an Leanna
Ardskenish
Tràigh nam Barc
Chapel (Ruin)
Burial Ground
Dun Cholla
Rubha Dubh
An Dubh Sgeir
Standing Stone
Garvard
Raised Beaches
L. Breac
Baleruminmore
Rubh' an Dùnain
Cùirn Mhòra
Meall an Arbhair
Eilean Leathann
Glas Eilean
Beinn Eibhne 321
Sgeir Bhiorach
Sgeir Leathann
The Strand
Port a' Chapuill
Hangman's Rock
Rubha Bagh nan Capull
Carraigean
Sgeirean Fada
Leac Bhuidhe
Eilean Mhugaig
Abhuinn a Chuirn
Poll Gorm
Rubha Bàn
Beinn Oransay 304
An Carn
Rubha Breac
Dun Domhnuill
Priory
Cross
Leaba Mhòr
Port na Luinge
Eilean Treadhrach
Oransay Farm
Bacastair
Dubh Eilean
Leac Bhuidhe
Eilean nan Uan
Leac nan Gèadh
Seal Cottage
Port na h-Atha
Frith Sgeirean
Druim Mòr
Raised Beach
Eilean Ghaoideamal
Raised Beaches
Rubha Caol
Caolas Mòr
Eilean nan Ròn
Eilean Treunaig
Caolas Mhic an Athar
Eilean an Eoin
Cubaig
Caolas an Iasgaich
Sgeir Leathann
An t-Sàil
Ceann Riobha

island with an enviable record for hours of sunshine. And there remains more, so much more, still to explore: perhaps even the farthest-flung of the Outer Hebrides, St Kilda, in splendid isolation miles from anywhere. But that's another story, for another time.

These islands off the west coast of Scotland harbour a strangely compelling enchantment: even from afar, they excite uncannily potent longings among those exiles, who feel that they still belong there, that the islands are truly home. The Gaelic words of the Canadian Boat Song carry the plaintive cry:

> Yet still the blood is strong, the heart is Highland,
> And we in dreams behold the Hebrides.

Details of ferry services and tours from Caledonian MacBrayne Ltd, The Ferry Terminal, Gourock. PA19 1QP, telephone: 0475 33755. Visitors will find Tourist Information Centres open in season on many of the Hebridean islands, and at ports on the mainland.

Part Three
Wales

Wales

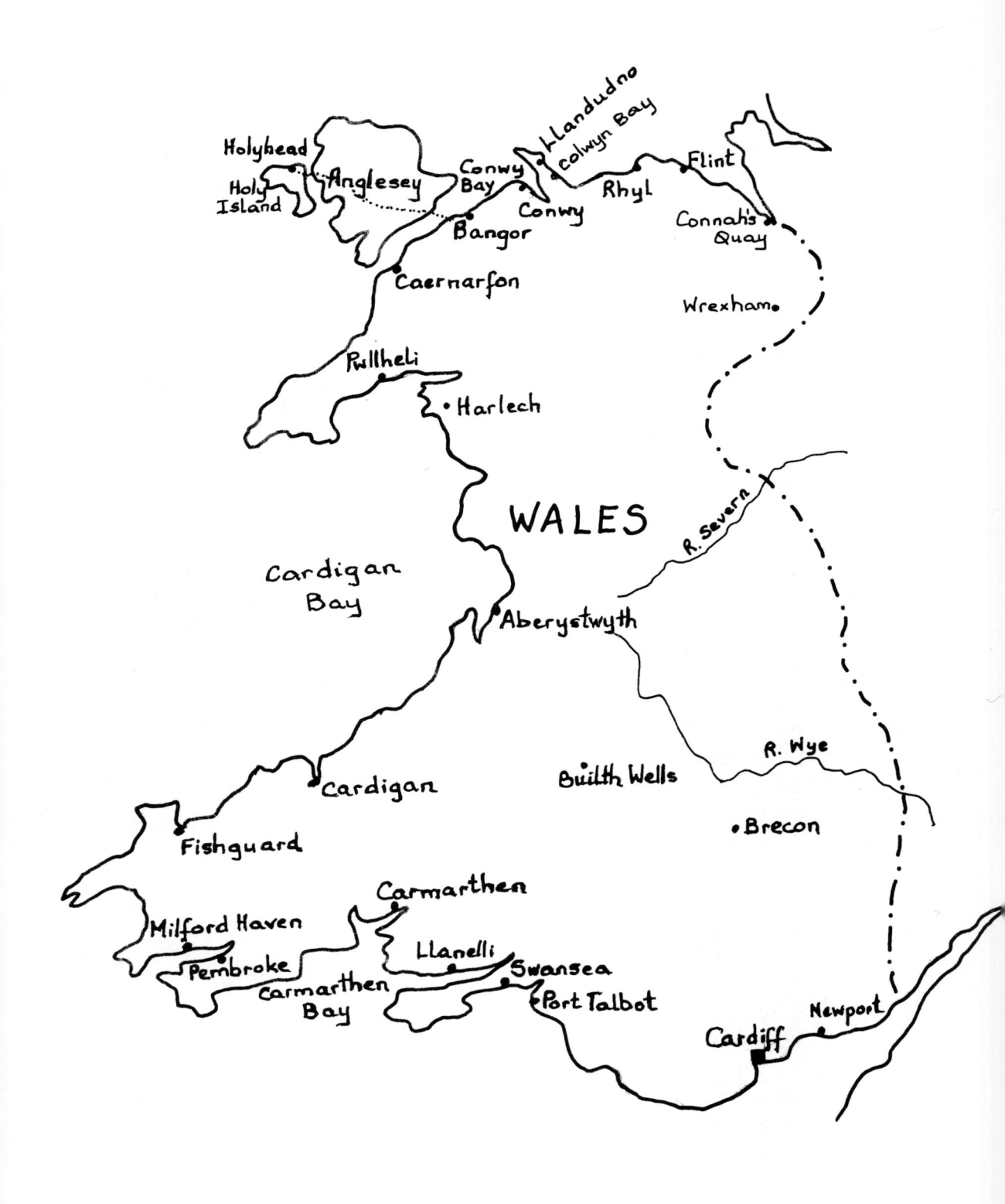

- Holyhead
- Holy Island
- Anglesey
- Conwy Bay
- Llandudno
- Colwyn Bay
- Conwy
- Bangor
- Rhyl
- Flint
- Connah's Quay
- Caernarfon
- Wrexham
- Pwllheli
- Harlech
- Cardigan Bay
- R. Severn
- Aberystwyth
- R. Wye
- Builth Wells
- Cardigan
- Brecon
- Fishguard
- Carmarthen
- Milford Haven
- Pembroke
- Llanelli
- Swansea
- Carmarthen Bay
- Port Talbot
- Cardiff
- Newport

Cara Wallia

> All westward, Wales beyond the Severn shore,
> And all the fertile land within that bound ...

Such was the lavish bounty promised to Owen Glendower, if we are to trust Shakespeare's account in *King Henry the Fourth Part One*.

Look at a map of Britain, then draw an imaginary line, running almost due south, from Liverpool to Bristol. On, or very close to that line which connects two great ports, are Chester, Shrewsbury, Ludlow, Hereford, Monmouth and Chepstow. These are border towns, guardians of the boundary which separates England from Wales, communities steeped in the history of this curious and fascinating region. To the west of the line, lies the Principality of Wales, a country of more than 8,000 square miles, with its own language, Welsh, spoken by more than a quarter of the inhabitants, its ancient rocks, the Cambrian Mountains, and its fierce national pride. Wales is bounded by sea on three sides: the Irish Sea to the north; westwards, beyond Cardigan Bay, St George's Channel; to the south, the Bristol Channel. Indeed, Wales provides travellers with convenient gateways to Ireland across the waters, from Holyhead, Fishguard, Pembroke and Swansea.

Although it has long been part of the United Kingdom, Wales retains its own distinctive character, inherited from Celts who were the earliest dwellers in this land. Their chronicles include accounts of continuing battles with their English neighbours, and warlike castles up and down the land are sufficient testimony to a turbulent past. Many of these strongholds owe their existence to Edward I, the English king who made successful conquest of Wales. It was during his reign, in 1282, that the Welsh prince, Llywelyn ap Gruffydd, was killed between Llanganten and Llanfair-ym-Muallt, now known as Builth Wells. That is a date remembered by every true Welshman.

Wales presents something of a mystery to most English people. The Welsh, along with Cornish folk, are survivors of the Celtic tradition in Britain, and their ways are not the ways of other inhabitants of the island. A Welshman is traditionally known as Taf, or Taffy. This is unlikely to be his real name. 'Dai Bach' is a greeting offered to 'little David', the use of the diminutive signifying affection or regard. 'Ap' simply means 'son of', the same meaning that 'Mac' has in Scotland and Ireland. There is something irresistibly attractive about the musical lilt of Welsh speech, which has a character 'most musical, most melancholy'.

Welsh nationalism manifests itself from time to time in demonstrations of hostility against anything to do with England. Holiday cottages belonging to English visitors have been burnt down, and English names erased from road-signs, leaving only the Welsh, so that if you do not happen to know that Abertawe is Swansea, and Caerdydd, Cardiff, you can easily miss your way. In 1301, King Edward I had his son proclaimed the Prince of Wales and, since that date, the eldest son of the reigning English monarch has held that title. In *King Henry IV*, we hear of 'that nimble-footed madcap Prince of Wales', but Shakespeare was writing of the youthful excesses of Prince Hal, in the company of that extraordinary character of dramatic fiction, Sir John Falstaff. Today, things are not quite the same.

Charles, the present Prince of Wales, is what one would call, without hesitation, a traditionalist. His views on modern buildings, vigorously applauded in some quarters, have not endeared him to some of today's architects. He also has something to say about the state of the English language: according to a report in *The Times* of 20 December 1989, he is convinced that it has become 'so impoverished, so sloppy and so limited that we have arrived at a dismal wasteland of banality, cliché and casual obscenity'.

The Prince of Wales who, when he accedes to the throne, will become Defender of the Faith, has very definite views on things ancient and modern, and on recent changes in the liturgy of the Church of England: 'Compare the courtesy of Cranmer's language with the crassness of the Alternative Service Book which spends much time telling the Deity what he must already know.'

What is worse, new versions of the Prayer Book and the Bible condemn to oblivion many of the memorable phrases of Cranmer, Tyndale and Wyclif, which have passed into the body of our speech and writing. For example, 'Give peace in our time', is watered down to 'Give your people the blessing of peace'; the prayer 'O Lord, save thy people/And bless thine inheritance', disappears altogether. What was memorable becomes, in its mode of expression, eminently trite and forgettable. One does not need to be a theologian, or even a believer, to enter into this argument. As Prince Charles is quick to point out, the King James Bible of 1611 and the Book of Common Prayer have for more than three hundred years been a part of English literature, a vital ingredient in literary expression. Some of us are convinced that it needed a Prince of Wales to say these things.

Wales is a place where language, literature and music matter: Welsh choirs are famous throughout the world; bards are crowned at the *Eisteddfod*; and who has not heard of Dylan Thomas? Wales is a land of legends, too: an early medieval tale, *Culwch ac Olwen*, tells of King Arthur and his knights hunting the boar Trwyth through the southern part of Wales. Then, for those seeking evidence of the warlike history of Wales, there are the great castles of Caerphilly (after Dover, the largest in England and Wales), Kidwelly, Harlech, Conwy, Caernarfon, Pembroke, Beaumaris, Flint and many others. From earlier times, there are burial chambers, like Pentre Ifan and Bryn Celli Ddu ('the hillock in the shadowy copse'), hill forts of the Bronze Age and Iron Age, solid evidence of Roman occupation and Christian symbols, like the 12th-century headstones at Strata Florida. In fact, this is where the curious traveller can begin to discover for himself the history of ancient Britain.

North Wales

Crossing into Wales near Chester, we drove into the busy little township of Mold, known further afield for its enterprising Theatre Clwyd, which has staged many admirable productions in recent years. In the town's main street, we found an excellent bakery, where we enjoyed what were advertised as genuine Welsh Cornish pasties. Certainly, they were very good, whatever their provenance. An 18th-century writer, Thomas Pennant, described the scene near Mold, so very close to the border with England:

'*Cambria* here lays aside her majestic air, and condescends to assume a gentler form, in order to render less violent her approaching union with her *English* neighbour.'

A friendly garage owner recommended that we should visit a nearby beauty spot, at Loggerheads. His pride in this local attraction was amply justified, as we discovered at a delightful site by the River Alyn. Much care has been taken in the restoration of Pentre Mill, with its water-wheel; there is a visitors' centre with a small shop and refreshment-room, and gentle, though occasionally muddy, walks through large areas of woodland, especially attractive when autumnal colours are at their most vivid.

Due north of Mold, looking out across the broad estuary of the river Dee towards England, is Flint. The castle, built by Edward I, is now a romantic ruin, yet substantial enough to occupy the visitor in fruitful contemplation for an hour or two. There, I met a man of Kent (or perhaps he was a Kentish man), who had come from the prosperous south-east of England, to set up a factory in Flint. 'I hope it's not going to spoil the view of the castle,' he remarked thoughtfully, as we inspected the keep. In fact, quite close to the castle is an industrial estate, and what appears to be an unofficial dumping ground for waste materials. 'They're going to clear all this up, make it all neat, with proper facilities for visitors.' My Kentish informant gestured towards the wasteland. We continued together through the echoing remains of Flint Castle. 'It sets the imagination going,' my companion observed. 'You get to wondering what it was like all those hundreds of years ago.' Indeed, it was at Flint Castle, in Shakespeare's play, *King Richard II*, that the king is forced to submit to the usurping Henry Bolingbroke, who summons him to appear in the castle's courtyard:

> In the base court? Base court, where kings grow base,
> To come at traitors' calls, and do them grace.
> In the base court? Come down? Down, court! down, king!
> For night-owls shriek where mounting larks should sing.

Holywell, one of the hallowed places of Wales, is true to its name: there is a legend that the 7th-century Saint Gwenfrewi (Winifred in English) had her head struck off by the importunate son of a chieftain, whose attentions she had spurned. Her uncle, St Bueno (so the tale runs), restored her head, and brought her to life again. She is said to have passed the remainder of her life as a nun. A spring appeared at the spot where Winifred's head was struck off, and in later years it became known as a healing-place, where the sick came to seek a cure. The 19th-century poet and Jesuit priest, Gerard Manley Hopkins, wrote poems about St Winifred; a visit with a friend to Holywell (Treffynon in Welsh) in 1874 moved him profoundly, as he recorded in his *Journal*.

> The strong unfailing flow of the water and the chain of cures from year to year all these centuries took hold of my mind with wonder at the bounty of God in one of His saints, the sensible thing so naturally and gracefully uttering the spiritual reason of its being (which is all in true keeping with the story of St Winifred's death and recovery) and the spring in place leading back the thoughts by its spring in time to its spring in eternity: even now the stress and buoyancy and abundance of the water is before my eyes.

There is a familial connection here between this part of Wales and a man who, though born in the south of England, thought of Wales as the land of his fathers. Britain is full of exiles, both willing and reluctant, people who feel that they really belong somewhere else than the place in which they are actually living. David Jones, one of the most distinguished poets and artists of his generation, was born on the outskirts of London, but from an early age, he felt a close affinity with Wales, the land of his father.

I first met David when he was in his 69th year, and living at Monksdene, a residential hotel close to the shopping centre of Harrow, Middlesex.

David Jones was born on November 1st, 1895, in Kent, son of James Jones and Alice Ann (nee Bradshaw). On his paternal side of wholly Welsh blood, his father being born in 1860 in Treffynon of a family from Ysgeifiog, in that north-east corner of Wales that had, historically, been a continuous cause of contention between the Earls of Chester, backed by the Crown, and the Princes of Gwynedd. James Jones had come to London in about 1885, and David was born ten years later.

'From about the age of six,' he said, 'I felt I belonged to my father's people and their land, though brought up in an entirely English atmosphere. So it was natural that when, sometime in the first decade of the twentieth century, I was taken to Gwenydd Wen, with the taut sea-horizon on the right, and to the left the *bryniau* and west, and further off, the misted *mynyddoell* of Arfon, I felt a Rubicon had been crossed, and that this was the land of which my father had spoken with affection and suppressed pride.'

'The Sleeping Lord', one of his finest poetic creations, points the reader towards the Welsh hill pictures which David Jones made in the mid-1920s when, according

Approaching Wales: Hereford Cathedral

David Jones, artist and writer

New Inn, Newbridge-on-Wye

River Wye

Caernarfon Castle

The gentle scenery of Wales

Brecon Beacons

Sunset off the coast of South Wales

to his own account, he was at last understanding something of the nature of the particular 'carpentry', that process of fitting together, which most sorted with his inclinations and talents. The tump by Honddu, the russet-hued mattress, the small, black horses, the couchant hills, the configuration of the land — all these images are reflected in his drawings: in them, as in 'The Sleeping Lord', he acknowledged his Welshness, which meant so much to him as an artist.

'In January 1915, being in a battalion of the Royal Welch Fusiliers, as part of the 38th (Welsh) Division, I found myself once more on the coast of Gwenydd, this time doing squad-drill on the esplanade at Llandudno. Then, early in December 1915, the Division embarked from Southampton for France. The various units of the Division were taking up positions astride the Estaires-La Bassée road, and there we remained from about Christmas, 1915, to early June 1916, when the long,long march south began, from the watery flats of Flanders to the wide, undulating chalkland of the Somme. It was those first six months in the trenches of the forward zone that I chose as the period and subject-matter in writing *In Parenthesis*. On July 10-11, 1916, in a confused attack on Mametz Wood, I was, along with many, many others of my unit, wounded and was evacuated to England.' *In Parenthesis*, published in 1937, was regarded by T S Eliot as 'a work of genius'.

The final scene of David's army career was one of near disaster, averted by a happy accident. On his way to the demobilisation point, David stopped to visit the lavatory, leaving his rifle outside, propped against a wall. When he came out, the thing was gone. He knew the loss of a rifle, in the army's book, to be a cardinal sin, and made his way forward with a sinking heart, until he chanced to pass an unattended pile of discarded weapons. He was able to seize a rifle, hand it in, and thus ensure his quiet and decent departure from the army. He asked me once not to repeat this story: 'They might still catch up with me!' he said.

In 1970, in Harrow, he suffered a stroke, and fell while he was carrying a pile of books. His subsequent account of the mishap was characteristically lively. After lying on the floor for some time, he thought, 'I can't stay here in this bloody draught.' From the days of the First War and his time in the trenches, he had hated draughts and 'the bloody damp'. So he dragged himself painfully over to the bed, and managed to manoeuvre himself into a sitting position. Then, curious to ascertain the extent of the injury, he removed his trousers to make an examination. It was at this point that he realised that it was just about time for the maid to come in to clean the room; almost simultaneously came recognition of the fact that he was unable to dress himself again in a hurry, and that it was quite likely that the young lady would enter, to be confronted with the spectacle of 'an old man sitting on the bed with his trousers down!'

The fracture that he had sustained necessitated an operation that was wryly reported by David to have been a 'technological success', but which was to leave him physically enfeebled for the rest of his life, and compel his removal from Monksdene to the Calvary Nursing home on Sudbury Hill. There, he continued his life, working on the completion of fragments of writing which, he hoped, were going to form part of a grand design. He was a great hoarder, and at the nursing-home things were piled on tables and chairs, pushed into drawers already crammed with other objects, hidden in cupboards, thrown into boxes. David had a fairly clear notion of what each heap contained, but the exact location of a single object often demanded a prolonged and, for him, exhausting search. Through long experience of these searches, which were orchestrated with groans, sighs and, if things were not going well, expletives of increasing force, I had learned to station myself strategically to field the debris as it spilled over the edges of tables, chairs and dressers, or was hurled in fury to the floor. Every so often, David would light upon something — not the object of his search — which afforded momentary and unexpected delight, and there would come a pause while he examined the treasure which had been rudely thrown to the surface, and explained its significance. Then the search would be resumed with increased intensity.

David had a horror of people going through his possessions in his absence. One of his fears was that, after his death, the contents of his drawers and cupboards would be disclosed to other eyes, and there would be found 'pork pies and letters from girls'. When necessity demanded, I used to take him to the dentist. It was not the easiest of outings: there were difficulties getting him into the car, and I usually had to tuck in a trailing leg or garment before setting off; then, after treatment, the return up the hill to the nursing-home, where he greeted the ramp leading to the side door as though it were his quarter-deck, and he the Lord Nelson returned from a spell of shore leave. On one memorable occasion, the struggle to alight from the car was more than usually prolonged, accompanied by determinedly patient groaning and gasping from David. At length, clinging precariously to the car-door, and then heaving himself laboriously to his feet, he exclaimed with triumph; 'Made it!' A nursing sister, attending on the ceremony said, 'Yes, but Mr Jones, your legs are crossed!'

Nobody who knew David could pretend that those last years in the nursing-home were happy ones for him. He gave way more readily to fits of depression; he missed the company of old friends, and of his books. But still he worked away. I saw him for the last time on 24 October, 1974, almost exactly ten years after our first meeting. The following weekend, he was told that he was to be moved to a room upstairs, a fate he had dreaded for some time, since he so hated change. In the early morning of Monday, 28 October, David was ready to receive his breakfast. Sister Joseph, of the Little Company of Mary, had just gone upstairs when a call came through for her on the internal telephone: 'Mr Jones has gone,' was the bleak message.

Mr Jones has gone, leaving to his friends and admirers a host of memories, memories of a man remarkable both as an artist and as a human being. His writings are available to all; his paintings are to be seen in galleries all over the world, with a fine collection at the National Museum of Wales in Cardiff, and his personal library and letters deposited at the National Library of Wales in Aberystwyth. I think that the Welsh are proud to number him among their poets. He was, as Tom Burns wrote in the obituary notice for *The Tablet*, 'a holy man'. *Dona ei requiem sempiternam.*

From Flint, the road runs along the coast of North Wales, through seaside resorts like Prestatyn, Rhyl, Colwyn Bay, Llandudno and Bangor. Southwards from Rhyl, the road leads to Denbigh. Coleridge was much taken with the sight of the place: 'At Denbigh is a ruined castle — it surpasses everything I could have conceived — I wandered there an hour and a half.' Due south of Bangor lies Snowdon, 3555 feet high, surrounded by some of the finest and most popular mountaineering country in Britain.

It was at a hotel in Bangor that we, late arrivals, hungry and tired after the crossing from Ireland, demanded sandwiches of a rather sleepy-looking night porter. In his own time, he delivered them to our room. As we chewed our way diligently through these offerings, we encountered pieces of polythene. On closer investigation, it transpired that the dozy porter, in haste to provide us with sustenance, had failed to remove the plastic wrapper from the cucumber, and this indigestible substance now formed part of our meal.

From Bangor, the way leads across the Menai Strait, and the famous bridge connecting the mainland with the island of Anglesey. The castle at Beaumaris, one of many built by Edward I towards the close of the 13th century, is a magnificent example of effective fortification: a double concentric wall enclosing the site, to ensure that an invader breaching the first line of defence does not have an easy passage through the next.

At the north-west point of Anglesey is the port of Holyhead, whence departs the Irish Mail, by ferry-boat to Dun Laoghaire, just south of Dublin. Jonathan Swift did not find Holyhead much to his taste; indeed, he cared little for

> ... this bleaky shore,
> Where loudest winds incessant roar,
> Where neither herb nor tree will thrive,
> Where Nature hardly seems alive.

Central and South Wales

A journey through the centre of Wales discloses a truly lyrical landscape. Memory can and does play tricks, but my recollection of expeditions in that region seems to place them all in autumnal days, when the countryside is a palette of rich colours, the shafts of sunlight imparting a luminous quality to the golden leaves. Tufts of trees on the rounded hillsides, silly sheep and docile cows in the gentle folds of green, upland pastures, and the soothing sight of running water coursing through streams and rivulets, all combine to the completion of a memorably pleasing and satisfying picture. Black and white cottages, dull in gloom and rain, carry a bright, clear visage under bright skies. Indeed a *plurabelle*, an assembly of beauties in which nothing jars, no element appears incongruous.

Aberystwyth was once described by the writer and broadcaster, Wynford Vaughan-Thomas, as 'the perfect town for the unambitious man'. A few miles to the east of Aberystwyth, in the high hills at the southern end of the Cambrian Mountains, is the source of the River Wye, Afon Gwy. Its course runs through some of the most beautiful country to be found anywhere. On our first excursion to this winsome region, we stayed most contentedly at the New Inn, Newbridge-on-Wye, telephone: 059 789 211. The river runs southwards for a little way, through Builth Wells, then turns eastwards, into England, through Hereford and Ross-on-Wye, before turning again to Monmouth, and southwards past the glories of Tintern Abbey to its journey's end, near the Severn Road Bridge. It was in lines composed a few miles above Tintern Abbey that Wordsworth owned to have felt

> A presence that disturbs me with the joy
> Of elevated thoughts; a sense sublime
> Of something far more deeply interfused,
> Whose dwelling is the light of setting suns,
> And the round ocean and the living air,
> And the blue sky, and in the mind of man.

For almost its entire length, the Wye offers untrammelled delights, and the peculiar solace conferred by scenes of rural tranquillity.

The Severn Bridge, an imposing example of modern engineering, carries the motorway over the water from England into Wales. The bridge itself has come in for a good deal of adverse criticism since the commencement of operations designed to strengthen its structure, operations which have certainly slowed the passage of travellers to and from the Principality. There is a charge for crossing the bridge, and a Welsh poet, Harri Webb, was quick to note the disadvantage in this arrangement, with

> ... all the tolls collected
> On the English side.

CENTRAL AND SOUTH WALES

Names of rivers, like Usk and Tawe, somehow seem to spell out a kind of enchantment which belongs to this part of Wales, but there is stark contrast between the rural splendour of the Black Mountains and the atmosphere of the industrial landscape of South Wales, what David Jones identified as 'the black pall of Merthyr'. The men of the valleys have played their part in the industrial history of the land, and the names of the townships, proud communities like Aberdare, Rhondda, Tonypandy, Pontypridd, Tredegar, Ebbw Vale, Pontypool, Abertillery, Rhymney and Merthyr Tydfil, give out a resonance proclaiming the annals of harsh toil and prolonged struggle, calling back to mind the almost-forgotten years of depression between the two wars, and evoking images of coal and steel which dominated life in the region. The poems of Idris Davies convey the temper of those days with accuracy, vividness and compassion.

Cardiff, capital of the principality of Wales since 1955, is a seaport, exporting coal, iron and steel, and importing timber, iron ore and grain. The city has an 11th-century castle and a university. Cardiff Arms Park has been the scene of many a famous encounter between rugby sides. The National Museum of Wales houses an outstanding collection, with many fine examples of Italian and Dutch painting; but the greatest strength is in 19th-century French works by Daumier, Millet, Corot, Courbet, Renoir, Pissarro, Boudin, Manet, Monet, Van Gogh, Sisley, Cezanne, Degas and Alfred Sisley, who painted briefly in Wales in 1897. British painting is well represented: following the death of David Jones in 1974, Cardiff was able to acquire a number of his very best works. In recent years, the Welsh National Opera has made a name for itself throughout the kingdom and beyond its boundaries. Their production of Wagner's music-drama, *Tristan und Isolde*, conducted by Reginald Goodall, provided for me one of the outstanding experiences of a lifetime of opera-going. Happily, those who missed it in the theatre can catch something of its quality from the complete recording of the work, made in Swansea's Brangwyn Halls by Decca.

Swansea was the birthplace, in 1914, of Dylan Thomas, one of the truly remarkable poets of this century. Today, he is best remembered as the author of that famous play for voices, *Under Milk Wood*, a magical evocation of a Welsh community, 'the small town, starless and bible-black', its inhabitants, and their lives and dreams. The boathouse at Laugharne (pronounced Larn), where Thomas did much of his writing, stands yet, looking out to where the waters run past Ginst Point and across Laugharne Sands into Carmarthen Bay. Dylan Thomas died, an alcoholic, on a lecture tour of the United States in 1953, but the poems survive in all their inextinguishable exuberance, even though electric pylons march now across Fern Hill, where once the poet

> ... was young and easy under the apple boughs
> About the lilting house and happy as the grass was green,
> The night above the dingle starry ...

The works of Dylan Thomas are among the many opulent gifts from Wales to the *corpus* of English literature. Like many writers before him, and many who will follow, Dylan Thomas has had his detractors; but in his writing there is, without question, something of the true voice of lyric poetry. There can be no mistaking the quality of such lines as these, from 'Poem in October':

> My birthday began with the water-
> Birds and the birds of the winged trees flying my name
> Above the farms and the white horses
> And I rose
> In rainy autumn
> And walked abroad in a shower of all my days.

We have spent blissful days exploring the Gower Peninsula, not far removed from Swansea, an area of interest to geologists and archaeologists, and decidedly a most restful and pleasing part of the country. During a brief and entirely agreeable stay at the Osborne Hotel in Langland Bay (telephone: 0792 366 274), I woke one morning to the realisation that it was February 14th, St Valentine's Day, and I had done nothing about it. Wandering disconsolately on the pebbly beach before breakfast, and wondering how to acquit myself of this dereliction of duty, I came across a pink stone in the shape of a heart. Clutching this piece of rock gratefully to my breast, I hastened to the reception desk, there to procure a felt-tipped pen with which to make a suitable inscription. With a justifiable air of triumph, I laid the object proudly on the breakfast-table a few minutes later, reassured that honour had, by this happy token, been retrieved. We still have fond memories of Langland Bay and its benevolent beach.

It is said that in some parts of Wales, if an Englishman enters a bar, the occupants immediately begin conversing in Welsh, even though they may have been speaking English before the stranger's arrival. This may well be true. Some years ago, I was making a recording with a minor Welsh poet in his little cottage in South Wales. At one point, I remember, his wife came in, and the poet addressed her in Welsh, a tongue of which I have no knowledge. After listening to what sounded like a reproachful tirade from her husband, the wife turned to me and said: 'My husband tells me that I am in the way, that you and he are busy, and that I must leave the room at once.' With those words, she departed, not to be seen again during my visit. Quite an embarrassing occasion, really, but the only instance I can cite of that particular practice.

Quite abruptly, as one journeys westwards, Wales seems almost to stop in the area around Pembroke: Welsh place-names give way to English ones, like Haverford West, Milford Haven, Fishguard, Johnston and Hook. The 17th-century chronicler, Thomas Fuller, has an explanation for this seeming oddity.

'A part of this county is peopled by Flemings, placed there by King Henry the First, who was no less politic than charitable therein; for such Flemings, being driven out of their own country by an irruption of the ocean, were fixed here to defend the land given them against the Welsh; and their country is called Little England beyond Wales.' We have frequently sailed from Pembroke to Ireland, passing the huge oil refineries at Milford Haven on our way. Pembroke Castle is an impressive pile, and we have enjoyed many an agreeable meal in the cosy restaurant of the Old king's Arms on the main street. There I had my first carpet-bag steak, a piece of succulent fillet stuffed with oysters. Very delicious, and entirely satisfying. It is a good place to stay, too: telephone: 0646 683611. The Pembrokeshire Coast Path, opened in 1970, with a length of 167 miles, was the third long-distance trail for walkers to be created in Britain.

There is a regular ferry service, which we have often used, from Fishguard to Rosslare, in Ireland. It was near Fishguard one day that I stopped at a little village store, in the hope of satisfying my wife's sudden craving for that exquisite Scottish delicacy, shortbread. Of course, I should have known better than to go looking for such a thing in Wales. Behind the counter was a youth whose countenance did not exactly radiate intelligence. 'Have you got any shortbread?' I asked. He stared at me as though I were speaking in a foreign language; perhaps, to him, I was. 'Shortbread,' I said again, but more loudly this time, just in case he happened to be deaf. I was anxious to cover all contingencies. This time, he repeated what I had said, but breaking the word up into two distinct syllables: 'Short bread.' After considering the implications of what he had heard and what he had repeated, the boy turned to the shelves, on which were displayed several loaves of bread, and began an elaborate and entirely serious pantomime of measuring them, to see which loaf was the shortest. This was almost too much for me, but when I had recovered a measure of equanimity, I tried again. 'No,' I said, still speaking loudly, as I had not yet ruled out deafness as a contributory factor in this absurd situation. 'Shortbread. It's a kind of biscuit.' And here I began to make what I now realise were entirely inadequate descriptive gestures with both hands. The boy looked more puzzled than ever, and turned in desperation to the loaves on the shelf. 'No,' I exclaimed. 'You won't find it there.' For a moment, something almost like an expression crossed his face, hinting perhaps that he thought it impertinent of me to presume to know the disposition of his stock. After all, how could I guess what might be hidden behind the loaves. 'Shortbread,' I repeated, for want of anything better to say. Clearly, the word meant nothing to him. It was at this point his mother appeared: at first sight, she looked a much more promising prospect than the son, bright, cheerful and clearly anxious to oblige. She asked what it was I required. 'Shortbread,' I replied. The son stood mutely by during this exchange, observing us both. A flicker of doubt came to the mother's face, to be dispelled immediately. Her head disappeared below the level of the counter, to reappear a few seconds later with a broad smile. 'Here you are,' she said. 'Shortbread.' She offered me a packet. I took it, and read the label. 'Shortbread Mix,' it announced.

'To make the perfect shortbread, follow these instructions carefully.' It then gave, in some detail, the method for creating shortbread by adding water to the powder which the packet contained and placing the resulting mess in an oven for a certain period of time. 'No,' I said despairingly. 'I want to eat the shortbread now. I want shortbread that's already made.' She looked at me with a pitying expression. 'Oh, then you're in a hurry,' she said. 'Well, I'm sorry, but I can't help you, this is all we've got.' Somehow, she managed to imply that it had been good enough for all her customers, and that it was quite unreasonable for me, an Englishman, to expect to find shortbread all ready and waiting for me, but she was too polite to say so. I left the shop, conscious of the son's baleful glare directed at my retreating figure, as I made my exit from Wales. *Ave atque vale!*

Part Four
Ireland

Ballycastle
Londonderry
NORTHERN IRELAND
Bangor
Belfast
Donegal
Omagh
Armagh
Newry
Balina
Carrick-on-Shannon
Achill Isle
Castlebar
Westport
Clifden
Athlone
Clara
Dublin
Galway
Galway Bay
Kildare
REPUBLIC OF IRELAND
Aran Is
Kilkee
Kilrush
Limerick
Kilkenny
Tipperary
Wexford
Tralee
Dingle
Killarney
Kenmare
Cork
Bandon
Bantry

IRELAND

I Am of Ireland

I am of Ireland,
And the Holy Land of Ireland,
And time runs on ...

Thirty years have gone by since I first set foot on Irish soil. It was, as I remember well, a pale grey October morning in Dun Laoghaire (pronounced Dun Leery), where everything appeared drab and unwelcoming, with not a hint of vaunted emerald to be seen anywhere. The night crossing from Holyhead established the mood: sleep was rendered out of the question by the unremitting labours of those strange, nocturnal beings regularly employed by shipping companies to drag chains across the decks of ships whose passengers fondly imagine that possession of a cabin aboard carries with it the right to undisturbed slumbers. After disembarkation, those of us going to what was then Westland Row Station (now Pearse), in Dublin were shepherded into a rather dingy train, whose doors were then locked from outside by a uniformed official. It was not, to tell the truth, a promising beginning, and sometimes I wonder why I have insisted on returning to Ireland every year since then. Perhaps it is the spirit of my great-grandmother tugging at the heart-strings. Her name was Isabella Costello, and that is just about all I can tell you about her until my genealogical researches are further advanced.

But I have the feeling that there are more reasons than one prompting those frequent journeys westward; perhaps the complex and subtle amalgam of seriousness and humour, of dark and light, in the Irish character has something to do with it. Then, of course, there are what an elderly Irishman was heard to call 'the sceneries'. So many fond memories there of majestic sights: the amiable Dingle peninsula, its winding roads occupied largely by donkeys and fringed with ancient beehive huts on the way to Slea Head, where the voyager looks out across the Blasket Islands; the riven surface of the Burren, alight in spring with a profusion of tiny wild flowers; the rich, autumnal glow that warms the Glen of Aherlow in County Tipperary; the untamed beauty of Connemara. Indeed, the scenic beauties defy description: the first sight of Killarney's lakes from Ladies' View, delightful roads hugging the jaggedly-indented coastline of West Cork and Kerry, with abundance of fuchsia hedges, the savage grandeur of the Cliffs of Moher which faced some wretched survivors of the Spanish Armada, the serenity of Coole Park and, nearby, the romantic setting of Yeats's Thoor Ballylee, the wildness of mountains and seascapes in Galway and Donegal. All these I have come to know and love, but still the account is incomplete, the fascination not entirely explained.

'People are more than places,' wrote the poet Ruthven Todd and, of course, he was right. Indeed, it is with people that abiding memories of Ireland begin and end. Some of the characters have departed this life: no more will those two wonderful people, René and Joan Hague (she a daughter of the artist, Eric Gill), entertain us with food, drink and dazzling conversation at Shanagarry House in County Cork; nor will Mary Cahir tell more tales of how she and her lady friends in County Clare used to beat their menfolk at cards by means of a little discreet cheating; nor shall we sit again around the dinner-table at Corofin with our dear friends Máire and Jack Sweeney, who now rest in the quietness of Ruan churchyard in Clare, while their bequest of pictures by Picasso, Paul Klee and Juan Gris is exhibited in Ireland's National Gallery, Dublin. Yet, as Tennyson observed, 'Tho' much is taken, much abides ...' and memories remain in all their vitality.

A willing addict since that first sight of Ireland, I have faithfully paid annual visits, latterly more like pilgrimages. Time was when early-evening passengers boarded their train, the Irish Mail, at Euston, reaching Holyhead in time for late supper aboard the *Hibernia* (or, with less enthusiasm, the much-abused *Princess Maud*). Those with cars were treated to the alarming experience of beholding their vehicles hoisted in and out of the ship's hold by crane. No drive-on, drive-off ferries in those days! All conspired to introduce the Irish tempo of life; but now, with shorter turn-around times to ensure maximum use of shipping. All is changed, changed utterly. Sadly, no terrible beauty is born. Unhappy sailors should know that the Irish Sea can be occasionally unfriendly, although of fifty crossings I recall only four distinctly rough. The shortest route is from Scotland, out of Cairnryan by P & O European Ferries, or from Stranraer by Sealink, to Larne in just over two hours. We found, for comfort and for catering, Sealink's refurbished ship between Holyhead and Dun Laoghaire most agreeable. Revised timetables in recent years occasionally dictate sailings at unsocial hours: 3.15 in the cold, dark morning is not the happiest of times to set off on a journey across the Irish Sea, especially if the ferry is late, and enthusiasm is cooled by a prolonged wait in the car park. Nor is it ideal, on the return voyage, to disembark at Holyhead or Fishguard some time after midnight. Many travellers from distant parts of Britain have enough to contend with, anyway, in terms of a long and tiring drive to any of the ports serving Ireland. Times have certainly changed, and holidaymakers should brace themselves against the shock of Ireland's high prices, especially for essential commodities like petrol and Guinness. Oh yes, there is one thing more: it rains frequently in Ireland. Gentle, persistent drizzle is optimistically classified as a 'soft day'. Such frequent irrigation helps to keep the grass green, as everyone knows.

So much for the bad news, which becomes utterly trivial when set against the fact that Ireland remains one of the most beguiling and intriguing of countries. Just when you think you have finally penetrated its essential mystery, something totally unexpected and unpredictable throws you off balance and, once again, a kind of beauty is born.

Like many other things in Ireland, the licensing laws have their peculiarities. I know not if the measure remains in force today, but there was a time when establishments serving intoxicating liquors had to close for one hour during the course of each day. Inevitably, this was known as 'the holy hour'. Once, a motorist found himself driving through a small market town at that time of day when the craving for a glass of stout makes itself felt. The visitor parked his car opposite a grocery which, as is often the case in Ireland, doubled as a bar. On trying the door, he was dismayed to find it locked. As he was turning away, disappointed in his quest, the door opened and the owner appeared. 'Can I help you at all?' he enquired solicitously. The thirsty traveller explained his need. 'Ah, well,' came the reply, 'I'm very sorry, but I can't do anything for you just now. You see, the bar is closed, it being the holy hour.' 'When will you be open again?' the stranger asked hopefully. 'Well, I've just now shut the bar, so it will be about another hour.' The prospect of hanging around the small town for another hour before liquid refreshment became available did not strike the traveller as an attractive proposition. But the host came up with a bright suggestion: 'Now, why don't you come in and have a drink while you're waiting?'

Ireland offers the joys of real conversation, at street-corners or in numerous little pubs. An eccentric, unpredictable, winsome place it surely is. The same epithets could equally well be applied to the inhabitants. Irishmen are sometimes addressed by well-meaning Englishmen as Paddy. Not all of them respond favourably to this appellation.

'Romantic Ireland's dead and gone,' announced Yeats, but I am happy to say that he was not altogether correct. For us, after many visits, the romance is still very much in evidence.

Ireland is a country whose history is inextricably bound up with that of Britain. 1 July, 1690, is a significant date for the Irish, for it was on that day, at the Battle of the Boyne, that James II was defeated by William III. There are many, in Ireland, in Britain and in the USA, who are convinced that the union of north and south must one day come to be a reality. That is their dream. There are others, in particular the Protestants who inhabit the Province of Northern Ireland, who are of the contrary opinion. Both views are held passionately and, as the world knows, have found expression in continuous and violent sectarian conflict. Unhappily, there seems to be no common ground between the parties to this dispute, and no immediate prospect of a resolution of their differences. That is the tragedy of present-day Ireland.

Information and useful guides and maps are available from the Irish Tourist Board, 14 Upper O'Connell Street, Dublin 1, telephone: 747733, and from the Northern Irish Tourist Board, 48 High Street, Belfast BT1 2DS, telephone: 0232 231221 or 246609.

Ferry operators include Belfast Ferries, 47 Donegall Quay, Belfast BT1 3ED, N Ireland, telephone: 0232 320364, or Brocklebank Dock, Bootle, Merseyside L20 1DB, telephone: 051 9226234; B & I Line, 16 Westmoreland Street, Dublin 2,

134   IRELAND

Ireland, telephone: 797977, or Reliance House, Water Street, Liverpool L2 8TP, telephone: 051 227 3131; Brittany Ferries, The Brittany Centre, Wharf Road, Portsmouth PO2 8RU, telephone: 0705 827701 or Tourist House, 42 Grand Parade, Cork; Irish Ferries, 2-4 Merrion Row, Dublin 2; P & O European Ferries, The Harbour, Larne, N Ireland BT40 1AQ, telephone: 0574 74321; Sealink UK Ltd, Charter House, Park Street, Ashford, Kent TN24 8EX, telephone: 0233 647047.

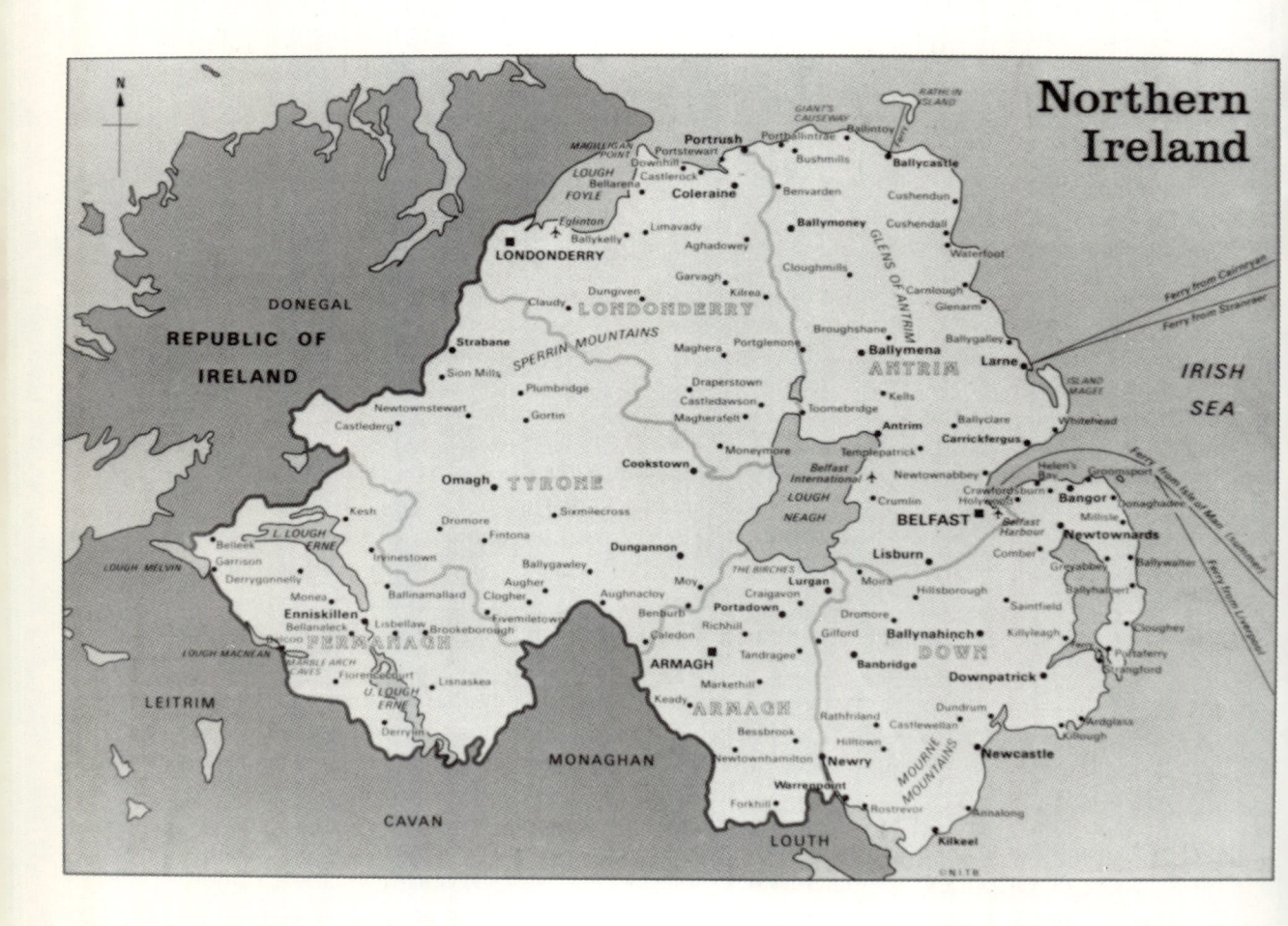

Northern Ireland

Sadly, the news which greets the outside world from Northern Ireland is mostly of a violent nature, the recital of events in a conflict which shows but little sign of resolution. That is the ugly side of life in Northern Ireland, but it is only part of the story of an area which holds so much to entice and charm the visitor.

Belfast has been called the Irish Liverpool, but Thackeray thought 'it would be better to call it the Irish London ... The houses are as handsome as at Dublin, with this advantage, that the people seem to live in them.' Northern Ireland's capital counts among its natives C S Lewis, Louis MacNeice and W R Rodgers. More than twenty years ago, in more tranquil days, I led a theatrical troupe, including Virginia McKenna, to the Queen's Festival, where we presented a programme of words and music which addressed itself to the subject of war. Today, we should be more circumspect in our choice of subject.

Tom Boyd, an amiable Ulsterman, manages a large hotel in Dunmurry, a fairly peaceful place on the outskirts of Belfast. He gave us a swift and fascinating tour of some of the city's attractions, among them Sir Thomas and Lady Dixon Park, famous for its roses, Stormont in its superb setting, Ulster Folk Park, and any number of fine buildings, including the City Hall, much admired by John Betjeman, and the Opera House. The Ulster Museum has an interestingly varied collection, in which British artists are well-represented, including paintings by Gainsborough, Turner, Sickert, Stanley Spencer, Paul Nash, Henry Moore, Barbara Hepworth, Ben Nicholson, Graham Sutherland and Francis Bacon. Nearby are St Anne's Cathedral and the charmingly sedate area containing the university. For the determined sightseer, there are the Botanic Gardens, Belfast Castle (1867), Cave Hill (with a grand view from M'Art's Fort), Ballylesson for the Giants' Ring, Lough Neagh, a dozen leisure centres, several good golf courses within easy reach, and the adventure of long-distance walking along the Ulster Way: so much to see and enjoy. Then, just to put things in perspective, Tom drove us past the shuttered fronts of buildings in the Shankill Road, where we were stopped and questioned at a checkpoint, before going on to the Falls Road and the Springfield Road, all melancholy reminders of Belfast's present.

Aldergrove Airport is fifteen miles to the west, and there is increasing use of Belfast Harbour Airport. Recently, we returned by sea from Belfast to Liverpool. It was a windy March evening when we presented ourselves at the ferry terminal, and I enquired of the man taking tickets at the gate what sort of crossing we might expect. He pondered the question seriously, and then said: 'Well, put it this way, sir, you'll know you're on a ship tonight.' He was right: it turned out to be quite a lively crossing, in storm force 10 winds.

To the north of Belfast is Larne, with a population of around 20,000, an increasingly busy port, equipped recently with two new weighbridges for heavy vehicles. There are up to a dozen sailings daily to Cairnryan and Stranraer on the Scottish mainland. From the rail terminal at the port trains run to Belfast, the town centre is within walking distance, and there is a small caravan park quarter of a mile away.

On my first landing at Larne, I was met by the Irish poet Seamus Heaney, whom I was to record reading his poems. My first thought was to find a convenient hotel, but Seamus, even with a new baby in the house, insisted that I stay with them: 'I'd have invited you by letter, but I thought you might be one of those balding imperialists!' he added. As for sightseeing, there are interesting churches in Larne (not to be confused, by the way, with Dylan Thomas's Welsh Laugharne, though pronunciations are identical). Then there is a ferry to Islandmagee, where the attractions include bathing, seabirds and a ruined castle. There are glorious changing sights on the Antrim Coast Road, past Ballygalley Head to the Antrim Glens, Cushendall for bathing, boating, fishing and scenery, and 55 miles away, the celebrated Giant's Causeway, an amazing mass of basalt columns, formed long ages since by volcanic activity.

Good hotels and restaurants are to be found in Northern Ireland. We can recommend Trusthouse Forte's Conway Hotel at Dunmurry, Belfast; the Ballygally Castle Hotel, where we spent a most pleasant weekend and enjoyed lavish and utterly delicious fried breakfasts; and a former stately home, Magheramore House, where we had an unashamedly traditional and generous Sunday lunch.

There are nightly crossings by Belfast Ferries from Liverpool, and frequent sailings by Sealink and P & O from Stranraer and Cairnryan; also by Isle of Man Steam Packet Seaways from Douglas, Isle of Man. By road from Belfast, Londonderry is 75 miles, Dublin 103, Sligo 129.

Dublin

Dublin, the Republic's capital, with a population of under a million, stands astride the River Liffey, which is said by connoisseurs to impart a conspicuous flavour to the local brew, Guinness, that dark and (so it is claimed) wholesome stout. Dublin is easy of access by sea from Liverpool or Holyhead, or by air, its airport conveniently situated only six miles from the city centre. Dublin is a city full of memories, as befits the country's capital. Our hotel on St Stephen's Green was a reminder of more gracious days, and also of Ireland's troubled history, for it was there, at the Shelbourne, that the 1922 Constitution was drafted, leading to the establishment of the Republic of Ireland, also known as Eire. From our window, we looked across an expanse of grass, trees and water, with a large population of contented ducks. A few doors away, a plaque announced that Oliver St John Gogarty, that distinguished man of letters, once had rooms there; impossible to escape literary associations in this place of 'grey, eighteenth-century houses'. The roll-call of Dublin-born writers includes Jonathan Swift, Dean of St Patrick's, Edmund Burke, Sheridan, Bram Stoker (author of *Dracula*), Oscar Wilde, Yeats, J M Synge, Sean O'Casey, James Joyce (who claimed that if Dublin were demolished, it could be rebuilt exactly as before by reference to his works), Brendan Behan and Samuel Beckett. Almost round the corner from Stephen's Green are the National Gallery, National Museum and Trinity College, whose library houses that marvellous 8th-century illuminated manuscript, the *Book of Kells*. Further sightseeing should certainly include the Gallery of Modern Art in Parnell Square, Swift's tomb in St Patrick's Cathedral, Phoenix Park, one of the largest in Europe and, if time allows, a visit to the theatre. The Abbey Theatre has a distinguished history since opening in 1904 with plays by Yeats and Lady Gregory. It was there, in 1907, that J M Synge's *The Playboy of the Western World* had such a turbulent reception that the occasion is remembered still. On the theatre's roll of honour are such names as Sara Allgood, Lennox Robinson, St John Ervine and Sean O'Casey. Following a fire in 1951, the company removed to the Queen's Theatre which was where, some thirty years ago, my father and I saw an unforgettably hilarious Irish comedy, *The Evidence I Shall Give*, followed by a short drama in the Gaelic tongue. The new Abbey Theatre opened on 18 July, 1966. In earlier years, the Abbey Theatre found itself with a rival, the Gate Theatre, run by distinguished men of the Irish theatrical scene, whose lifestyles were, for those days, considered somewhat unorthodox. Someone (nobody seems absolutely certain who), dubbed the Gate and Abbey Theatres 'Sodom and Begorrah'.

Looking for a quiet refuge outside city limits, we were very happy at the Green Isle Hotel, Naas Road, Clondalkin, telephone: 593406. In the city, Patrick Guilbaud's French restaurant has a Michelin rosette: 48 St James's Place, off Lower Baggot Street, telephone: 764192; and *The Good Food Guide* mentions the Park Restaurant, Main Street, Blackrock, telephone: 886177.

138 IRELAND

It is worthwhile taking the short excursion to Howth Castle's rhododendron gardens, although golfers may prefer a visit to the Portmarnock course. Limerick is 123 miles, Galway and Sligo equidistant at 135 miles by road from Dublin.

Just a little way south of Dublin, the port of Dun Laoghaire has two crossings daily by Sealink from Holyhead, a voyage of 3 hours. Sightseeing in the area could take in Bray, 8 miles distant, the Powerscourt Demesne at Enniskerry 12 miles away, with extensive gardens and walks, the Wicklow Mountains, Stepaside and Killakee viewing points, the Sally Gap, Glendalough with its Round Tower and St Kevin's Cross, and an inviting stretch of sand which we had to ourselves one fine day at Brittas Bay.

Wexford and the South-east

Rosslare is quite the most pleasing of Irish ports, with a population of just a few hundred. By road from Rosslare, Dublin is 90 miles away, Cork 130 and Limerick 131. There are sailings by B & I from Pembroke Dock, by Irish Ferries from Cherbourg and Le Havre, and by Sealink from Fishguard. We have made this last crossing on many occasions, in fair weather and foul. Once, with my wife and father, we were feeling peckish but not ravenous, and persuaded the dining-room steward to serve us with the children's menu to preserve our funds and comfort our digestions. I placed our order with trepidation, since we were clearly not children, but no problem presented itself until I had the temerity to ask for a bottle of claret. 'Ah, you can't have a bottle of claret with the children's menu!' pronounced the steward, with the air of a man who has just laid his ace on the table. Certainly, he had us there.

On another occasion, a minor mishap to our car on the overnight ferry from Pembroke to Rosslare had disabled a windscreen wiper, and when we landed, as we might have expected, it was what the Irish call 'a soft day'. That is to say, it was raining, gently but persistently. It was also just after six in the morning, and still quite dark. Not altogether hopefully we enquired of a passer-by where we might obtain assistance. The reply was distinctly encouraging: 'Oh, just up the road a way, then turn left, and at the first house on the right you ask for Jim Ryder. He's the best man in the parish for this sort of thing.' 'But won't he be asleep at this hour?' I asked. Back came the response my informant knew I craved to hear: 'Oh, no. He sleeps very little. He's usually awake.'

We followed the directions, and came to what we judged to be Mr Ryder's home. (By the way, that is not his real name.) The house was in darkness, no sign of light, or life, or activity of any kind. So we settled down to wait in the rain. There was nothing else we could do. After an hour or so, pale signs of dawn began to appear in the sky. It was still raining. A cyclist appeared out of the grey dampness, and I thought it best to ascertain whether or not we were in the right place. For all I knew, we might be outside the residence of the parish priest.

'Is this the home of Mr Jim Ryder?' I began warily, prepared to learn that we had mistaken our destination. 'Oh, it is,' said the cyclist, with reassuring conviction. Then, I know not why, I asked one of the silliest questions that has ever passed my lips: 'Do you know if he is likely to be up and about soon?' Now, how on earth could a passing cyclist be expected to know the habits of Mr Ryder, nocturnal or matinal? But his reply was calculated not to disappoint me. 'Oh, you'll see him any minute now. If you watch that gate,' (he pointed vaguely towards the yard), 'you'll see it open and you'll see himself going across the field.'

We resumed our vigil. Eventually, a light appeared in an upper window, and there came to us the sound of children's voices. This we took to be an auspicious sign, but another half-hour passed without further developments. By this time we were quite cold, hungry and not in the best of spirits, so my wife decided on direct attack, and went to knock on what looked like the front door. After an age, it opened and she disappeared inside. Another half-hour passed without incident, and then my wife returned. It transpired that she had been taken into the kitchen by the lady of the house, told the entire life story of the Ryder family, and then been solemnly assured that himself would be down in a very few minutes. I do not have to tell you here that another half-hour passed without incident, nor do you need to be told that it was still raining. But the story has a happy ending: at long last, Jim Ryder himself appeared with tool-kit, and in a few minutes he had repaired the windscreen-wiper. I offered to pay for his services. 'No, no,' he said firmly. 'Take it as a blessing. Now, be on your way!' We drove off, and it was not until we were some miles further on that my wife asked, in tones of some bewilderment: 'If he has just got up, why was he so very dirty?' There was no answer to that.

Among our greatest delights each year is a visit to the Wexford Festival, in the south-east corner of Ireland. Usually, we stay a few miles away, at Rosslare Harbour where, at the Hotel Rosslare, there used to be a noteworthy night-porter, D J Black, who will refuse your tip, but gladly sell you a copy of his collected poems. These verses, rather in the style of McGonagall, are in praise of things Irish and, in particular, the qualities of the Rosslare Hotel, telephone: 053 33110. With identical sea-views, Tuskar House is comfortable and less expensive, telephone: 053 3363. In Wexford itself there are two notable hotels, the Talbot, boasting swimming-pool and hairdressing salon, and White's, where we have often taken refreshment. It was there, at dinner one evening, that I was much tempted by one item on the menu: 'Fresh Dublin Bay sole,' it announced. But how much would this delectable dish cost me, I wondered? All the menu said was, 'Market price.' I consulted the waitress. 'Excuse me, miss, but what is the price of the Dublin Bay sole?' 'It'll be on the menu, sir,' she replied. 'Oh, no,' I said, believing that I had the better of her in this exchange. 'No, all it says there is market price.' But she was too good for me. 'That'll be exactly it, sir,' she returned swiftly, and went on her way to the next table.

Jonathan Swift was distinctly scathing in his comments on the inhabitants of Wexford: 'They say the cocks and dogs go to sleep at noon, and so do the people.' Of the place itself, he remembered best 'clean sheets, but bare walls'. Yet each autumn, this little town in the south-eastern corner of Ireland rouses itself to mount a famous festival. Wexford's operatic feast comes just about last in the calendar of Europe's major musical gatherings — a marvellous way to round off the year — and punt for pound and note for note, probably provides its customers with as good value as can be found at, let us say, Covent Garden. At least, such is my impression, relying as I must on fading memories of those far-off days when I was

Brittas Bay, near Wicklow

Glengariff, Bantry Bay

Healy Pass, between Cork and Kerry

Near Waterville, Kerry

Ballinskelligs Bay, Kerry

A scene in Clare

A road in Clare

Thoor Ballylee, home of W B Yeats

able to afford seats at that grand establishment on London's Bow Street.

By contrast, Wexford's Theatre Royal is probably the least imposing of the world's opera houses, set as it is in a row of rather drab houses, whose doors open directly on to the street. Yet, as at Glyndebourne, evening dress is strongly recommended to patrons. Inside, it is small, even intimate, one could say, though recently enlarged to the extent of another 156 seats, making 550 in all, and an extended foyer. Even so, the conductor has to make his way through the auditorium and open a little gate to obtain entrance to the orchestra pit. In the course of many years since we were first lured to Wexford, we have found much to enchant us. Perhaps the most vivid memory is of Massenet's delightful, if sentimental, opera, *Le Jongleur de Notre Dame*, which tells of the inmates of a religious house offering their gifts, their talents, to the Blessed Virgin Mary. The jongleur has only his tricks, his juggling, and when he attempts to present them as his tribute, the brothers intervene, intending to drag him away and prevent what they regard as an undignified spectacle. Just at that moment, the statue of the virgin becomes animated, and the efforts of the jongleur receive an unmistakable sign of approval from above. A rather absurd little tale, true, but the score is unfailingly inventive, and the performance, under Yan Pascal Tortelier, with Patrick Power and that splendid Russian baritone now well-known in Britain, Sergei Leiferkus, was really something to cherish. Among other rarities, we have enjoyed the opulent vocal writing of Rossini's *Tancredi*, superbly conducted by Arnold Östman, and the melodramatic absurdities of Catalani's *La Wally*, even though the heroine does turn out to be something of a wally herself. We missed the sublime hilarity of one performance of Spontini's *La Vestale*, when a steeply-sloping stage was polished to such an extent that none of the cast could retain a foothold. Happily, the event is faithfully chronicled by Bernard Levin in his book, *Conducted Tour*, and we live in fervent hope that some day we may encounter an equally extraordinary Wexford happening. Over the years of its existence, there have been ups and downs in the financial fortunes of this remarkable and adventurous enterprise, and more than one real crisis, but stern resolve and an uncompromising determination not to lower standards have ensured the survival of the annual festival.

For us, Wexford is a place to revisit, for its musical, scenic, social and gastronomic attractions. Nobody with a real interest in opera should be put off by the esoteric appearance of the repertoire, since Wexford so often strikes pure gold in its daring selections. More conventional entertainment is provided by morning programmes of operatic scenes in White's Hotel, where budding young singers, cast in smaller roles in the main operas, are given the opportunity to attempt larger parts from the standard repertoire. We have always had immense enjoyment from these presentations, one of the many excellent ideas to come from the festival's energetic and perspicacious director over many years, Elaine Padmore. Throughout the festival, a full and varied programme of events, including late-night concerts, ensures that there is something to please everybody, be his brow high or low. Box office is at the Theatre Royal, High Street, Wexford, Ireland, telephone: (from Britain) 010 353 53 22144. A word of warning here: tickets for the operas, especially at weekends, are snapped up eagerly by the early birds.

Wexford, once a Viking settlement, later sacked by Cromwell, is today the most sociable and hospitable of places. Regulars from year to year greet each other cordially as they pass in the busy, narrow streets. Not so long ago, my wife and I were invited before the opera by Bernard Levin, himself a notable Wexford enthusiast, to drink champagne at the Talbot Hotel. Champagne seems to flow freely, too, in the intervals at the Theatre Royal, and both before and after the performances there is good eating to be had. Good conversation, too. We eavesdropped at the oyster bar, just down the road from the theatre, and heard the following fascinating account of an American tourist in Rome, visiting the Vatican, and anxious to see the Sistine Chapel. 'Well, she was told that it was closed, and when she asked why it was closed, she was told that they were repainting the ceiling!' The conversation then took a different tack, and someone mentioned the name of Lord Longford, that well-known defender of moral standards, whose investigations into lurid goings-on in certain European cities attracted some publicity years ago. 'I just hope and pray that I shall outlive him,' the lady announced, 'because I have devised the perfect epitaph for him: "A terrible duty is porn!"'

A word of explanation here for those who may not be thoroughly acquainted with the works of William Butler Yeats: in one his most famous poems, 'Easter 1916', there occurs thrice the memorable line, 'A terrible beauty is born.'

Beyond city limits, there are numerous and varied attractions in the county of Wexford, and its neighbouring shires. The coastline rewards explorers and bird-watchers on gentle excursions by way of Lady's Island, a place of pilgrimage where once stood an ancient monastery dedicated to Our Lady, Carnsore Point, where we watched strutting oyster-catchers, and Kilmore Quay, just a few miles from Ireland's largest bird-sanctuary on the Saltee Islands. As a diversion, we visited Johnstown Castle, a 19th-century Gothic mansion, with extensive grounds which are especially attractive in autumn. Since this is Ireland, it goes without saying that there is good golfing all around. Westward lies the village of Ballyhack, where folk really in a hurry can use the ferry to take a short cut to destinations further west, thus avoiding a long detour by road. Anyone interested in the origin of commonplace phrases may pause awhile to test the local explanation of 'by hook or by crook', Hook and Crook being the names of two settlements in that area.

At Ballyhack, hungry travellers can find ease and refreshment at the Neptune, whose menu offers such temptations as avocado and cucumber sorbet, hot crab

Brehat, scallops in garlic butter and hot, buttered lobster. On our first visit, being rather pressed for time, I asked whether we could just have a snack before pursuing our way. My request was readily granted, but such haste in Ireland is unseemly, and in the end we succumbed to three tempting courses which, in my case, consisted of oysters, baked crab and ice-cream flavoured with Bailey's liqueur. As I was settling the bill, the Neptune's amiable and hospitable proprietor, Pierce McAuliffe, remarked: 'If that's your idea of a snack, pray God you come here for dinner one day!'

Cork and Kerry

Cork is Ireland's second city after Dublin, with its own international airport. Swansea-Cork Ferries, who suspended operations recently, are back in business again; this has been, for so many years the most convenient crossing for access to the west of Ireland, allowing a comfortable night's rest in either direction. We even managed to sleep right through a fierce storm on one particularly rough night, only to hear about it when we appeared for breakfast the next morning. It is to be hoped that this service will now continue on a regular basis. In season, Brittany Ferries sail to Cork from Roscoff in Brittany.

Cork is a pleasant enough city, although navigation can present some difficulties in rush-hour traffic. We have often stayed at Moore's, Morrison's Island, telephone: 021 271291/2. There, one October, I put my watch forward rather than back at the end of Summer Time, and in consequence descended to the lobby at 5 o'clock in the morning, thinking it to be 7 o'clock and time for breakfast. The night-porter was at first startled, but then showed himself friendly and understanding. I have to report that my wife did not follow his example.

We halted one evening for drinks and liked the look of Fitzpatrick Silver Springs, Tivoli, telephone: 021 507533. Sightseeing trips from Cork should not fail to include Blarney Castle and its famous stone, 6 miles distant. Cobh, known as Queenstown in Victorian times, is 15 miles from the city centre, Passage West 7 miles, Monkstown Castle, Crosshaven 13 miles, and there is always Ram's Head for a fine viewpoint.

Cork is gateway to the spectacular scenery of Ireland's south-west. Kinsale lies about 12 miles south of Cork International Airport. Winner of the 'Tidy Town' contest in 1986, it is a compact, cheerful place, with several characterful restaurants and taverns, and a museum in the 17th-century courthouse. From our hotel, the view was over a pleasant stretch of water and a flotilla of small boats. On the way out of Kinsale, we stopped to enquire directions from a charming young lady. Her instructions seemed of some complexity, so I asked whether the road was signposted. 'It is indeed,' returned the lass. 'It says "Yield".'

The farther west one travels in Cork, the more beautiful the landscape, all the way through Clonakilty, Castletownshend, Schull and Barleycove, down to Mizen Head, or northwards, to Bantry Bay, Glengariff and, just offshore, warmed by the Gulf Stream, Garinish Island, with its amazing display of exotic plants. There is spectacular scenery around Roaring Water Bay, jolly little villages like Ballydehob, rivers, lakes and mountains.

Kindness and hospitality are qualities seemingly present in abundance amongst the Irish. Once in Schull, a small town near the south-west corner of the country, almost in the shadow of Mount Gabriel, and with a fine prospect over Roaringwater

Bay, I entered a chemist's shop in search of film for my camera. It soon became evident that the particular film I required was out of stock, but long after all reasonable hope had been exhausted, the chemist continued his search, shaking boxes of aspirins, peering thoughtfully into jars of pastilles, and exploring similarly unlikely avenues in a desperate attempt to stave off the inevitable admission of defeat. In the end, determined not to disappoint me, he telephoned ahead to the next village on my route, and made sure that a supply of film would be awaiting me there. And so indeed it was.

Ireland's most westerly county is Kerry, with its noble scenery, perhaps Ireland's finest. Here are Killarney, the Ring of Kerry, Tralee Bay and Dingle, where John Doyle's Seafood Bar provides a gastronomic experience not easily forgotten: telephone: 066 51174. Once, when we had expressed particularly keen appreciation of one of his many delectable seafood dishes, John not only gave us his recipe, but donated the wherewithal to make it for ourselves, a bag of fresh mussels. From Dingle, a winding road runs westwards, past prehistoric beehive huts (*clochans*), to Slea Head, as far west as you can go in Ireland without falling into the sea. From Dunquin, there are boat-trips to the uninhabited Blasket Islands. Another route goes north, over Connor Pass, with its stunning panorama from Dingle Bay in the south to the broad sweep of sands northwards near Tralee.

We renewed acquaintance with the Church of Ireland in Dingle. There we came to a church that had no organ, nor even a tinkling piano to be our guide, but contrived a form of accompaniment for the hymns by means of scratchy gramophone records, which would every so often fall victim to a repeating groove, putting the congregation into some disarray. On the next visit, we decided to throw in our lot for the time being with the Catholics, who had a much larger church anyway, and a fine organ, as might be expected. It was on a Wednesday, if I remember rightly, that I ambled into the porch to see if there might be a service on that evening. However, in typical Irish manner, all notices displayed there referred to events which had taken place (or, perhaps, had failed to take place), months, and even years before. There was a convent at hand, and I made to enquire of one of the sisters about the evening's arrangements. 'Oh, to be sure, there is Mass at half-past seven,' said the amiable creature who came to answer the door. Then she beamed at me, and delivered herself of a startling remark: 'And it's a fine thing to see a good man like yourself around these days.' As the door closed on me, I walked away, wondering whether I should feel flattered or guilty at such unexpected commendation.

One of the remarkable things about churchgoing in Ireland (and in France, Spain and Italy, too, for that matter), is the complete lack of self-consciousness about dutiful attendance at worship. People come into weekday services laden with shopping, or with tools of their trade, as though it were the most natural thing in the world. Indeed, so it should be, and there is a good lesson to learn in this. In remote villages, scattered over the lush landscape of the west of Ireland, simple folk attend to their devotions as faithfully as their parents and grandparents did before them. Indeed, on Sunday mornings, it is often difficult to find parking space in streets around the churches.

Kerry's appeal is enhanced by its gentle, often balmy, climate, the abundance of attractive beaches warmed by the waters of the Gulf Stream, almost empty roads lined by fuchsia hedges and leading to such delectable scenes as Killarney's lakes and fells, Macgillicuddy's Reeks, with frequent sight of snow on the high peaks, Waterville, where Charlie Chaplin was a frequent visitor, and Ballinskelligs Bay, where the spectacle of the sun setting behind the Skellig Rocks far out to sea is one of undeniable splendour. A regular car ferry across the Shannon from Tarbert to Killimer opens the way northwards to Clare, a county for which we cherish a deep and abiding affection.

Clare and Galway

Ennis, about twenty minutes' easy drive from Shannon Airport, is the principal town of Clare, boasting a 13th-century abbey, carefully restored some 35 years ago. Bunratty Castle, best known for medieval banquets, lies nearby, on the road to Limerick; also within easy reach are the cliffs of Moher which dismayed wretched survivors of the Spanish Armada, who were eventually washed up on those shores, and found no mercy at the hands of the local inhabitants, Kilfenora, with its 12th-century high cross and Burren Display Centre, Lisdoonvarna, where folk go to take the waters, Yeats's Thoor Ballylee and Coole Park, with its woodland walks. Ennis is a jovial, bustling place, with tight streets, and a host of pubs, many offering traditional Irish music along with traditional Irish beverages. The Old Ground Hotel is a comfortable, well-run establishment which carries reminders of the days of gracious living. Telephone 065 28127 for reservations. We have been fortunate enough to have lived graciously on our frequent visits to this part of the world.

Northwards from Ennis, through Gort, the road leads towards Galway City. Regularly, we have turned off the main route near Kilcolgan, to head towards the waters of Galway Bay and Moran's Oyster Cottage. A humble establishment when we first came to know it, the restaurant has been enlarged to accommodate the influx of visitors from near and far, who have heard of Moran's and the choice fare to be had there. At our table, tucked away from general gaze in the cosiness of the log cabin, we have paid proper respect to dishes of crab, oysters, mussels and smoked salmon, and delighted in the best of company. After such feasts, we have taken the leisurely coastal route back to Corofin, through Kinvara and Ballyvaughan, with sightings of the Aran Islands westwards. Those were days to cheer the heart.

I sometimes wonder what happened to the man I met early one morning in a country lane in Clare. It has long been my practice while staying in Ireland to take a brisk bicycle ride before my hosts are stirring, and on this occasion I had a camera with me, having been asked by friends in the publishing business to provide photographs of typically rural life in Ireland. As I rounded a corner on my Dawes King-Pin, the perfect picture was before me: a horse and cart, halted at a farm gate where stood a milk-churn, and the driver carefully ladling milk from the churn into his jug. As I aimed the camera at this charming scene, he turned around; one glance at me and my camera sufficed. Whipping his horse furiously, he sped off down the lane. It took me some minutes to come to the realisation that the poor fellow was engaged in stealing his morning supply of milk; probably he had been observing a similar routine for years, but now, at an hour when most of Ireland was still asleep, he had been caught in the act by a silent intruder upon his peace, who had actually attempted to photograph the crime at the moment of commission. Once discovered, did he, I wonder, ever dare to return to the scene, or has he now discovered another source of supply?

Early mornings in Ireland can present unexpected problems. One autumn morning, I flew into Shannon from New York, having taken the precaution of reserving in advance a hired car. My flight arrived on time, customs clearance was unexpectedly swift, and very soon I was at the car-hire desk in the main concourse. But I was there alone, for the position was unattended, and remained so for such a length of time that I was constrained to make enquiries of a uniformed official. 'Excuse me,' I said, 'but doesn't this desk open at eight o'clock?' 'Oh, it does, sir,' replied the worthy fellow; the Irish have this in common with Italians, that they will often return to a stranger the answer they think he wants to hear, rather than the strictest truth. 'Well,' I continued, 'there's nobody here.' The official consulted his watch, and then gave tongue: 'Well, no, there wouldn't be. You see, it's only half-past eight yet.' Time and motion studies are not easily accomplished in Ireland; at least, such is my experience. When I enquired about times of the car ferry service across the Shannon, a route which saves a long detour through Limerick, I was told that it sailed 'every half-hour on the hour'.

It has been a long time since we first attended a Church of Ireland (that is to say, Protestant) service; it was in the village of Corofin, County Clare. The congregation was small, the prayer books had an odour of mustiness suggesting infrequent use, and we felt uncomfortably like conspicuous intruders into some private rite. Not long after our visit, the building was converted for use as a folk museum, and thereafter we fell into the habit of accompanying our hostess to Mass in the Catholic church, which occupied a rather isolated position on the road to Ennistymon. A curious sight there was that of menfolk, uncomfortable in baggy suits and sober ties, standing sheepishly apart at the back of the church throughout the service, while their womenfolk and children went forward to sit in the pews.

On one visit to Clare, I had to take my wife to see a doctor. In Ennistymon, we found a most amiable and helpful physician, who did what was necessary, but said that he would like to see my wife again the next day, just to make sure that all was well. We asked what time we should come. 'Oh, in the morning, I think,' he said. We thought this was rather vague, and our expressions must have betrayed our sentiments, for he added: 'I don't use the appointment system, you see. It doesn't work in Ireland.'

For almost twenty years, we made regular visits to dear friends, Máire and Jack Sweeney who took up residence in a fine house they had built on an eminence overlooking the waters of Inchiquin with its population of resident swans, and the rounded limestone slopes of the Burren. Jack, who taught for many years at Harvard University, became friend to a number of celebrated writers; his wife, Máire, daughter of the Gaelic League's co-founder, Eoin MacNeill, worked for a time with the Irish Folklore Commission, and was author of a comprehensive and absorbing introduction to Irish folk-lore and legend, *The Festival of Lughnasa*. Their house was a mile or two from the village of Corofin, reached by a winding and narrow road skirting the lake. There, in one of the loveliest settings imaginable, the Sweeneys cultivated, assiduously and generously, good companionship and good conversation. Friendship is a special commodity in Ireland, and here it was displayed liberally: late one autumn evening in Corofin, a knock at the door announced an unexpected visit from Ted Hughes (now Poet Laureate). He had been out fishing, had spied from afar a friendly light in the Sweeneys' home, and knew the welcome there would be warm.

Returning from an autumn visit to Corofin, it was odd chance that led us to book a ferry crossing from Ireland to Britain at two o'clock in the morning, on the very day and at the very hour that Summer Time officially came to an end and clocks were due to be put back. When, we wondered, would the ship scheduled to depart at 2 am pull away from its moorings? The first 2 am, or the second? 'Oh, there's really no problem at all,' a representative of the shipping company assured us. 'We leave as soon as it's two the first time, and then we just go around the harbour until the time catches up with us.' I am ashamed to confess that I do not recall exactly what did happen.

Eventually, even in Ireland, time catches up with the visitor, and the hour comes for departure. For us, travellers late in the year as we often are, we say farewell to Coole Park when, indeed,

> The trees are in their autumn beauty,
> The woodland paths are dry,
> Under the October twilight the water
> Mirrors a still sky ...

Even now, steeped in the atmosphere of this strangely enchanting land, our hearts have not grown old. Perhaps the influence of my great-grandmother, Isabella Costello (God rest her soul!), attends upon me still. I can wish visitors to Ireland no richer gift than to be as blessed in good fellowship there as we have been for so many years.

Last Words

> In the sun that is young once only,
> Time let me play and be
> Golden in the mercy of his means ...
>
> Dylan Thomas, 'Fern Hill'

Very gently, very gradually in most cases, life prises open our grip on beloved objects. Places once dearest to the heart begin to assume a quality of remoteness, the area of operations becomes ever more circumscribed. Slowly, the light begins to fade, as inevitably it must for each human creature that treads this earth. Yet, for most of us, there is time allowed for a sort of celebration, space for the accumulation of memories. As R S Thomas puts it so very aptly in a poem called 'A Day in Autumn', these memories provide

> ... something to wear
> Against the heart in the long cold.

My hope is that, as the years roll on, I may continue to say, with Tennyson's Ulysses,

> ... my purpose holds
> To sail beyond the sunset, and the baths
> Of all the western stars, until I die.
> It may be that the gulfs will wash us down:
> It may be we shall touch the Happy Isles,
> And see the great Achilles, whom we knew.
> Tho' much is taken, much abides; and tho'
> We are not now that strength which in old days
> Mov'd earth and heaven; that which we are, we are:
> One equal temper of heroic hearts,
> Made weak by time and fate, but strong in will
> To strive, to seek, to find, and not to yield.

In the end, the poets give us the clearest and the purest view of the lands they inhabit or visit: their visions of Britain and Ireland will remain, bright and untarnished, so long as there are still those who love 'place, time, demarcation, hearth, kin, enclosure, site, differentiated cult ...' Thus it comes about that I give pride of place to the poets, who have guided me through the wonders of these journeys more surely than any navigator with sextant and compass, and whose poems have revealed to me so much about these islands. I can find no fitter valediction to the reader than these lines from T S Eliot's 'Little Gidding':

152 LAST WORDS

We shall not cease from exploration
And the end of all our exploring
Will be to arrive where we started
And know the place for the first time.

THE END

Select Bibliography

AA Members' Handbook, Automobile Association, annual publication

Abse, Joan. *The Art Galleries of Britain and Ireland*, Robson Books, 1985

Ancient Monuments of Wales, HMSO, 1973

Bede. *A History of the English Church and People*, Penguin, 1955

Benn, Ernest, *Blue Guides*, separate volumes for England, Scotland, Wales, Ireland and London

Bord, Janet & Colin. *A Guide to Ancient Sites in Britain*, Latimer New Dimensions, 1978

Cameron, Kenneth. *English Place-Names*, Batsford, 1961

Clifton-Taylor, Alec. *The Cathedrals of England*, Thames & Hudson, 1967

Country Life Book of Castles and Houses in Britain, Country Life Books, 1986

Davies, Idris. *Collected Poems*, Gomer Press, Dyfed, 1972

Dunn, Michael. *Walking Ancient Trackways*, David & Charles, 1986

Eagle, Dorothy, & Carnell, Hilary. *The Oxford Literary Guide to the British Isles*, Oxford University Press, 1977

Eperon, Arthur. *Travellers' Britain*, Pan Books, 1981

Evans, Rosemary. *The Visitor's Guide to Northern Ireland*, Moorland Publishing, 1987

Ferrier, Winifred. *The Life of Kathleen Ferrier*, Hamish Hamilton, 1955

The Good Food Guide, Consumers' Association, annual publication

Great Britain and Ireland, Michelin, annual publication

Grossmith, George and Weedon. *The Diary of a Nobody*, various editions

Guest, John (ed). *The Best of Betjeman*, Penguin and John Murray, 1978

Guide to Gardens in Britain, Ordnance Survey and Hamlyn, 1986, subsequent revisions

Guide to Historic Houses in Britain, Ordnance Survey and Hamlyn, 1987, subsequent revisions

Graham, Cuthbert. *Portrait of Aberdeen and Deeside*, Robert Hale, 1972

Guest Accommodation, Irish Tourist Board, annual publication

Hinde, Thomas (ed). *The Domesday Book*, Hutchinson, 1985

Hoskins, W.G. *The Making of the English Landscape*, Hodder & Stoughton, various volumes

Houlder, Christopher. *Wales: An Archaeological Guide*, Faber, 1974

Housman, A.E. *Collected Poems*, Cape, 1939

Hudson, Kenneth, & Nicholls, Ann. *The Cambridge Guide to the Historic Places of Britain*, Cambridge University Press, 1989

Johnson, Paul. *Castles of England, Scotland and Wales*, Weidenfeld and Nicolson, 1989

Kee, Robert. *Ireland*, Weidenfeld & Nicolson, 1980

Kerr, Nigel & Mary. *A Guide to Medieval Sites in Britain*, Grafton Books, 1988

SELECT BIBLIOGRAPHY

Kiek, Jonathan. *Everybody's Historic England*, Quiller Press, 1988
The Landmark Trust Handbook, Landmark Trust, annual publication
Larkin, Philip. *High Windows*, Faber, 1974
Levin, Bernard. *Conducted Tour*, Cape, 1981
Long-Distance Footpath Guides, HMSO for the Countryside Commission, various titles
MacNeill, Máire. *The Festival of Lughnasa*, Oxford University Press, 1962
Mee, Arthur. *The King's England*, Hodder & Stoughton, 40 county volumes
Mercer, Eric. *English Vernacular Houses*, HMSO, 1975
Moody. T.W. & Martin, F.X. *The Course of Irish History*, Mercier Press, Cork, 1967
Muir, Richard. *Traveller's History of Britain and Ireland*, Michael Joseph, 1983
The National Trust Book of Long Walks, Pan Books, 1981
The National Trust Handbook, National Trust, annual publication
Naylor, Peter. *Discovering Lost Mines*, Shire Publications, 1981.
Nicholson, Norman. *Selected Poems*, Faber, 1966
Nicholson's Guide to English Churches, Robert Nicholson, 1984
Nicolson, Adam, & Morter, Peter. *Prospects of England*, Weidenfeld & Nicolson, 1989
O'Brien, Edna. *Mother Ireland*, Weidenfeld & Nicolson, 1976
Ordnance Survey Guide to the Waterways, Robert Nicholson and Ordnance Survey, regional volumes for England: South, Central, North, River Thames
Ordnance Survey Leisure Guides, Automobile Association and Ordnance Survey, various titles
Ordnance Survey Maps, Motoring Atlas, 1:50 000 *Landranger* series, 1: 25 000 *Pathfinder* series, Ordnance Survey, periodic revisions
Pevsner, Nikolaus (ed). *The Buildings of England, Ireland, Scotland and Wales*, Penguin, individual county volumes
Piggott, Stuart. *The Druids*, Thames & Hudson, 1968
Place Names on Maps of Scotland and Wales, Ordnance Survey
Prince of Wales, HRH. *A Vision of Britain*, Doubleday, 1989
Protz, Roger (ed). *Beer, Bed and Breakfast*, Robson Books, 1986
Read, Herbert. *Collected Poems*, Faber, 1966
Read, Herbert. *The Contrary Experience*, Faber, 1963
Red Guides, Ward Lock, individual volumes covering Britain and Ireland
Sanger, Andrew. *Exploring Rural Ireland*, Christopher Helm, 1989
Scotland, Scottish Tourist Board, accommodation guides, annual publication
Stonehouse, Bernard. *The Aerofilms Book of Britain from the Air*, Weidenfeld & Nicolson, 1982
Thomas, Dylan. *Under Milk Wood*, Dent, 1954
Thomas, Dylan. *Collected Poems*, Dent, 1966
Thomas, Dylan. *The Collected Stories*, Dent, 1983
Thorold, Henry. *Collins Guide to Cathedrals, Abbeys and Priories*, Collins, 1986

Touring England, Automobile Association, various titles
Trevelyan, G.M. *English Social History*, Longmans, 1944
Trueman, A.E. *Geology and Scenery in England and Wales*, Pelican, 1949
Tucker, Alan. *The Penguin Guide to Ireland*, Penguin, 1989
Wainwright, Alfred. *Fellwalking with Wainwright*, Michael Joseph, 1984
Wainwright, Alfred. *Wainwright on the Pennine Way*, Michael Joseph, 1985
Wainwright, Alfred. *Wainwright's Coast to Coast Walk*, Michael Joseph, 1987
Wales: Hotels and Guest Houses/Self Catering/Bed and Breakfast (separate volumes), Wales Tourist board, Cardiff, annual publication
Walker's Britain, Pan Books & Ordnance Survey, two volumes, 1982 & 1986
Where to Stay, English Tourist Board, various versions, revised annually
Where to Stay, Northern Ireland Tourist Board, Belfast, annual publication
Wilkinson, L.P. *A Century of King's*, King's College, Cambridge, 1980
Wilson, John G. *Follow the Map*, A & C Black and Ordnance Survey, 1985
Wood, Nicola. *Scottish Place Names*, Chambers, Edinburgh, 1989
Wright, Christopher John. *A Guide to the Pembrokeshire Coast Path*, Constable, 1988
Young, Geoffrey. *The Best Views of Britain*, Partridge Press, 1989